The Container Gardener's Bible

The Container Gardener's Bible

A Step-by-Step Guide to Growing in All Kinds of Containers, Conditions, and Locations

**Joanna K. Harrison
and Miranda Smith**

RODALE®

A QUARTO BOOK

Published by Rodale Inc.
33 East Minor Street
Emmaus, PA 18098-0099

Library of Congress Cataloging-in-Publication Data

Harrison, Joanna.
The container gardener's bible : a step-by-step guide to
growing in all kinds of containers, conditions, and locations
/ Joanna Harrison and Miranda Smith.
p. cm.
"A Quarto book."
Includes index.
ISBN-13 978–1–59486–958–7 paperback
ISBN-10 1–59486–958–8 paperback
1. Container gardening. I. Smith, Miranda, date II. Title.
SB418.H38 2009
635.9'86--dc22   2008040544

This book was conceived, designed,
and produced by
Quarto Publishing plc
The Old Brewery
6 Blundell Street
London N7 9BH

Plant Directory by Miranda Smith

Editor: James Harrison
Assistant editor: Emma Poulter
Proofreader: Rachelle Laliberte
Art director: Caroline Guest
Designer: Tanya Devonshire-Jones
Photographer: Vivien Shelton
Illustrator: Richard Palmer
Picture research: Sarah Bell
Indexer: Dorothy Frame
Creative director: Moira Clinch
Publisher: Paul Carslake

Cover photo taken at Longwood Gardens,
Kennett Square, Pennsylvania, by Rob Cardillo

Color separation by Modern Age Repro House Ltd,
Hong Kong
Printed by 1010 Printing International Ltd, China

2 4 6 8 10 9 7 5 3 1 paperback

CONTENTS

DESIGN

Designing your container garden is the combination of personal taste with practical considerations. This chapter helps you to navigate around the seemingly limitless combinations of containers and plants by coming to grips with fundamental design guidelines. The first thing you should ask yourself before you purchase pot and plant is: What do I want from my containers? How do I want them to look? And where am I going to place them? You will find the answers easier if you take an holistic approach, that is, seeing the pot not just on its own but viewing it in the context of your home and outdoor space. Ultimately, your design is a reflection of your own personality—be it fun, frivolous, or formal.

Containers: *A potted history*

It is reassuring to know that all the pleasures of container gardening have been experienced by green-fingered gardeners as far back as ancient Rome and very likely beyond.

Many of the principles of designing and planting in containers are as relevant now as they were in antiquity. Back then, terra-cotta pots were used for practical purposes—propagating plants and growing seedlings, for instance—by the ancient Egyptians, Greeks, and Romans, especially in regions with long, hot summers and dry, impoverished soils. Excavations in Crete have unearthed remains of terra-cotta pots probably used by the Minoans (as the inhabitants were called about 5,000 years ago) for planting shrubs such as figs and pomegranates and flowers including lilies and roses.

In his book *De Agricultura* (about 160 B.C.), the Roman writer Cato the Elder described how terra-cotta pots were used for propagating tree roots. When the new trees were planted, the pots were smashed and then buried with the roots. Archaeologists excavating at the ancient Garden of Hephaistos (460–420 B.C.), which once overlooked the Agora in Athens, uncovered evidence of decorative planting in a line of flowerpots running parallel to a line of columns along the side of the temple.

The earliest window boxes and hanging baskets

As time went on, the notion of decorating rooftops and balconies with colorful flowerpots on a more permanent basis took hold.

This custom quickly caught on, and soon decorated roofs and terraces emerged in Rome and Pompeii. In Pompeii, where buildings were extremely cramped and water needed to be conserved, large window boxes began to proliferate "so that every day the eyes might feast on this copy of a garden, as though it were a work of nature" (Pliny the Elder). Plants such as pomegranates, figs, olives, and laurel were also grown in pots or baskets.

Perhaps the most famous of the early rooftop gardens were the legendary hanging gardens of Babylon. King Nebuchadnezzar II had them created in the 6th century B.C. to please his homesick wife Amyitis, who pined for the trees, flowers, and mountainous terrain of her homeland, Media.

Islamic gardens

About A.D. 800, beautiful Islamic gardens were being created in what is now Iran, Iraq, and Syria. These courtyard gardens were sensual places of fragrance and color in hot and inhospitable places. Designed around cooling pools of water and geometrically laid-out flowerbeds, tubs were planted with carefully restrained trees such as almond, apricot, and cypress. Roses, vines, jonquils, wallflowers, and tulips were also grown. These earthly paradises provided a quiet and contemplative spot from the outside world. The Islamic garden was adopted in Spain during the 700 years of Arab political influence on the Iberian

Formal container framing
A mid-17th century oil painting by Theodoros Pulakis
entitled *David Watching Bathsheba Bathing* (c.1650)
shows a formal European garden setting
featuring terra-cotta pots.

Time-honored trellising
A 16th-century illustrated manuscript shows Indian cress scrambling over a trellis planted in a blue and white pot. The design for training climbers and vines in pots has changed little in 400 years. This watercolor drawing (c.1589) is taken from an early catalog of plants called *Camerarius Florilegium*.

Peninsula, which ended in 1492. Spanish courtyard gardens became places for relaxing and socializing. One of Europe's oldest surviving gardens can be found at Cordoba's Orange Tree Courtyard at the Grand Mosque, where many of the courtyards are dotted with fountains and pools and filled with flowers grown in pots.

Medieval roots

The European roots of container gardening in the Middle Ages (about A.D. 750–1270) can be found in abbey and monastery gardens, where fruit, vegetables, and herbs were cultivated not only for culinary but also medicinal purposes. Many flowers, such as the rose, lily, and iris, were grown for their religious symbolism and used as altar decorations.

In the mid-13th century, pleasure gardens attached to great households became more common. They were in many ways similar to monastery gardens, with enclosed walls and fruit, vegetables, and herbs grown for ornamental as well as practical purposes. A favorite feature was the turf bench, a wooden or brick container filled with earth and then planted with grass and sweet-smelling herbs for sitting on.

Medieval tapestries, manuscripts, and engravings are renowned for depicting garden scenes, many of which include plants in pots both inside and outside the house. Scented plants such as carnations and wallflowers were particularly popular. Ceramic pots were generally used for planting, and woven baskets were used for moving plants from place to place, as famously depicted in a 15th-century painting of the fictional French romantic figure Renaud de Montauban.

About this time, explorers and merchants were traveling the many routes that made up the Silk Road to the Far East and crossing the oceans to the Americas with seeds and potted plants of new and exotic specimens. Plants became an important commodity for trading and collecting. Many of the traded plants were tender, lending themselves to being planted in containers over which frames were built in winter to protect them.

In the 17th century, French landscape architects were hugely influenced by the then classical style of the Italian Renaissance. Many pots were planted with tender plants such as anemones, narcissus, foxgloves, and tulips, as well as citrus and evergreens, so the garden would be filled year-round with ever-changing color and greenery, regardless of season or climate.

André Le Nôtre, a great French landscaper, designed many gardens and parks but most notably planned and constructed the massive gardens at the Palace of Versailles. Between 1686 and 1687, he used 250,000 containers for the more tender shrubs and 3,000 for trees.

Italianate inspirations

In the early 1800s, the Italian style became fashionable in Britain, thanks largely to architect-designer Sir Charles Barry, who, after a tour of Italian villas and gardens, showcased it in many grand gardens. The style emphasized geometric designs with large terraces and reintroduced formal rows of pots, giving height and structure to the newly laid gardens. Victorians filled their conservatories with exotics such as potted palms and orchids, and mass production of cast

POPULAR POTS

A particularly popular form of container was the Versailles box (presumably inspired by Le Nôtre and his handiwork), a square wooden box with a hinged door allowing easy access to its metal liner. Thanks to its elegance and practicality, the Versailles box (right) remains one of the most popular styles of containers.

In 18th-century England, the continued introduction of exotic plants from around the world generated great new possibilities for gardeners, despite the move from formal gardens to more naturalistic landscapes. Many of these tender plants had to be confined or overwintered in orangeries, leading to a renewed interest in containers, many of them made of lead or stone.

RIGHT: **Versailles box**
A modern "take" on the 17th-century original.

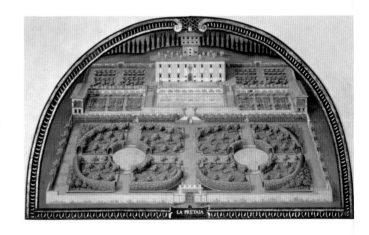

ABOVE: **Classical containers**
In Giusto Utens' painting of the late 16th-century Tuscan villa Petraia, planted ceramic pots are placed geometrically in rows and at the corner of parterres to enhance the overall design.

TOP: **Softening the boundaries**
The use of terra-cotta pots filled with flowers at the Belvedere, Villa Piatti, Rome (painted here by George Samuel Elgood), lends a personal touch to the more formal setting.

Container for contemplation
This late 19th-century oil painting by the American Impressionist painter Frederick Childe Hassam (1859–1935) shows a woman tending a potted geranium.

iron and cement led to a far wider range of containers and styles. With people enjoying more leisure time than ever before, visits to parks became increasingly popular, encouraging park gardeners in a new trend of "bedding out." Enormous numbers of plants were grown under glass in pots to be planted out into flowerbeds and then replaced at each season. Winter bedding included evergreens that were planted out, pots and all.

Transatlantic potting

The tradition of pot making in America is a long one, dating back to the 1750s and even further—Spanish settlers' pots predating Colonial New England gardens by 100 years or so have been uncovered. The use of ornate and glazed pots became fashionable in the Civil War era. In the early 20th century, immigration and travel led to a fairly strong Italian influence in the United States. Landscape designer Beatrix Farrand used European themes in her gardens and, through her friendship with craftsman Eric Soderholtz, created pots and urns that could withstand the cold Maine winters. In the 1920s, she also designed the arbor garden at Dumbarton Oaks in Washington, DC, which is filled with an array of plants grown in containers. Meanwhile, Irving Gill pioneered low-cost, modernist-style housing in California, using window boxes and potted plants to offset the minimalist white walls and create a zenlike feel of graciousness.

20th-century style statement

From the late 19th century, England's most influential garden designer, Gertrude Jekyll, used pots of plants to add color and textural accents to her 100-plus gardens. She was particularly fond of potted hostas (or, as they were known at the time, funkia). In the 1930s, Vita Sackville-West used many containers in her garden at Sissinghurst in Kent. She happily explained: "I like the habit of pot gardening…I know it entails constant watering, but consider the convenience of being able to set down a smear of color just where you need it." She also pioneered the use of old copper washtubs as plant containers. Another famous English plantswoman, Beth Chatto, wrote at the close of the 20th century in her *Garden Notebook* while on holiday in France: "Many years ago, I was fascinated by the use of plants in all kinds of containers and situations [especially] the unexpected sight of great leafy hostas among fountains of fuchsias."

In the 1950s, a modernist and minimalist approach to garden design led to renewed interest in container gardens. Its legacy sadly has been the swathes of bleak and largely neglected concrete containers seen in shopping malls and parking lots everywhere.

A more recent and more welcome trend has been the idea of the garden as an extension of home interior design—and containers are highly integral to this. Containers lend themselves wonderfully to instant makeovers, providing a practical and stylish way to update the contemporary garden.

Concrete and steel
This rooftop garden features strategically placed modern
steel containers and concrete urns containing single-species
plantings of silver birch and spiky-leaved succulents.

Why use a container?

Imagine a Moroccan or Manhattan city rooftop without stylish containers, or a country garden where no elegant urns grace the terrace. What would it be like to walk down a cobbled street in Spain without vibrant geraniums tumbling over windowsills and balconies?

CHECKLIST

- *Grow your own vegetables and herbs in containers and save money.*
- *Cheer up a tired corner of a garden instantly.*
- *Add color and fragrance to an otherwise paved or concreted area.*
- *Insert instant style and privacy to your garden with minimum input.*
- *Create focal points in key areas of your garden and your house.*
- *Attract wildlife to your back door or patio.*
- *No garden? Not even a balcony? How about a windowsill!*

WHEN NOT TO USE A CONTAINER

- *All containers require some degree of maintenance. A neglected container is a dismal sight. If it really is all too much, just buy a beautiful Cretan pot and forget the plant.*
- *A clash of ill-assorted plants struggling to escape is also an unpleasant sight. In these situations, containers detract from rather than enhance the setting.*

Bunches of color
Well-planted containers provide instant color, style, and maturity to a graveled garden area. These spring copper containers are planted with tulips including *Tulipa* 'Apricot Beauty', *T.* 'Black Hero', and *T.* 'Negrita'.

Without a doubt, containers are the icing on the cake when it comes to gardening. Whether you have a large garden, a small yard, or just a windowsill, there is a plant and a container for every space. Containers allow you to unleash your innate creativity, while adding a stylish accent to your garden. You can grow fragrant and colorful flowers, provide tasty herbs and fresh vegetables (right next to your kitchen door), attract birds and butterflies, and even grow trees and shrubs. The most important aspect of container gardening is to have fun—and this book will help you do just that.

Versatile solutions

- If you have a shady basement passage or terrace, use a mix of pots to soften hard edges and bring color to the spot.
- If something unsightly is on the other side of the garden fence, screen it instantly with trees or bamboos in pots.
- If you have noisy traffic next to your paved yard, grow grasses in containers and catch the sound of the wind.

Do you need containers?

- Do you want to draw attention to pathways or boundaries or even your own front door? Then containers provide the perfect framing to do this.
- Do you love gardening but don't have time for all that digging and weeding? Then go for containers.
- Do you want to grow organic fruit and vegetables, but the soil in your garden is polluted? Containers offer the ideal way to overcome this problem.

Dos and don'ts

• Always consider the safety aspect when placing a container.

• Consider the climate that the container will be exposed to.

• Don't place your best where they might easily be stolen. (Garden ornament theft is no joke.)

• Make your low and wide containers less attractive to cats, if you have them. Try taking branches from a thorny plant and laying them in a lattice pattern on the container, then plant in the gaps, or create an outside sandbox for a more appropriate alternative for felines.

• Commit to a little love and tenderness so your containers will thrive, not die. All containers need a degree of maintenance.

• Avoid posing a danger to passersby. The sharp barbs of cacti can be extremely painful, and the sap of euphorbias can cause skin irritation.

TOP RIGHT: **Catch the wind**
Containers not only provide a portable color palette for any would-be garden designer, they soothe other senses too: For example, the rustle of ornamental grasses catching the wind on a roof garden counteracts the noise of the traffic below.

RIGHT: **Relaxing, not gardening**
As indoor living is extended to the outdoors, containers bring the garden to your back door. These low-maintenance echeverias in a container beside the stylish chairs on decking prove the point.

Unwanted, unloved
Neglected pots are worse than no pots at all: This one's surface is covered in liverwort *Marchantia polymorpha* (below). Be prepared to put some effort into planting and maintaining your pots!

TIPS AND HINTS

• It is better to go for quality rather than quantity when choosing a container.

• If you have a small backyard, forget lawns and flower beds and try paving and containers instead.

• If your garden is looking tired and you're preparing for a special occasion, plant your containers with fresh, colorful foliage and flowers to add extra glamour and sparkle.

SEE ALSO
Chapter on low maintenance gardening, page 60.

1 Reflect your personality
A container garden is a reflection of your personality. Have the confidence to express yourself creatively.

2 Consider context
Be aware of the surroundings in which your container is placed. Are they formal or informal? Modern or old-fashioned? Try to link the color, materials, and design of your containers with those of your home's exterior so they relate in terms of shape, color, and purpose.

8 GUIDELINES FOR: Designing with

Push the boat out
How about an old rowboat for a creative container? Be adventurous and go for the unusual—as with this small urban garden at the side of a house in New York.

5 Picture proportion and scale
Don't forget to to consider how large potted plants will be when fully grown. Will they be trailing or upright? How will they relate to the shape and size of their container?

Creating focal points
Stylish urns filled with restrained planting punctuate this gravel path lined with Nepeta 'Six Hills Giant'.

It's hip to be square
Quite a statement comes from this lead and rusty metal container planted with *Buxus*—a boxwood table designed by Tony Ridler.

3 Set a style

Have a clear vision of what you want from your garden and how it will look. A container can make an instant bold statement, so be careful. The choice and style of your container should be in harmony with the plants you choose to put in it and vice versa.

4 Serve a purpose

What are you going to use your pots for? Are they for structure? Giving color? Growing herbs or vegetables? Attracting wildlife? Buy a container with an eye to where you will place it and how it will serve a particular purpose.

containers

6 Think outside the box

Rules are made to be broken. A big pot with a small layer of clipped boxwood can look fabulous. An extra-large container in a small garden can give a sense of space. However, always be aware of the overall center of gravity—a container should have a central pull, and a planted container should, whatever the design, look stable and secure.

Raised awareness
Tall ceramic containers filled with lavender (*Lavandula* spp.) provide a stylish raised border and heighten the aromatic impact of these plants.

7 Have an eye for aesthetics

Container plants tend to be closer at hand than those in flower beds, so go for the more sensual varieties, not for color alone. Consider taste, texture, fragrance, and sound. The more visible your container will be, the more you should invest in quality and style.

8 Know your limitations

Before you start, think carefully about not only how much work and commitment you are prepared to put in but also whether your proposed container can cope with the limitations of the intended site. Be realistic; otherwise, the outcome might be both depressing and expensive.

Basic planting shapes

Consider the space that you wish to fill with a container. What plants will be most suitable for your chosen location, and which shape of container will show them off to their best advantage—as well as accommodate the way they grow?

SHAPING UP YOUR CONTAINER

- *When considering a container at a nursery, take it to the plant section to try out various combinations before committing yourself. Too many of us buy plants and pots separately instead of first seeing them together.*
- *Trust your own eye and sense of design. If you are unsure, try sketching your intended plant shape with the shape of your container to get an idea of whether they'll work together.*
- *For visual excitement, contrast the shape and texture of the plant to that of the container. For example, put a round-headed standard bay tree, Laurus nobilis, in a square Versailles box, or try a spiky, succulent agave in a round, polished metal container.*

It is essential to know your preferred plant's habit—whether, for instance, it is upright or trailing—and its likely eventual size and height. As a first step, check the label details attached to the plant you're thinking of purchasing (and consult the directory at the back of this book). One of the container gardener's most valuable skills is the ability to visualize a display's growing stages through to maturity. The eventual shape should be harmonious both with the intended pot and its surroundings.

Right pot, right plant, right shape

To achieve a sense of balance and proportion, it is useful to be aware of basic planting shapes. On the next pages are key planting shape outlines to guide you.

Matching plant and container
When choosing plants for a container, trust your eye and go with what looks best. These aggressive-looking architectural plants look perfectly at home in the heavy geometric shaped container that has been chosen for them.

Tall

A tall container demands attention. The height can make a modern, stylish statement and works well with a neat topiaried shape. A tall container such as a Grecian urn on a plinth can bring height and interest to an otherwise flat garden and is ideal for decorative trailing plants. It also allows for aromatic and fragrant plants to be lifted for better impact.

Rectangular

The typical shape for window boxes and troughs is a rectangle. For a long trough or window box, it is best to have symmetry to the planting, however formal or informal, to avoid a lopsided look. Abundant colorful planting will soften the lines into an informal and relaxed display.

Oval

Rounded shapes create a mood of informality, calm, and stability. When choosing a container for a central position, a round pot would work especially well. Choose plants with a relaxed symmetrical habit, so that the pot will look good from every angle.

Plant and container ideas

- Tall terra-cotta container planted with ball-shaped boxwood (*Buxus* spp.) (*above*)
- *Stipa tenuissima* (a.k.a. *Nassella tenuissima*) in a tall, sloping, galvanized-metal container
- *Lilium regale* in a terra-cotta long-tom
- Cardoon (*Cynara cardunculus*) and 'Lady Plymouth' scented geranium (*Pelargonium* spp.) in a stone Grecian urn on a plinth

- A window box display draped with pink and purple petunias, geraniums, blue convolvulus, pinkish-mauve lobelia, and brachycome (*above*)
- Boxwood ball (*Buxus* spp.), cyclamen, viola, and trailing ivy in a wooden window box
- *Pennisetum orientale* 'Karley Rose'—a fountain grass in a contemporary galvanized-metal trough
- Purple cabbage, French marigolds (*Tagetes patula*), and nasturtiums in a stone trough

- Container with *Heuchera* 'Silver scrolls', American alumroot (*Heuchera americana*), and black mondo grass (*Ophiopogon planiscapus* 'Nigrescens') (*above*)
- Dwarf Japanese maple (*Acer palmatum* 'Atropurpureum') in a glazed oriental container
- Groups of round-leaved hostas (*Hosta tokudama*) and wavy-leaved hostas (*H. undulata*) in rounded terra-cotta pots
- Blue fescue (*Festuca glauca*) in an oval, polished-metal container

Flat

Shallow pots are best observed from above, so use plants that look best when viewed that way. Place them near the house where they can be appreciated up close. Wide and shallow pots are particularly good for displaying low-level plants that do not require much soil for their roots.

Fan-shaped

With this most traditional container shape, the lines of the pot are continued by the spreading habit of the plant. Make sure the display does not become too top-heavy, either visually or otherwise, as it will be in danger of becoming unstable.

Bell-shaped

Choose plants with mound-forming foliage and upright flowers for height and trailing foliage and flowers to soften the edges. Save money also by buying a cheaper container for this display, since most of it will be hidden from view.

Plant and container ideas (continued)

- Sempervivums in a wide and shallow terra-cotta dish (above)

- Variegated lemon thyme (Thymus citriodorus 'Variegata'), planted with Iris reticulata and yellow crocus bulbs in a low wooden container

- Thrift (Armeria spp.), moss phlox (Phlox subulata), and Saxifraga spp. planted in gravel in a stone sink

- Osteospermum and Heuchera 'Plum Pudding' in a low container

- An assortment of alpine plants such as cranesbill and gentians in a stone trough

- Small narcissi and Anemone blanda

- Block planting of saxifrages

- Marguerite (Argyranthemum spp.) in a terra-cotta pot (above)

- Clipped boxwood ball (Buxus spp.) in a traditional terra-cotta container

- Oxeye daisy (Leucanthemum vulgare), Anthemis tinctoria 'Sauce Hollandaise', Geranium himalayense 'Plenum', cordyline, and purple petunias in an oak half barrel

- Sweet fennel (Foeniculum vulgare) in a half wooden barrel

- Curry plant (Helichrysum italicum)

- Fan palm (Chamaerops humilis)

- Heuchera 'Cappuccino', Hedera helix 'Light Fingers', and black mondo grass (Ophiopogon planiscapus 'Nigrescens') in a terra-cotta container (above)

- Marguerites, osteospermums, petunias, verbenas, and gray-leaved licorice plant (Helichrysum petiolare) in a wicker basket lined with plastic

- Variegated ivy, Pelargoniums, trailing fuchsia, bush fuchsia, and lime-green-leaved licorice plant (Helichrysum petiolare) in a hanging basket

- Strawberries in terra-cotta pots

Architectural

Architectural plants such as ferns and palms are best planted on their own so that their distinctive shapes are shown to their advantage. Sharp angles also look more edgy and modern and can be well complemented by the sharp angles of succulents and cacti. Use them as a focal point.

Freestyle

Break all the rules, and try something new and exciting that will bring vitality and quirkiness to your garden. It might be a modular geometric shape; a shiny, cast-iron texture; or a combination of materials such as treated oak with polished decorative stone. Alternatively, you can recycle containers to create cheap and easy planters out of virtually anything—old paint cans, wicker baskets, large olive oil cans, and even old wheelbarrows. If the reused pot looks too garish, hide it by growing trailers. If it looks good, complement it with an upright plant that will not detract from the pot.

- *Agave americana* in a polished stainless-steel container (*above*)
- Topiaried plants such as yew (*Taxus* spp.) or boxwood (*Buxus* spp.) in a Cretan clay pot
- Cordyline in a terra-cotta pot
- Bamboo in a rubbed zinc trough

- Copper cone container with dwarf Japanese maple (*Acer palmatum dissectum* 'Crimson Queen') (*above*)
- Single echeveria in large seashell
- Colorful tulips in a child's seaside bucket
- A thick rope or chain coiled to hide an inner pot

- An old wheelbarrow makes an excellent container for growing vegetables (*above*)
- Potatoes in an old garbage bin
- Strawberry plants growing in a recycled chimney pot
- Tomato plant in a recycled potting mix bag
- Drought-resistant sempervivum, variegated London pride (*Saxifraga* spp.), and sedum growing in kitchen castoffs
- Thyme or oregano in old galvanized watering cans

Using color

Everyone has a favorite color—you need only look in your own closet for proof. Of course, not everyone will share your taste, and the same goes for container plants. But whatever your personal preferences, you want to make the most of your chosen color scheme.

PLANT COLOR TIPS

- *Purple and mauve are the most versatile of colors. For example, Verbena bonariensis goes well with more or less everything.*
- *The most difficult colors to blend are orange, salmon, and pink. So use with care.*
- *For a more sophisticated and contemporary color scheme, use lime greens and acid yellows such as lady's mantle (Alchemilla mollis) or Euphorbia × martinii instead of warm yellow.*
- *Always try to use colors that suit the season.*
- *In the bleak winter months, do not underestimate the color contribution that berries, bark, and twigs can make to containers.*
- *If you are only using a single-color scheme, introduce different shades of that color in both foliage and flower for extra interest (see mauve-themed planting, page 26).*
- *Use containers with plenty of green foliage to cool hot colors (see opposite page).*

Color is a highly personal choice, especially when choosing plants for containers. Someone favoring a mauve and pale yellow display might view your orange and purple pots with alarm, but these are your containers, and they are there to please you and not your neighbors. Just bear in mind that you want to avoid ending up with a strident and unattractive clash of colors or shades inappropriate for their surroundings. By understanding certain well-tried-and-tested rules, you can avoid those pitfalls and use flower colors that bring out the best in each other and their settings. With a simple grasp of color harmonies and contrasts, you will confidently try out new and exciting combinations of plants.

Color wheel

To understand how to put certain colors next to others, study the color wheel (see image), a concept used by artists. Colors can be divided into sections. First come the three primary colors—red, blue, and yellow. These colors do not share common pigments and are the purest form of color. When these colors are combined, they produce other colors: Red and blue mixed become purple; blue and yellow produce green; yellow and red create orange. These colors are known as secondary colors.

Using the color wheel

As a gardener, understanding and applying the basic color principles illustrated by the artist's color wheel will enable you to select colors that not only work well together but are in keeping with your desired look.

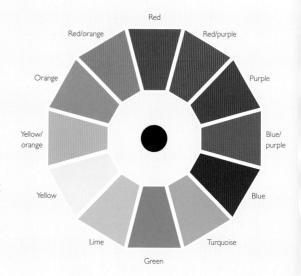

Red
Red/orange
Red/purple
Orange
Purple
Yellow/orange
Blue/purple
Yellow
Blue
Lime
Turquoise
Green

LEFT: **Shades of violet and blues**
Terra-cotta spring containers with *Crocus tommasinianus* 'Whitewell Purple' and *C.* 'Flower Record' with *Iris reticulata* 'Harmony' behind show that colors close together on the color wheel harmonize well. The yellow daffodils enhance the complementary mauve of the irises.

GO GREEN

BORROW FROM NATURE

Look around your natural environment for color schemes and flower combinations. This will not only help you harmonize your containers with the natural environment outside your garden but also attract bees, butterflies, and other pollinators indigenous to your area.

Complementary colors

The most harmonious, safest colors are the analogous colors that share pigments and sit near each other on the color wheel. The pigments that are diametrically opposed are the most contrasting, such as yellow and purple. These are called complementary colors. English landscape painter John Constable always placed a little piece of red to heighten the green in his landscapes. The French Impressionists used complementary colors in much the same way, strategically placing tiny dots of mauve to make yellow appear more brilliant. By putting complementary colors together, you too can create vibrant combinations that are easy on the eye.

Hot colors

Hot colors such as red, orange, and pink demand attention and bring glamour to the garden. Most hot-colored flowers are sun lovers and look their best in bright light. However, they can be unrestful and constricting in a small space. For a really eye-catching effect, choose two or three closely harmonizing hot colors (for example, red, orange, and yellow), and then add a complementary hue from the opposing end of the spectrum (such as blue) and watch those colors zing. Try not to place pastel colors next to bright colors, however, as they will disappear into insignificance alongside their showier cousins.

ABOVE: **Blues to purple**
Combine flowers of complementary colors in the same pot. The orange of the tulips is vividly accentuated by the violet-blue underplanting in these unusual floating containers.

ABOVE: **Hot-colored terrace**
A striking display of hot-colored plants stands tall in these terra-cotta containers: *Canna* 'King Humbert', *C.* 'Wyoming', *Dahlia* 'Grenadier', and *D.* 'David Howard'. The blue windows and lighter blue paving behind provide a soothing contrast. This display also highlights a useful tip: Unless you want a hot-colored container to be a focal point, try to keep vibrant displays close to the house.

CONTAINER
COLOR TIPS

• *Harmonize your containers with your house and garden color schemes.*

• *Play it safe: Terra-cotta looks good with most colors.*

• *Reflective and silver-leaved plants look particularly effective in contemporary metal containers.*

• *Choose colored glazes that enhance rather than dominate (see chapter on containers).*

• *If you are going to buy a colored container or paint your own pot, make sure it works well with your chosen planting scheme.*

• *If you want your planting scheme to dominate, use the more natural "old style" colors, as opposed to bright, modern, synthetic colors. The color wheel principles still apply (see page 22).*

Green and gray combined
A contemporary courtyard garden in which the predominantly gray panels, terrace, pond, and black containers are perfectly accented by the *Festuca glauca* 'Blue Glow' and other foliage plants. The overall effect is peace and tranquillity.

Cool and pastel colors

Pastel colors, including creams and white, may be easier to work with. Unlike hot colors, random mixes of cool colors will nearly always harmonize well. On a warm summer's evening, there is nothing more pleasurable than relaxing on the terrace surrounded by pots filled with fragrant lavenders and white-and-pink-striped *Lilium regale*. The colors are restful on the eye, and the white flowers will continue their magical, luminous glow long after the sun has set.

Soft colors

Soft colors give an illusion of space and work well in small, enclosed gardens or shady corners. Choose pastel colors that sit close together on the color wheel for a harmonious display. A pastel color of a complementary hue will add a stylish and sophisticated accent. Combine different shades of the same color, such as mauve and purple.

Foliage

Foliage often plays as important a part of the display as the flowers themselves. Sometimes it provides a foil for flowers to be shown off at their best; at other times, it can be the focal attraction itself. Soft gray-green foliage can cool a hot display of flowers, while sharp acid greens make hot colors even more vibrant. Evergreen foliage adds a formal note. Plants with dark, richly colored foliage can add a bold and agreeable note to any garden by creating depth and drama as well as a calming effect on the brighter, hot-colored flowers.

Dark-colored plants also go well with the more contemporary galvanized metal and glazed bronze containers. However, too many dark containers can be oppressive. They should be used sparingly in a small garden or as a backdrop for silvery or brighter foreground plantings. Silver foliage is far more restful on the eye than the darker colors and gives the illusion of space, especially on a patio. Shades of pink are particularly harmonious with both silver and purple foliage. When designing a foliage-only container, follow the rules and principles of the color wheel just as you would for a color planting with flowers.

Mauve-themed planting
An old white enamel bowl is a perfect receptacle for this mauve-themed planting of mixed petunias, fuchsia, lobelia, and *Isotoma*. These pretty mauve flowers of the same hue harmonize well but are saved from being too monotonous by the addition of the dark purple petunia and the pale mauve lobelia.

Color in action

Burgundy

STAR PLANT:
Ajuga
'Burgundy glow'

Description: The rounded dark burgundy leaves of the ajuga contrast beautifully with the fresh vibrant green and yellow sword-shaped leaves of the *Iris pseudacorus* 'Variegata'. Both plants prefer semishade and a moist soil.

Season of interest: The ajuga has evergreen foliage and produces pretty spikes of blue flowers in April and May.

Companion planting: For early and late summer color, plant with *Allium* 'Purple Sensation' and *Nerine bowdenii*.

Other great burgundies: *Heuchera* 'Plum Pudding', *Helleborus orientalis*, *Lilium nepalense*, *Tulipa* 'Burgundy'

Red

STAR PLANT:
Camellia japonica
'Barbara Morgan'

Description: The sumptuous bright red flowers with their intense yellow stamens contrast beautifully with the dark, glossy, evergreen leaves of this potted camellia.

Season of interest: The attractive foliage provides year-round interest, which is particularly useful in winter. The beautiful jewel-like flowers in spring are a bonus.

Companion planting: The hardy soft shield fern *Polystichum setiferum* 'Pulcherrimum Bevis' goes well as does the snowdrop *Galanthus* 'Atkinsii'.

Other great reds: *Dahlia* 'Grenadier', *Crocosmia* 'Lucifer', red-twigged *Cornus alba* 'Sibirica', and *Imperata cylindrica* 'Rubra'

Orange

STAR PLANT:
Acer palmatum

Description: Known as Japanese maple (of which there are over 400 varieties), *Acer palmatum* is a small, hardy, deciduous tree with many dwarf cultivars that are ideal for containers. The *Acer palmatum* var. *dissectum* 'Atropurpureum' Group and *Acer palmatum* 'Osakazuki' both have brilliant orange and crimson foliage and are very well suited to planters.

Season of interest: In fall its leaves turn glorious shades of red, scarlet, orange, and yellow.

Companion planting: Best on its own, but looks great next to *Iris sibirica*, hostas, and oriental plants such as hakone grass (*Hakonechloa macra*).

Other great oranges: 'Fiesta Gitana' pot marigolds (*Calendula officinalis*), 'Alaska' nasturtiums, and 'Golden Bunch' crocuses (*Crocus ancyrensis*)

Yellow

STAR PLANT:
Tulipa 'West Point'

Description: The yellow of these spring tulips in a decorated terra-cotta container is highlighted by the complementary mauve-blue of the forget-me-nots (*Myosotis sylvatica*) that are grown as companions.

Season of interest: Spring

Companion planting: *Erysimum* 'Primrose Monarch', dark blue or mauve pansies such as *Viola* 'Blue Blotch', as well as blue fescue grass.

Other great yellows: Citron daylily (*Hemerocallis citrina*), *Argyranthemum* 'Jamaica Primrose', *Petunia* 'Prism Sunshine', *Helianthus* 'Teddy Bear', and *Crocus* 'Romance'

Color in action *(continued)*

Green

STAR PLANT:

Nicotiana 'Lime Green'

Description: The fragrant *Nicotiana* 'Lime Green' is planted here in a terra-cotta pot with golden Creeping jenny (*Lysimachia nummularia* 'Aurea') and 'Limelight' licorice plant (*Helichrysum petiolare* 'Limelight').

The subtle pastel hues of green foliage and flowers are very soothing on the eye. This is a good example of colors that sit closely together on the color wheel being especially harmonious.

Season of interest: Summer

Companion planting: *Cordyline australis*, a crimson *Pelargonium* variety such as 'Paul Crampel', or as underplanting for tall *Nicotiana sylvestris*

Other great greens (flowers): Pineapple lily (*Eucomis bicolor*) and *Zinnia elegans* 'Envy'

Blue

STAR PLANT:

Blue grape hyacinths
Muscari armeniacum

Description: A white, oval, enamel kitchen bowl neatly offsets the blue grape hyacinths (*Muscari armeniacum*). The true primary blue of the grape hyacinths is highlighted by the complementary yellow narcissus in the background.

Season of interest: Midspring

Companion planting: *Narcissus* 'Tête-à-tête', cowslips (*Primula veris*), lesser periwinkle (*Vinca minor*), and *Fritillaria pyrenaica*

Other great blues: *Clematis* 'Perle d'Azur', *Hyacinthus orientalis* 'Delft Blue' or *H.* 'King Codro', and *Convolvulus sabatius*. Also *Lobelia erinus* 'Riviera Sky Blue', and *Campanula* 'Takion Blue'

Purple

STAR PLANT:

Deep purple iris
Iris spp.

Description: The velvety texture and rich color of deep purple bearded irises, such as *Iris* 'Matinata' or *I.* 'Titan's Glory', are well-suited to a large barrel-shape container. The flowers are saved from being too somber by the pastel gray-green of the foliage. Try mixing with orange and acid-green foliage and flowers for a punchy effect.

Season of interest: Early summer

Companion planting: Blue oatgrass (*Helictotrichon sempervirens*), *Euphorbia griffithii*, *Heuchera* 'Plum Pudding'

Other great purples: Alliums, *Geranium wallichianum* 'Buxton's Variety', *Verbena bonariensis*, 'Ping Tung Long' eggplant, *Sempervivum* 'Purple Queen', and *Viola* 'Penny Violet Flare'

Mauve

STAR PLANT:

Lavandula stoechas 'Papillon'

Description: Mauve is the gentlest of all the colors, and this French lavender, with its gray-green aromatic foliage, must be one of the most soothing and delightful shrubs available for the container garden.

Season of interest: June through July, when the flower heads will attract a mass of nectar-loving insects

Companion planting: Try underplanting olive and bay, or grow next to other aromatic plants such as purple sage or the curry plant (*Helichrysum italicum*).

Other great mauves: *Erysimum* 'Bowles' Mauve', *Lobelia erinus* 'Waterfall Light Lavender'

Pink

STAR PLANT:
Cyclamen coum

Description: An attractive stone sink container shows off the bright feminine fuchsia pink of some of these cyclamen. They are nicely softened by the paler variety. The two pink hues are also reflected in the variegated gray-green leaves, which harmonize well with the flowers.

Season of interest: Spring

Companion planting: Blue and purple crocuses, *Primula* 'Miss Indigo', and echeverias

Other great pinks: *Gladiolus communis* ssp. *byzantinus*, *Osteospermum jucundum*, and bleeding hearts (*Dicentra* spp.)

White

STAR PLANT:
Agapanthus

Description: The pure white flowers of this elegant agapanthus contrast spectacularly against the dark green foliage of the yew hedge in the background. Though you might think it best to buy a lovely big pot at the outset, agapanthus plants flower best when their roots almost completely fill the container.

Season of interest: Late summer

Companion planting: Best grown on its own, but place against *Crocosmia* 'Lucifer', *Nicotiana sylvestris*, hedged boxwood, or lavender.

Other great whites: White snapdragons (*Antirrhinum majus*) and *Lavatera trimestris* 'Mont Blanc'

Black

STAR PLANT:
Viola 'Molly Sanderson'

Description: This is one of the few plants to have nearly black flowers, making it unusual and eye-catching. It has a neat but slightly trailing habit and so works best on its own, especially as the tiny flowers can get lost in a mixed color scheme. To enhance the deep-purple flower color, try placing near yellow planting schemes; this will also echo the vibrant yellow "eye" of this jewel-like viola.

Season of interest: Early summer

Companion planting: Trailing verbena 'Tapien Violet' and golden creeping jenny (*Lysimachia nummularia* 'Aurea')

Other great blacks: *Iris chrysographes*, black mondo grass (*Ophiopogon planiscapus* 'Nigrescens'), and *Aeonium* 'Zwartkop'

Brown

STAR PLANT:
Carex buchananii

Description: Mix all the colors on the color wheel and you will produce the most under-rated color of all—brown. It is probably the most natural of colors, and instead of identifying it with dead and dying plants, we should learn to appreciate its wide and subtle range of tones. These sit in perfect harmony with the natural environment and cycle of life. Brown comes in many shades, from pale beige to a dark walnut brown, and is beautifully expressed in most of the ornamental grasses, such as leather leaf sedge grown here in a metal container.

Season of interest: Late summer; fall

Companion planting: *Verbena bonariensis* and *Helenium autumnale* 'Moerheim Beauty'

Other great browns: *Panicum virgatum* and *Acer griseum*

Texture

Visually, plants can offer a huge range of textures—from the soft, furry velvet of lamb's ears to the sharp prickles of cacti. A pot planted for texture alone can be the ultimate expression in container sophistication.

PLANT LIST

Agave	Spiky
Boxwood	Neat
Cacti	Prickly
Cannas	Waxy
Ferns	Feathery
Grasses	Silky
Lamb's ears	Velvety
Moss	Soft
Poppies	Papery
Succulents	Fleshy

It's all too easy to associate container gardening with lavish displays of colorful flowers. And why not? Color cheers. But color alone can be indigestible—rather like too much fast food. As the container gardener gains more experience and confidence, the delights of foliage and texture become more important and pleasing than an abundance of color.

Try juxtaposing textures to create visual excitement. Or use similar textures together—spiky for energy and rounded for a more relaxed look. Leaf size is important, too. Combine the stiff, straplike leaves of the cordyline with the light, frothy fronds of the maidenhair fern, or the fleshy round hummocks of sempervivums with the shiny narrow leaves of black mondo grass for a stunning display.

Texture is not just confined to the plant but applies to the container, too. Try contrasting textures—rough with smooth, shiny with matte, and so on.

Some textures are visually stimulating and also provide a sensual treat for touching. Try patting a soft mound of moss before the spring bulbs push their leaves through or stroking the fuzzy velvet of lamb's ears (*Stachys byzantina*). A tall ornamental grass grown on its own is almost like fireworks exploding out of the earth, and who can resist running their fingers through the silky stalks?

LEFT: **Soft and velvety**
Tiny standard lavender bushes grow side by side in square containers on a leaded window sill. The soft, downy moss provides a miniature landscape from which the small lavender standards emerge. It's almost impossible to pass a pot covered with moss without stopping to give it a soothing pat. Gathering moss from the woods will deprive invertebrates of their natural habitat, so why not use the recipe provided (*right*) to make your own?

LEFT: **Long and spiky**
This spiky *Dasylirion glaucophyllum* explodes from its well-proportioned container, contrasting boldly with the smooth, fleshy leaves of the surrounding succulents.

BELOW: **Prickly and smooth**
A tableau of terra-cotta containers planted with dwarf pine and grasses enhances the decking in a seaside garden. The contrasting soft needles of the pine, silky stalks of the grasses, and chalky smoothness of the terra-cotta pots create a visually exciting grouping.

GO GREEN

MAKE YOUR OWN MOSS

Try this recipe for growing moss in or on a container for a natural look.
1 Put a handful of desired moss into a kitchen blender (get rid of unwanted dirt first).
2 Add half a teaspoon of white sugar or buttermik and a can of beer.
3 Briefly blend, then spread the pureed mixture over the area where you want the moss to grow—either on the container itself or on rocks placed on the top of the container.
4 Keep it out of the sun, and keep it moist by very gently spraying with distilled water.

Sharp and firm
An arrangement of *Pachyveria* 'Glauca' succulents embedded in gravel mulch makes a formal composition in a contemporary metal container. The neat order creates an assured, stylish statement. The pointed, smooth rosettes of leaves are contrasted by the gritty mulch and echoed in the rounded pebbles reflected in the polished metal container.

High-impact containers

The only way to create a dramatic container is to be brave and think big. It pays to be bold when planning your container garden—after all, most gardens benefit from a design statement. This display will be a focal point, talking piece, and star attraction in your garden. A favorite plant combination in a container will draw attention to itself rather than get lost in the hurly-burly of the flower bed.

6 RECIPES FOR: Planting

PLANT LIST

Brugmansia *spp.*
Cannas
Cordyline
Dahlias
Dicksonia antarctica
Fatsia japonica
Lilium longiflorum
Melianthus major
Miscanthus sinensis
  'Morning Light'
Phormium

1 Simple and striking

This purple glazed container is planted with *Allium giganteum*. These alliums thrive in full sun. Plant the bulbs in fall for an impressive showing in early summer. They will need a well-drained soil mix with extra sand or grit. These alliums can reach up to 5 feet tall, and, if you are lucky, you can get away without staking. The more you plant, the more they will support each other. Try also to keep the container sheltered from the wind. When the flowering is over, let the foliage die back naturally so that it will flower again next year.

LEFT: **Purple glazed container planted with *Allium giganteum***
The tallest of alliums make a stunning focal point. They look particularly stunning when planted with ornamental grasses or used as part of a Mediterranean planting scheme. Containers can be planted with spring bulbs through which the alliums can emerge for an early summer flowering.

LEFT: **Unusual companions**
An exciting and eccentric combination of two spectacular grasses: potted Japanese blood grass, *Imperata cylindrica* 'Rubra', with black mondo grass, *Ophiopogon planiscapus* 'Nigrescens'.

HIGHLIGHTING YOUR CONTAINER

- Placing the container is key: Try to position it where pointers, such as paths, walls, and pergolas, will lead the eye toward it.
- If your container is small, use a plinth to give it height.
- If you are going for a large display, avoid using narrow-based containers that might be unstable when it is windy.
- Spend as much as you can afford on a really spectacular or stylish container made of high-quality materials.
- Large terra-cotta pots, Versailles boxes, and Grecian urns all lend themselves particularly well to dramatic plantings and in themselves create visual impact.
- If you decide on single-specimen, use plants that have a distinctive shape.
- If you have neither the large pot nor confidence to go big, try staging groups of smaller pots in tiers so together they make a unified whole.
- There are many creative ways to customize a container—for example, painting the pot the same color as your front door.

2 Over the top

Potted Japanese blood grass, *Imperata cylindrica* 'Rubra', is combined with black mondo grass, *Ophiopogon planiscapus* 'Nigrescens'. This spectacular combination thrives in well-drained, moist, and fertile potting mix. The plants prefer full sun but will put up with a little shade. Do not cut back in the winter, as they will continue to give structural interest. Place where the late summer sun can light up the beautiful red leaves of the Japanese blood grass.

3 Classic and calm

Annuals in large stone decorative containers. Appropriately restrained but pretty planting of annuals will show off gorgeous cast stone urns to their best advantage, without the distraction of excessive foliage and flowers.

4 Authoritative and statuesque

An impressive container topiary display of boxwood, with fall plants including cyclamen, is featured in this public garden. While it may be overly formal for a home landscape, it shows the classic "mother hen and chicks" grouping. The boxwood ball containers alternate with pots of cyclamen and grasses, adding color and texture to the formality of the arrangement. The centered topiaried boxwood has been planted in a large terra-cotta pot to give extra height and authority.

LEFT: **Standing guard**
Topiary display of *Buxus*—boxwood with fall planting including cyclamen.

ABOVE: **Show-off**
A splendid brugmansia makes an impact in this terrace setting. Be warned: The plant is toxic, so pets and young children should be kept away.

5 Big and bold

The container-grown brugmansia demands attention with its exotic fragrant flowers. This tender species needs sun as well as fertile, well-drained soil. For best flowering results, use potting mix high in nitrogen.

6 Stage and set design

If you cannot afford or have no access to big containers, try creating a theater with small potted plants using old seats, shelves, and small ladders to create a tiered effect. Put the taller plants at the back.

Single-species planting

Single-species planting in containers is the essence of formal and contemporary design. In addition to making a bold statement, it allows the foliage, flowers, and form of the plant to be fully appreciated.

PLANT LIST

Flowers
Agapanthus
Lilium regale
Tulips

Foliage
Ferns
Hostas
Phormium
Tree ferns

Shrubs
Boxwood
Hydrangea

Grasses
Bamboos
Ornamental grasses

Trees
Dwarf mugo pine
Japanese maple

The effect looks particularly good when repeated in rows or pairs, creating an instantly sophisticated visual rhythm. The best plants for single-species planting have strong architectural form and distinctive character and look attractive from every angle. A single-species planting need not be confined to larger plants. Smaller species of plants such as cyclamen, sempervivum, thyme, and allium look marvelous when grown in blocks. Delicate fall and spring bulbs are often overshadowed by showier companions.

When planted in shallow bowls, they can be positioned to make maximum impact and be fully appreciated. Have fun, too, by placing bowls together as you experiment with color combinations.

LEFT: **Fresh white** Petunia 'Conchita Blossom White' looks great underplanted with standard roses, and is also perfect for covering an unattractive pot.

Hints and Tips

• Plants with particularly fibrous roots, such as lilies and agapanthus, positively prefer to be grown on their own.
• Plants that spread by root runners or grow too large for the smaller garden (such as phormiums) can be contained in pots.

GO GREEN

Petunias have to be one of the easiest annuals to grow. Their neat, rounded habit covers pots and hanging baskets, and they are a magnet for hummingbirds, butterflies, and bees.

6 SEASONAL Single-planting schemes

Spring

TULIPS

Tulipa 'Ballerina'

Description: The reddish-orange, lily-flowered *Tulipa* 'Ballerina' looks most impressive in a container when densely planted in a block. It can grow up to 22 inches. Another stunning orange tulip is *Tulipa* 'Prinses Irene', which is streaked with red and hints of purple and green and grows to 12 to 14 inches.

Setting: For maximum effect, place pots where flower heads will be set off by the complementary blues of forget-me-nots (*Myosotis sylvatica*) or the acid greens and yellows of background flowers and foliage. A stunning example is *Euphobia × martinii*.

Container: A galvanized metal container with handles lends a contemporary feel and is practical as well.

Tip: Plant tulip bulbs densely, with as many as 15 bulbs in each pot, in the fall or early winter.

Early summer

LEMON BALM

Melissa officinalis 'Aurea'

Description: In early summer, this terra-cotta pot planted with variegated lemon balm (*Melissa officinalis* 'Aurea') creates a fragrant focal point that looks good from every angle. It grows from 24 to 48 inches.

Setting: Place the plant where you will brush against it—the leaves smell strongly of lemon when touched.

Container: Ideally suited to a kitchen or herb garden, lemon balm looks best planted in a classic terra-cotta pot.

Tip: Pour boiling water over a few picked leaves to make a relaxing herbal tea.

GO GREEN

The tiny white flowers of lemon balm will attract bees and other insects.

Seasonal single-planting schemes *(continued)*

Summer

AGAPANTHUS
Agapanthus 'Purple Cloud'

Description: Agapanthus always look best grown on their own; besides, the tough fibrous roots inhibit the growth of companions. They are particularly eye-catching when planted in rows of containers on a paved surface. This *Agapanthus* 'Purple Cloud' will flower from August to September and requires a sunny south-facing site. It can grow up to 35 inches in height.

Setting: Coming from South Africa, they love the sun.

Container: These containers give the plants height and status, but beware—the roots can crack a poorly made pot.

Tip: In cold areas, mulch containers well over the winter, and place them in a frost-free place such as a shed or greenhouse.

Late summer

MEXICAN SAGE
Salvia leucantha

Description: Such a stunning profusion will get everyone guessing as to its identity. This is in fact the graceful Mexican sage (*Salvia leucantha*). It flowers in late summer and fall and is extremely easy to grow, being both drought and pest tolerant. It reaches between 2 and 4 feet in height and about the same width.

Setting: Full sun is best; otherwise, the plant might get leggy.

Container: A tall container allows for the plant's natural draping over the sides.

Tip: Prune back in early summer to promote bushier growth. Allow plenty of space for summer growth (the flowers bloom in late summer).

GO GREEN

Salvia is a magnet for butterflies and hummingbirds.

Fall

CORNUS
Cornus spp.

Description: Red-twigged dogwoods (*Cornus* spp.) have excellent year-round interest with white flowers in May and leaves that turn red-purple in fall.

Setting: The stems are bright red, and the plant should be placed where it can catch the late fall sun.

Container: This makes a great winter-interest container, with its red shoots especially complementing terra-cotta pots.

Tip: Try mulching with pine needles, as it prefers an acid soil.

Go Green

Dogwoods' berries provide food for birds from summer through to winter.

Winter

TOPIARY
Boxwood

Description: Kangaroos, rabbits, and cockerels have been sculpted using topiary. They add a humorous statement to any terrace and are a terrific conversation starter.

Setting: Sculpted boxwood topiary works best when used as a focal point.

Container: The container shown in this example is the nursery-bought one for transport only. A permanent evergreen plant requires something that will not only lend stability but also be appropriate for its prominent position. A heavy, frost-proof terra-cotta or glazed ceramic pot would make a suitable long-term container.

Tip: Many topiary shrubs prefer a sunny position, but some, like boxwood, will tolerate shade.

Formal planting

The formal garden attempts to create order and beauty with the use of a symmetrical framework and geometric points.

PLANT LIST

Flowers
Lilium regale
Roses
Tulips

Foliage
Hostas

Shrubs
Lavender
Portugese cherry laurel
Privet
Topiaried boxwood
Topiaried yew
Santolina

Trees
Citrus trees
Conifers
Standard bay trees

Climber
Trailing ivy

Formal gardens often feature traditional hard landscaping materials, as well as carefully planned and tended flower beds and containers. Planted containers are an essential part of the formal garden, both to accentuate a formal design and provide that all-important focal point. They can also give an illusion of space when placed in rows along prominent pathways and create a visual rhythm when repeated. Containers might also be utilized to accentuate a geometric pattern—even a circular design— or "carve up" spaces and lead from one area to another. The best types of containers for formal settings tend to be large, old-style, Italianate terra-cotta pots; stone Grecian urns; and wooden Versailles boxes.

Pointers

• Paired containers are particularly effective at giving weight and importance to a feature—from a bench to a front door.
• Try to use containers that are identical or at least of a similar style and material.
• Large containers can be used to frame a particularly attractive view and, in some cases, draw the eye away from an eyesore in a neighboring garden.
• Containers can also be used to mark a change of level in the garden—or tall pots can add height and drama in a flat garden.

Topiary is tops

When it comes to planting, the absolute essence of a formal garden is topiary. Well-pruned boxwood, yew, and privet in containers will create instant formality in any garden, as will aromatic lavender and santolina.

In a formal garden setting, dense evergreen plants such as yew, privet, and boxwood make great cover for protecting the more vulnerable species of wildlife from predators.

CREATING ORDER AND BEAUTY

Large terra-cotta pots planted with the graceful white lily–flowered *Tulipa* 'White Triumphator' direct orderly attention through a pergola and toward a formal yew-hedged archway.

Setting: This elegant tulip looks particularly good not only in formal situations but also in a more natural setting when planted with spring grasses.

Container: Plant the bulbs tightly together in fall in fertile, well-drained potting mix. The plant grows to 24 inches.

Tip: The white tulip flowers stand out well from the dark green foliage behind them. Plant the bulbs 15 or more to a pot for maximum effect.

GIVING THE ILLUSION OF SPACE

This is a classic example of formal positioning of identical containers and plantings to create a visual rhythm.

CREATING A FOCAL POINT

A graceful combination of verbena, lobelia, and petunia cascades from this elegant stone urn, the soft pastel colors harmonizing with the gray of the stone.

GIVING IMPORTANCE AND WEIGHT

The *Stipa tenuissima* (a.k.a. *Nassella tenuissima*) in these terra-cotta containers are sensitive to the slightest breeze. The movement of the grass in the wind cleverly reflects the sway and texture of the water.

Setting: These large decorated terra-cotta pots, planted with clipped boxwood balls, draw attention to a change of levels in the terrace. They also give the illusion of the area being larger and more important than it would otherwise appear.

Container: This type of large terra-cotta pot goes back to antiquity and gives the garden an instant sense of culture and history.

Tip: Boxwood balls in containers look at their best when repeated, creating both harmony and structure.

Setting: Placing the urn on a plinth elevates the container above the surrounding flower beds and creates a commanding focal point. The evergreen hedge in the background provides a perfect backdrop for the delicate floral planting that could be lost in a busier scene.

Container: The height of this urn allows the flowers and foliage to trail gracefully over its edge, keeping them off the ground.

Tip: Placing containers higher makes plantings easier to maintain.

Setting: Formal positioning anchors the design, giving it extra weight and importance.

Container: Wide-bottomed containers give stability as the plants rustle and sway with the wind.

Tip: The seed heads in winter provide a valuable food source for finches and other seed-eating birds.

INSTANT GRANDEUR

HINTS AND TIPS

Try to use containers made out of traditional materials such as marble, slate, and terra-cotta. It's hard to beat a natural, elegant stone urn for instant grandeur.

FRAMING A FOCAL POINT

These containers of *Argyranthemum* on the steps of the Moat Walk at the most famous 20th-century garden in England—Vita Sackville-West's Sissinghurst—not only give importance to the steps but also soften the hard edges of the brick walls behind them.

Setting: The flowers are repeated at the top of the steps to draw attention to the Edwin Lutyens seat.

Container: In a frost-prone area, *Argyranthemum* should be moved to a protected location in winter.

Tip: If you do not have a greenhouse, buy semimature plants at the end of May.

DEFINING A SPACE

Italian-style potted conifers in large terra-cotta containers help define the perimeter of the terrace.

Setting: They add a Tuscan feeling as well as a sense of privacy and security by drawing the eye away from the garden beyond.

Container: It is best when planting conifers in containers to choose those that are drought resistant and cold-hardy (especially the roots), such as 'Skyrocket' Rocky Mountain juniper (*Juniperus scopulorum* 'Skyrocket'). Even then, you may need to insulate the containers with straw or a horticultural fleece.

Tip: Choose conifers that have a compact habit for container growing to avoid frequent pruning. Columnar conifers in containers break up awkward spaces and add height and structure to any design.

CREATING FORMALITY

Small pots of boxwood stand beside a larger, formal, lead cistern container planted with a garland of ivy and a *Ligustrum* standard.

Setting: The formal arrangement is somewhat spoiled by its inappropriate placement in front of a window.

Container: It is best to give a container of this size and weight a permanent location. Placing smaller pots around this ornate water tank helps soften its otherwise dominating appearance.

Tip: A large container will allow you to plant a shrub or small tree that would not ordinarily thrive in your soil type, such as an acid-loving blueberry in a location where soil pH is naturally high.

Informal planting

Informal container gardening is relaxed and fun. There's no need to agonize about what container to use—anything that holds enough soil and is relatively attractive will do.

PLANT LIST

Annuals
Annual flowers
Pelargoniums
Trailers
Vegetables

Foliage and perennials
Cacti and sempervivums
Grasses
Herbs and
* aromatic plants*
Wildflowers and
* native species*

Trees and shrubs
Climbers
Fruiting shrubs
* and plants*
Olive trees

GO GREEN

An unkempt garden is undoubtedly better for attracting wildlife than an orderly one. Wild patches are especially valuable for nesting bumblebees—all the more important as their population has been in decline for the past 50 years.

One of the great pleasures of gardening is the spontaneous purchase of a desirable or intriguing plant at a roadside stand or farmers' market, and then rummaging around at home for something to plant it in—an old wooden crate, perhaps, or even an unused log basket. Old farm buckets, worn-out cowboy boots, rusty wheelbarrows, empty wholesale olive oil cans, and even creaking rowboats can be converted into containers. Anything goes. Of course, your choice may not be to everyone's taste, but if it allows you to feel that very elemental joy of growing plants—and to express your creativity—then does it really matter? And, of course, it saves money and recycles old items just lying around.

Informal groupings

However informal, there should be some kind of structure in the way containers are placed. If they're just randomly plunked down, they'll look chaotic. A very effective look is the "mother hen and chicks" grouping, with small pots grouped around a central large one. Try to keep a rhythm as you place your pots. "Rhythm" doesn't necessarily mean straight lines; it could be found in meandering curves.

Unlike the more restrained order of the formal garden, the informal garden can be a riot of color and plant combinations. For instance, why not mix herbs with flowers, and grow vegetables by the kitchen door? When fall comes and the flowering is over, leave the old flower spikes so that the birds can eat the seeds.

USING A RECYCLED CONTAINER

If you cannot lose it, use it! Cottage garden-style flowers, planted in wooden window boxes attached to the doors, have transformed this unsightly old auto.

Setting: This retro car creates a haven for wildlife, providing shelter and protection.

Container: This is the ultimate recycled container.

Tip: A less junky recycled container possibility is a burlap coffee bag. If you can get one from a coffee shop it's a lightweight and attractive way to add recycled gardening space to your yard.

GROUPING A "MOTHER HEN AND CHICKS"

Here's a classic example of a "mother hen and chicks" grouping of winter pots.

MIXING FLOWERS AND HERBS

This cottage garden is packed full of flowers, fruit, and vegetables in rustic containers. There is 'Tom Thumb' lettuce in an old saucepan and sweet basil in a bucket, while onions, Johnny-jump-ups (*Viola tricolor*), calendula, and purple Brussels sprouts fill other assorted pots.

CREATING A HEAVY METAL BASKET CASE

This metal basket holds echeveria, the most tolerant of all container plants. Echeverias can withstand long periods of neglect.

Setting: Because of their interesting texture and compact habit, these plants are ideal for low-level design.

Container: The metal basket makes a refreshing change and ideal container especially for echeverias, which require a well-drained soil.

Tip: When planted in blocks, the symmetrical blue-green rosettes of echeveria make a particularly attractive container grouping.

Setting: Without the large centered "mother" pot, the other four would be without a sense of purpose and simply look footloose.

Container: The "mother" container is planted up with *Cornus sericea* 'Cardinal' and winter heath (*Erica carnea* 'Winter Snow'), and the "chicks" contain *Carex dipsacea, Heuchera* 'Can Can', *Pinus heldreichii* var. *leucodermis* 'Schmidtii', and winter heath.

Tip: When placing plants in small groups, it is aesthetically preferable to use odd numbers, such as threes and fives.

Setting: This kitchen-garden arrangement is best placed near to the back door for easy pickings when cooking.

Container: This is an attractive way to recycle old kitchen hardware such as saucepans, tin buckets, and colanders.

Tip: Don't forget to drill holes in the bottom of kitchen containers to allow for drainage.

GO GREEN

- An informal container garden, with its vast range of pots and planters, provides living and hibernating habitats for a variety of invertebrates, amphibians, and animals.

- Try not to be too tidy. Don't sweep up leaves and sticks that settle around the containers, as these will provide shelter in the cold winter months. An untidy garden is a welcome home to a wide array of wildlife.

THINKING CREATIVELY ABOUT CONTAINERS

An old white enamel bread bin is filled with a summer blend of pink, purple, and mauve petunias and lobelia, proving that anything can used to grow plants, so long as it can hold soil and has good drainage.

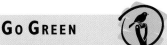

Setting: An upturned log makes an excellent natural plinth, giving the tin container prominence.

Container: A pretty, nostalgic planting echoes a bygone era.

Tip: Tin will rust pretty quickly, so avoid using a container you do not want spoiled.

Go Green

- Look around your natural environment for inspiration and ideas for attracting native wildlife into your garden.
- Grow annuals and wildflowers in pots to attract wildlife.
- Leave in seedlings of attractive self-sown wildflowers rather than weeding them out.

DISPLAYING CONTRASTING SHAPES

This group of terra-cotta containers planted with a variety of colorful tulips, yellow pansies, and grasses provides an especially effective display of contrasting shapes and textures.

Setting: A diverse collection of unglazed terra-cotta pots achieves a sense of unity as a grouping and shows how containers can work well in paved areas. The warm browns provide an excellent foil for the attractive and colorful arrangements.

Container: The large terra-cotta container with pink tulips holds this disparate display of pots together. The contrasting shapes of the plants—the wispiness of the ornamental grass against the rigidity of the tulips—create a visually exciting display.

Tip: If you want to show off an ornate or attractive pot, use a simple plant. If you want show off an interesting or exotic plant, then use a plain container.

CREATING A NATURAL LOOK

This heavily foliaged garden has been fittingly furnished with mostly natural materials, such as the wooden table and container. The planting is tactile and textural—and highly effective in its simplicity.

Setting: Informal within a structured setting, strong posts support a pergola (out of view) that provides shade and hanging basket support.

Container: The moss at the rim of the hollowed-out wooden container borrows from nature and adds a zenlike calm to the setting.

Tip: Ferns and moss will soften a shady softwood setting. Purchase native woodland plants from a reputable nursery—do not collect them from the wild.

Contemporary planting

Contemporary container gardening is a reflection of how we live our lives today—even though the basic principles have changed very little throughout the centuries.

PLANT LIST

Flowers
Agapanthus
Alliums
Cannas
Irises
Lavender
Lilium

Foliage
Bamboo
Ferns
Ornamental grasses
Phormium
Tree fern

Succulents
Agave
Sempervivum

Shrubs
Boxwood

Trees
Birch
Olive tree

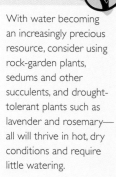

GO GREEN

With water becoming an increasingly precious resource, consider using rock-garden plants, sedums and other succulents, and drought-tolerant plants such as lavender and rosemary—all will thrive in hot, dry conditions and require little watering.

Gardens are no longer either a chore or something to be simply admired from a distance. They have become outdoor extensions of the home—places where people can relax and entertain—with such diverse influences as Moorish courtyards and Japanese Zen gardens. With land at a premium, contemporary gardens often enhance the limited space available with clean lines and lack of clutter. Containers play a pivotal role as stylish accessories, echoing contemporary materials—stainless steel, granite, stone veneer, and wood—found in the modern house. They can also accommodate the vogue for exotic planting.

The principles of placing contemporary containers are not unlike those used in formal container gardening, adhering to repetition, geometry, and use of space. For instance, a line of large, identical, contemporary containers, placed with precise geometry in relation to their surroundings, can create a sense of space, order, and sophistication.

Modern plantings similarly tend to be uncluttered—emphasizing single-specimen plants such as boxwood, phormium, and olives—with special attention given to texture rather than color. Easy-maintenance plants such as sempervivum and ornamental grasses have become popular for those with busy urban lifestyles. Topiary is also favored for a clean, crisp look.

MODERN APPROACHES

HINTS AND TIPS

- To reflect the clean, uncluttered look, use as few varieties of plants as possible.
- Block planting in large containers is highly effective.
- Cover any exposed potting soil with natural materials that are sympathetic to the plant's natural growing habitat—large polished pebbles with agave, for example, or seashells and stones with grasses. This will also act as effective mulch, inhibiting weeds and conserving water.
- Use particularly choice specimen plants that offer something interesting by way of color, texture, or form, such as arctic fern.
- Continue the container theme into the home, if possible.
- Uplighting or spotlighting of architectural plants is particularly effective when viewed in areas for social gatherings, such as patios and roof terraces.
- Swivel casters, found on some modern containers, allow for easy maintenance and portability for impromptu rearrangements.
- Try to relate the materials used in the hard landscaping and garden furniture to that of the containers for a unified look.

PLANTING FOR OUTDOOR LIVING

Large terra-cotta containers planted with boxwood balls are the perfect backdrop for this contemporary dining area. They not only define the space but also give a feel of luxury and sophistication.

Setting: Uplighting draws attention to the formality of the arrangement and creates a welcoming invitation to eat out in the evening.

Container: Note that the size and height of the containers make the terrace appear larger than it really is.

Tip: To avoid the expense and weight of filling a large container with a potting medium, place pieces of Styrofoam or other lightweight fillers in the base beforehand.

CREATING A SENSE OF ORDER

Shallow containers planted with sedums appear to float in an orderly fashion on the water of this contemporary rill.

Setting: Where other plants would wilt in the midday sun, these sedums love the baking-hot seaside setting and soften the modernist water feature.

Container: Because sedums have shallow roots, these elegant, low-level bowls make perfect containers.

Tip: Sedums generally do not need regular watering—once every week or 10 days is enough in drought conditions.

ULTIMATE EASY MAINTENANCE

The *Carex buchananii*
(leather leaf sedge) in this
tire-shaped steel container
is very eye-catching.

Setting: The wispy
explosion of grass provides
a textural counterpoint
to the smooth, shiny
metal container.

Container: This polished
steel container is as much
a rim as a bowl. Despite
being made of modern
material, its shape is inherently organic.

Tip: In nature, plants in the genus *Carex* (sedges) are generally
bog or waterside plants and therefore prefer a moist soil.
Avoid exposure to the hot midday sun.

MULTIPLYING SPIKY NUMBER FOUR

The spiky architectural shapes of *Agave americana* are accentuated
by the mirror image from the water below.

Setting: Placed four in a row, they create a modern linear
arrangement, while the pointed gray-green leaves make a
sculptural statement.

Container: These Cretan pots are similar in form, but, being hand
thrown, each one displays its own distinctive character.

Tip: The seductively curvy leaves of agave can be very sharp, so
either surround them with pots full of softer plants, or place them
where they will not get in way of passersby.

USING CUSTOMIZED CONTAINERS

In the contemporary garden, the container is becoming increasingly
a style statement and even an art form—in some cases, more
important than the planting.

Setting: On this smooth decking surface, these containers
combine style with practicality. The casters allow them to be easily
rearranged for different purposes, such as screening or partitioning.

Container: Sheet metal is particularly versatile, not only because of
its contemporary look, but also because it can be made into many
shapes and sizes.

Tip: Containers filled with sun-loving plants can be easily rolled to
temporarily brighten a shady area.

NATURAL STONE MULCH

Smooth, rounded pebbles contrast beautifully with the rough texture of the olive's bark and the shiny surface of the galvanized metal container.

Setting: The pebbles emulate the natural conditions in which a terraced olive tree would traditionally grow. It all makes for a harmonious combination.

Container: Silver metal containers are especially complementary with plants that have silvery blue-green foliage, such as lavender and olive trees.

Tip: Stone mulches help conserve water and suppress weeds. Try placing either a layer of newspaper or a pierced (for drainage) plastic sheet under the stones for extra protection.

RELAXING GREEN ROOFS

There are thousands of acres of unused rooftops the world over that could be planted and utilized as a natural environment. Sensibly planted containers can attract indigenous wildlife and help counteract air and noise pollution.

Setting: Rooftop containers planted with ornamental grasses create protection and privacy from the outside. They frame desirable views while screening less appealing scenes.

Container: Contemporary metal containers look great, but beware: They can overheat plant roots, especially on an exposed roof terrace where there is little shade (see chapter on containers).

Tip: Planters, especially when watered, can be extremely heavy; before you start placing them on rooftops, seek out the advice of a qualified structural engineer.

GO GREEN

Save money, and put a neglected area with possibly contaminated soil to good use, by growing tasty organic vegetables in containers.

Balconies

The balcony offers an elevated extension of your interior living area. Containers can help create an attractive year-round microenvironment that can be appreciated from both inside and out.

Shoreside balcony
These seaside plants are ideal for exposed balconies. They can cope with the wind and a little bit of neglect. In this bleached-wood container are *Armeria maritima*, saxifrage, sempervivum, and *Veronica teucrium*.

PLANT LIST

Wind-tolerant trees
Hawthorn
Maple

Climbers
Actinidia spp.
Clematis
Crimson Glory Vine
Ivy

Screening
Griselinia littoralis
Holly, evergreen
Hornbeam
Privet

Evergreen shrubs
Boxwood
Hebe 'Autumn Glory'
Inkberry holly
Mexican orange blossom

Perennials
Armeria maritima
Daylilies
Pelargonium

Balconies offer scope for versatility, whether it is urban chic in the middle of the countryside or, conversely, a taste of rural France in the heart of the city. Anything's possible with a few containers and a little bit of imagination.

Safety for balcony containers

However, it is important to have your balcony checked by a good builder or structural engineer. Containers, particularly when watered and planted, can be extremely heavy, and the balcony must be able to withstand the weight.

Always place the container near load-bearing walls or over a joist. Put the largest containers at each end of the balcony, where it is likely to be strongest.

Secure all containers—window boxes, hanging baskets, and containers on ledges or at the edge of the balcony—so that they cannot fall and hurt either you or the people below.

Check railings for stability, particularly if you intend to attach window boxes to them. The weight will increase dramatically once the boxes are filled and watered, so use sturdy railing brackets to secure them.

All pots should be on raised feet and have adequate drainage. Place bowls or trays underneath to catch excess water. If you are concerned about weight, consider using lighter synthetic containers for larger plantings or groups of smaller ones to spread the load.

Design ideas
Before you start lugging containers to your balcony, use a sketchbook to plan different options. If your drawing skills are not up to it, take a photograph, place tracing paper on top and, using basic shapes such as spheres and cubes, draw rough outlines of your options. Here are three different balcony options.

relaxing

formal

privacy

Hot and high maintenance
Pelargoniums in pots and window boxes have been planted en masse for vibrant color, more rewarding, perhaps, for the passerby.

ORIENTATION

CHECKLIST

- What microclimate exists on your balcony?
- What direction does your balcony face?
- Does it get the morning or evening sun, or none at all?
- Is it windy or sheltered?
- Is it polluted?
- Do you need screening?

Taking all these factors into consideration, choose plants that are suitable for the situation of your balcony. Your plants need to look their very best, as they will be on show at all times, not only from the outside but also from within.

Cool and contemporary
Deep, galvanized metal containers allow for a more varied and lower-maintenance approach to planting, giving this balcony a natural contemporary setting in an urban environment.

TIPS FOR BALCONY PLANTING
Design
- If the style of your balcony reflects your interior living space, it will make the overall area appear more spacious.
- In a confined area, round containers waste more space than rectangular ones.
- Use deep pots—they dry out less rapidly.
- Create year-round interest by planting evergreen shrubs such as boxwood.
- Make the pots work at their maximum potential by interplanting with spring and fall bulbs.

Screening
- Use climbers that grow up well-secured trellising, railings, and supports to create privacy and shelter.
- Plant a yew hedge in a trough to function as a screen.
- As an alternative to screening, use deciduous climbers growing up a trellis, creating less wind resistance than evergreens.

Wind and exposure
- For windy balconies, work out the most constant direction of the wind, and use screening to create shelter.
- Use wind-tolerant shrubs such as boxwood or privet to obscure unwanted views or as a windbreak.
- Try not to use very tall plants, which could become unstable in the wind.
- Place less hardy plants within the shelter of a trellis, or use plants tolerant of exposure.

Watering
- In the summer, balcony plants will need more watering than those on the ground. If you have a large collection, it might be worth investing in an irrigation system (see chapter on watering, page 122).
- Water the containers all year round (except when it freezes), particularly if the balcony is sheltered overhead.
- Reduce water loss by using nonporous containers made from fiberglass, plastic, or metal.
- Use a lightweight soilless planting mix rather than a soil-based mix to reduce weight.

Roof terraces

High-rise buildings and apartment blocks are fast becoming sites for creative outdoor gardens. There is no reason a garden cannot be transplanted to new heights, especially with the use of containers.

PLANT LIST

Wind-tolerant trees
Dwarf mugo pine
English holly
Escallonia
Hawthorn
Trident maple

Wind-tolerant evergreen shrubs
Atlantic white cedar
Boxwood
Griselinia
Hebe (especially the small-leaved varieties)
Inkberry holly
Juniper
Pittosporum

Wind-tolerant deciduous shrubs
Roses, including Rosa rugosa, Rosa *'Sarabande',* R. *'Alberic Barbier',* R. *'Rene Andre'*
Spirea
Sea buckthorn

Evergreen palm
Dwarf fan palm

Wind-tolerant perennials
Agapanthus
Armeria maritima
Phormium
Daylilies

It's simple, really: The ground area taken up by a building is transferred vertically to the roof space. A roof terrace is no bar to a green or productive garden, nor does it prevent you from mimicking the natural environment to encourage indigenous insects and birds. In addition to providing sanctuary away from the hustle and bustle of the busy urban or suburban life below, roof gardens can enhance air quality and trap airborne particles. Containers provide the frontline troops in this transformation.

Safety, however, is the most important consideration when planning a roof garden. Containers can be extremely heavy when filled with soil, plants, and water. It is essential that you get an expert to survey how much weight your roof can support and the best places to site your containers safely. It is also worth checking whether you need local planning consent. Try to place containers near load-bearing walls or over a joist.

Overexposure

Rooftops by definition tend to be exposed sites, so try to use plants that are appropriate. Particularly good choices include plants that thrive by the seaside, such as drought- and wind-tolerant ornamental trees and grasses, low-growing shrubs, and those with waxy leaves.

In an exposed site, containers will dry up very quickly. Plants such as drought-tolerant sedums, or gray- and small-leaved plants including lavender and santolina, would be suitable selections. It might also be wise to consider an irrigation system.

Design ideas
These sketches give an idea of the styles that can be obtained on a roof garden space depending on whether you want to grow vegetables, relax, or entertain.

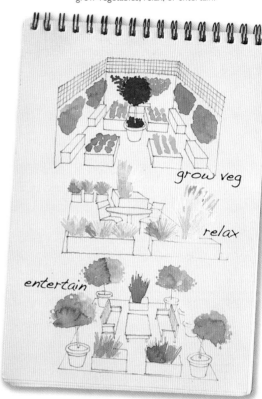

Tropical terrace
This aerial view of a roof garden shows some imaginative tropical planting.

Whispering grasses
Metal containers give height to the ornamental grasses on this roof garden. You can almost imagine a beach beyond rather than a long drop to a busy main street below.

CONTAINER CHOICES

• Use containers that are as large as is safe and practical.
• All containers should be secured against wind gusts; otherwise, they can either break or become a serious hazard to those on the roof or the street below.
• Avoid any containers with narrow bases, as they will be unstable unless secured.
• All pots should be on raised feet and have adequate drainage.
• If your terrace has a particularly good floor, try lining the pots with a fine cloth to prevent soil leaking from the drainage holes.
• Instead of lining the bottoms of tall containers with gravel or broken pots, use a lightweight filler such as Styrofoam peanuts. This will reduce the total weight of large containers—essential on a roof garden.
• Although terra-cotta containers are more stable, they are also more likely to dry out than plastic or fiberglass, which are lighter as well. This is an important consideration when dealing with a roof terrace, so consider plastic copies of terra-cotta as an alternative.
• Metal containers are very durable while also being aesthetically pleasing in a contemporary setting. However, in an exposed or sunny situation, they can heat up fairly quickly, drying out the soil mix and possibly damaging the roots. Ideally, you should line a metal container for this kind of location with a double layer of bubble wrap,

prior to filling with potting mix—this should help to protect against both heat and cold.
• Go for an overall theme rather than an eclectic mix of pots, which can look messy.

PLANTING

• In a contemporary setting, structural plants such as phormium, hosta, agave, and bamboo look particularly appropriate.
• Use soilless planting mix made with peat or a peat substitute, such as coir, because it's lighter than a soil-based one. Add perlite and vermiculite to improve drainage.
• Bear in mind that reducing its weight will make a container less stable. A well-draining pot will also dry out very quickly and consequently need more watering.
• Check your containers at least twice a year to ensure plant roots are not overcrowded.
• If you are growing permanent plants in exposed conditions, choose those that are generally hardier than what grows locally in your region.
• Trees and shrubs not only give shelter but can divide the roof space into rooms. Evergreens such as boxwood, yew, and juniper in long, tall containers make excellent screens while protecting less robust plants.
• Trellises can be attached to containers, and climbers such as grape, ivy, or even tomatoes can be grown. These also make excellent screening and windbreaks.
• Shrubs should be grown close to a wall to protect them from the elements.

Wind break and screening
This Pinus (above) is reasonably hardy and tolerant to pollution and winds, creating an evergreen windbreak as well as screening for privacy on this roof garden. Both trees are underplanted with hostas and azaleas.

Sunken gardens

Believe it or not, there are advantages to container gardening in a sunken space. Not only will more tender and shade-loving plants thrive in a sheltered area, but care and maintenance will be far easier than with those more demanding plants and pots out in the sunlight.

PLANT LIST

Perennials
Aspidistra
Easter lily
Ferns
Helleborus
Heuchera
Hosta
Lilyturf
Rodgersia
Viola

Annuals
Impatiens
Nicotiana

Bulbs
Cyclamen
Narcissus
Snowdrops
Tulips

Climbers
Clematis
Climbing hydrangea

Shrubs
Boxwood
Camellia
Euonymus
Flowering quince
Fuchsia
Mexican orange blossom
Pyracantha
Winter jasmine

Trees
Holly

Grass
Carex
Hakonechloa

For container-grown subjects growing in sunken gardens, the shade will not only keep the soil from drying out, but some larger shrubs will grow at a slower rate and stay more compact than they might in bright sunlight.

Light and access are the first two considerations when planning containers for a below-grade garden. Some sunken areas have very limited light, and this will affect your choice of plants that will grow successfully. Take note of where and when the light falls so you can plant accordingly. Luckily, there's an enormous range of shade-tolerant plants that can transform a dingy space. The other key factor is ease of access, which will determine the size of the container. If the sunken space is restricted, it's best to buy as large a container as possible and plant a low-maintenance shrub that will require only occasional watering and springtime fertilizing (for long-term planting, use a soil-based potting mix).

If the space is a busy thoroughfare, use rectangular containers that take up less room, and go vertical by growing climbers, which are invaluable for hiding some of the gloomier aspects of a subterranean space as well as brightening up even the darkest wall. A good example is clematis, most of which are well adapted to growing in semishade. Although the paler clematis varieties won't flower as freely as those grown in the sun, they'll keep their color far longer.

Most climbers need some kind of support, such as a trellis, but others are obligingly self-clinging, including the climbing hydrangea, which endears itself even further to low-maintenance gardeners by requiring little or virtually no pruning.

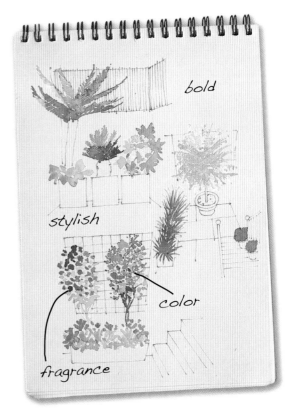

Design ideas
For a sunken space, you might consider making a bold statement such as a jungle theme, creating a stylish and restrained setting, or introducing color and fragrance.

STYLE HINTS

- To create a sense of space and style, it's worth spending money on one large container or a particularly attractive matching pair and single planting with a specimen tree or evergreen for a dramatic statement.
- If a luxuriant green jungle is more your style, fill the space with pots planted with exotic shade-loving plants such as ferns, rodgersia, or Easter lily (*Lilium longiflorum*).
- Contrast round-leaf forms such as hosta and begonia with the spiky leaves of grasses.
- Never underestimate the beauty of soft, sensual moss. Use it as a mulch for freshly planted pots, on its own in a shallow bowl, or even in the hollow of peeled bark for a natural effect.

TIPS FOR SUBTERRANEAN CONTAINERS

- All containers should be on stands to prevent them becoming waterlogged.
- Color can be provided by seasonal pots of bulbs, perennials, and annuals.
- Buy light-reflecting containers made of mirror, polished steel, and aluminum to create a sense of light and space.
- White and pale-colored flowers will lighten the area and make it feel less cramped than those with hot colors.
- Use plants with light-reflecting leaves, such as chartreuse hostas and coleus, or variegated hydrangea.
- Avoid sun-loving silver-leafed plants if your space is dark.
- Most herbs thrive in the sun; however, mint, chives, and parsley all will grow in shade.
- Use plant-filled containers to screen unsightly objects such as trash cans and recycling bins.

ABOVE: **Shade loving**
This evergreen polypodium fern will thrive in a pot in any shady sunken area. It will soften hard edges and brighten a dark corner.

BELOW: **Sunken treasure**
In this basement garden, a luxuriant planting of calla lily (*Zantedeschia* spp.) and bamboo softens and greens a stark area, making it a pleasant place to relax.

GO GREEN

Pyracantha will grow happily in a shady, below-grade garden. It not only has masses of white flowers in spring that are attractive to bees but also an abundance of red or orange berries in fall. Its dense screen of foliage makes an ideal nesting place for birds and other wildlife.

GO GREEN

Recycle vegetable waste into compost by vermicomposting (using worm bins). You can purchase a kit from garden mail-order suppliers or angling stores (where they're sold as bait). Feed your worms—usually red wigglers (*Eisenia fetida*) or earthworms (*Lumbricus rubellus*)—on raw or cooked vegetable waste from the kitchen. They'll turn it into a nutrient-rich, natural fertilizer and soil conditioner. This is ideal for small spaces such as below-grade sites.

Passageways

It's easy to overlook the importance of passageways. Too often they're cluttered with trash cans and other household stuff. Yet these narrow spaces are often the main access to your home. A cleanup and some containers can transform this neglected area.

PLANT LIST

Color for shade
Begonia
Bird of paradise
Cyclamen
Fuchsia
Impatiens
Japanese camellia
Lobelia erinus
Nicotiana
Primrose
Viola

Shrubs and ferns that tolerate deep shade
Aspidistra
Japanese holly fern
Kuma bamboo grass
Northern maidenhair fern
Skimmia × confusa 'Kew Green'
Wood ferns

Perennials for deep shade
Helleborus
Heuchera
Hosta

Plants for wildlife in shade
Carex
Holly
Ivy
Melittis melissophyllum
Pyracantha

Plants for fragrance in shade
Camellia sasanqua
Lily of the valley
Lonicera × purpusii 'Winter Beauty'
Mexican orange blossom (Choisya 'Aztec Pearl')
Mahonia japonica
Nicotiana
Scented hostas such as 'Royal Standard'
Viburnum

Sketchbook
These three rough sketches suggest a formal focal point to break up the length of a high wall; informal mixed aromatic planting to soften a low wall, and bamboos to screen an unsightly wall and provide privacy.

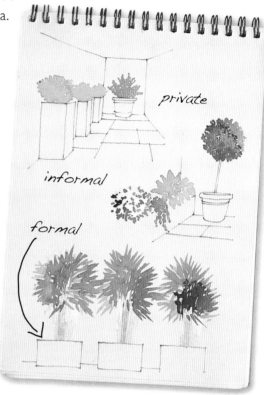

Passageways can be rather gloomy, with a high house wall flanking one side and fencing on the other. They're usually paved, concreted, or graveled or have dry, compacted soil, which is why containers can be especially effective in opening up planting possibilities.

To create a feeling of space, position identical pots with a simple repeated planting scheme at regular intervals along the path. A row of boxwood balls in metal pots, for example, would create a strong year-round structure. Interspace more relaxed seasonal containers for color and contrast.

At the end of a passageway, try placing a large, striking container as a focal point.

This will help draw the eye away from the narrowness of the passageway.

When placing pots of different plants together, group those that thrive in similar growing conditions—for example, woodland plant combinations such as ferns, foxgloves, and hostas.

The climbing rose 'Zephirine Drouhin' is particularly well suited for growing in a narrow passageway. Not only does it have a wonderful old-fashioned fragrance and tolerate some shade, but this deep-pink bourbon rose is also thornless and can climb to 10 feet or more with a good spread. Other good shade-tolerant roses are the hardy, disease-resistant climber 'New Dawn' and Knockout shrub rose.

GO GREEN

Slugs and snails are attracted to cool, damp places such as passageways. Rather than have them eat your container plants, put an old carpet or plank on the ground overnight. The next morning, turn it over, and there will be a ready-made breakfast of slugs and snails for the birds.

BELOW: **Punctuation pots**
These clipped boxwood balls lead the way along a meandering brick path toward the house. They add a touch of formality to an otherwise informal planting scheme.

ABOVE: **Home jungle**
Ferns, hostas, and bamboos planted in pots transform a side passage of a house into an exotic environment. The decking made from recycled floorboards completes the natural setting.

TIPS FOR PASSAGEWAY CONTAINERS

- If your passageway is particularly narrow, use rectangular containers—they hold more potting soil yet take up less space.
- Avoid cluttering your space with too many pots, and allow at least 3 feet clear from side to side to give room for access.
- Rather than have bushy shrubs that grow outward and obstruct the way, plant climbers and shrubs that can be trained to grow up the walls.
- At the base of the wall, choose plants that are best suited for semishade—for example, woodland plants such as ferns and cyclamen.
- Avoid very spiky or prickly plants.
- Break up the space of a long passageway by placing a group of containers two-thirds of the way down.
- The wall space is a great area for hanging pots. Try to use pots of a uniform shape and design; otherwise, the display can look very messy. The higher the pot, the more light it will receive; plant accordingly.

Patios

When thinking about buying plants and containers for a patio, take a long, hard look at the living space to which it is linked. Ask yourself the following questions: Is your interior decor contemporary or classic? What color schemes do you prefer? Is your style rustic, sophisticated, or cutting edge?

PLANT LIST

For attracting butterflies
Frikart's aster
Heliotrope

For a closed habit
Holly or bay

For evergreen screening
Bamboo
Mexican orange blossom

For long flower display
Hydrangeas
Lavender

For an open habit
Olive tree

For perfume
Nicotiana
Scented lilies

For semishade
Pelargonium

For shade
Impatiens

For structure
Boxwood
Skimmia
Yew

For sun
Petunias

For texture
Artemisia
Blue fescue grass

Your patio should reflect and link in with your interior space. As with all container gardening, assess the microclimate and exposure of your patio, as this will affect your choice of plants. Try always to position your pots so that hardier species give shelter to more tender ones. Why not use larger containers for permanent plantings, and smaller ones for annuals giving seasonal color.

A patio without plants can look hard and unforgiving. Containers are an excellent way of softening sharp edges and giving the area an aesthetic and inviting appeal. They also define boundaries and give a sense of security or privacy. Areas for dining and relaxing can be marked out and unappealing views screened. If the patio can be viewed from the interior living area, a permanent planting of evergreens in containers will give year-round structure and interest.

If you have a small patio, avoid bushy plants that take up a lot of space. Go for either topiary evergreens, such as boxwood or yew, or those with vertical growth form—for example, juniper.

If you want to use your patio for relaxing, put fragrance at the top of your list for flower choice, and the color will take care of itself. Pale-colored flowers tend to be the most fragrant and visually relaxing. Night-scented flowers are particularly valuable, not only for their delicious fragrance that carries so much farther than daytime scents, but also for their pale-colored flowers that glow long into the night. For unbeatable fragrance, grow scented lilies and *Nicotiana sylvestris* or *N. alata*. Aromatic plants such as

Design ideas
These design ideas (*below*) for a patio include a simple approach using grasses, a high impact arrangement with topiaried evergreens, and a relaxed mix of plantings.

simply stylish

hi-impact

relaxed

lavender and scented geraniums, which release their fragrant aromatic oils when brushed against, are also ideal (see pp. 98–99). For seated areas, don't forget texture. It's lovely to run one's hands over the aromatic silver filigree foliage of *Artemisia* 'Powis Castle'. For the ultimate stress reliever, try gently combing the soft leaves of blue fescue grass.

Avoid mixing too many styles of containers, and make sure the materials blend with the surface on which they stand. Terra-cotta, for example, looks great on stone and brick, while polished metal is perfect with decking.

FUNCTIONALITY

CHECKLIST

- Grow a large pot of basil next to your container-grown tomato plants for an instant and tasty salad.
- It is handy to have pots of herbs near your barbecue not only to be able to sprinkle herbs on your meats and salads, but also to give your outdoor grilling an instant, aromatic fragrance.
- Create "rooms" with your containers, so children can have a place to play while giving the parents an area of their own to relax and socialize.
- Fill pots with strawberries and blueberries to encourage young would-be gardeners and delight even the fussiest of eaters.

BELOW: **Triple effect**
A tabletop grouping of small, potted sedums and violas provides a focal point to this patio.

ABOVE: **Singular statement**
A large terra-cotta pot planted with a boxwood ball makes a small terrace look bigger while creating vertical interest in this flat patio dining area.

TIPS FOR PATIOS

- Don't use too many containers; they will create a busy, restless feeling and require a lot of work for an area that's supposed to be relaxing.
- Use planted containers to either enhance or distract from the rest of the landscape. If you want to fix attention on the patio, go for denser plantings that will obstruct the view. To draw attention to the garden beyond, use more open "see-through" plants.
- One way to secure larger pots from accidental damage is to drive a stake through the drainage hole (before filling the pot) so that at least half the stake is fixed into the paving mortar or flower bed.

Walls

Walls provide a blank canvas on which pots can be displayed and offer an invaluable extra dimension, especially in a smaller urban yard. Containers can transform a potentially stark, oppressive area into an all-year-round colorful, eye-catching feature.

PLANT LIST

East facing
Arum lily
Cherry (Prunus spp.)
Climbing hydrangea
Flowering quince
Honeysuckle 'Graham
  Thomas'
Tasmanian tree fern

North facing
Camellia
Clematis 'Nelly Moser'
Cotoneaster
Forsythia
Rosa 'New Dawn'
R. 'Zephirine Drouhin'
Silk-tassel bush

South facing
Fruit trees
Pelargonium
Roses
Star jasmine
Winter daphne
Wisteria

West facing
Camellia
Ceanothus
Jasmine
Magnolia
Roses

In many outdoor small spaces, a wall can take up as much surface space as the floor, if not more, so why not make use of it?

When planning for containers against a wall, things to consider are:
1 Which way the wall faces—north, south, east, or west.
2 How much sun and shade it receives throughout the day.
3 How exposed it is to the elements.
4 What shape container to choose. Bear in mind that rectangular containers hold more soil than round ones and take up less space.

Each wall has its own microclimate and can be a potential suntrap, shady spot, or windy thoroughfare. Remember that a south-facing wall is on the north side of a garden and vice versa.

Exposure

West-facing walls: Most plants, particularly roses and fruit trees, do well with warm, west-facing walls, which are also sheltered from northeast winds.

South-facing walls: In a sheltered area, a south-facing wall can protect some of the more tender species. Hot-colored flowers such as pelargoniums and silver-leafed Mediterranean plants (typically, lavenders and herbs) will thrive in the heat of such a spot. However, you'll need to mulch well to prevent the pots drying out too quickly.

East-facing walls: Hardier forsythias and flowering quince are better choices for this situation, which is prone to frost and the abrupt change in temperature brought about by the early morning sun.

Design ideas
Try securing 3 pots of aromatic herbs under a window. Soften the top of a wall with a trough of plants, or cover up an ugly wall with evergreens interspersed with colorful annuals.

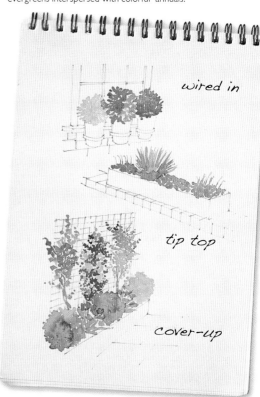

wired in

tip top

cover-up

This can damage more delicate, early flowering specimens such as camellia, fruit trees, and clematis.

North-facing walls: Many plants suitable for north-facing walls have pale or white flowers that show up well in the shade and will lighten a dark corner. Woodland plants such as foxgloves and ferns will do well in this exposure. Gooseberry can be grown as a standard or bush or trained against a wall. The Morello cherry is one of the few fruit trees that will grow well in the shade. Many sun-loving plants, such as winter jasmine and some honeysuckles, are tolerant of a northern exposure.

ABOVE: **Local color** Recycled tin cans of pelargoniums on elevated sidewall steps recreate a near-eastern courtyard setting.

BELOW: **Aromatic entrance** Galvanized containers planted with herbs make this dingy basement area into a kitchen garden.

SAFETY AND WATERING

- Any wall-mounted container should be well secured. A falling container filled with heavy soil, particularly if wet, could cause serious injury. All fixings must be sound (see Container safety, page 103).
- Wall-mounted pots can present watering problems. Make sure that you have a safe and accessible method of caring for your containers, as they'll need regular attention to look their best. If your container drips, make sure this does not affect whatever lies beneath it. Or else place another container underneath to catch any excess water.
- If watering is a problem, invest in a drip irrigation system. Or, you can try organic water-retaining gel with natural nutrients to keep your potted plants, window boxes, and hanging baskets moist. (See Watering page 122–123.)
- Try tying a cane to your hose to create a rigid watering hose for highly placed wall plantings or hanging baskets.

TIPS FOR CONTAINERS

- A wide variety of containers can be used for dressing a wall, including troughs, hanging baskets, wire half baskets, wall-mounted pots, and decorative tins or watering cans.
- Free-standing pots and planters can be placed at the base of the wall. If space allows, try to place containers away from the wall so they catch the rain.
- If you intend to plant climbers at ground level, you'll need to attach a wooden trellis or horizontal wires to the wall. If possible, mount the trellis on 1-by-2 wood strips away from the wall to allow air to circulate.
- An alternative to climbers is the use of trailing plants secured in troughs to the top of a wall (if it is not too high).

Entrances and steps

The entrance to your house says more about your style and personality than you might realize. Choosing the right containers and plants to show off or enhance your front door entails careful planning.

SAFETY FIRST

• *Steps in a garden, however attractive, can be hazardous if not negotiated properly, therefore plantings must not get in the way of safety:*

• *Containers should not obstruct steps and certainly should not be used on fire escapes. Easy access to steps and entrances is essential, especially with regard to elderly visitors. Conversely, containers can draw attention to steps and level changes that might otherwise be overlooked and can also create a psychological barrier where there is no handrail.*

• *Avoid bushy or prickly plants if your steps are narrow or if your entrance is restricted.*

Choose types of plant already suggested for patios (see page 58).

Entrances are all about impact: They are spaces for passing through rather than for lingering or relaxing. Containers can help you make an instant statement that doesn't rely on a high-maintenance front yard. It's well worth taking a long, hard look at your front door space and the architecture of the facade: Is it brick, stone, concrete, or wood? Is it traditional or contemporary in style, rustic or sophisticated in look? Is there a predominant color scheme going on?

Formal for fronts

Generally, a degree of formality and structure is well suited to the front yard. Containers must look in tiptop condition so choose low-maintenance plants for impact. For example, clipped evergreens such as yew and boxwood will look consistently good all year-round. A pair of identical containers flanking either side of a front door will give an entrance extra focus and gravitas. Standard clipped bays in Versailles boxes or boxwood balls in tall containers frame a doorway particularly effectively. You can add extra color by underplanting with seasonal plants such as bulbs in spring, cyclamen or pansies in winter, and nasturtiums or lavender in summer. In winter, small evergreen trees and topiary can be decorated with lights for a welcoming and atmospheric display.

For a more informal look, plants such as gray santolina (*Santolina chamaecyparissus*), also called cotton lavender, or artemisia can be clipped into neat shapes to make a textural and aromatic statement. Climbers including repeat-flowering fragrant roses,

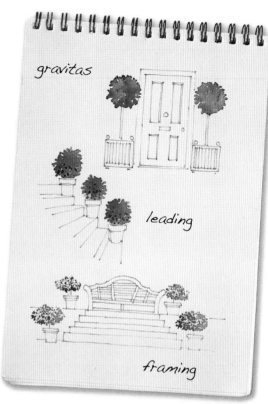

Design ideas
Visualize any of these areas without containers and you can immediately see how much these hard spaces are enhanced and embellished by careful placement.

honeysuckle, or jasmine can be trained to grow around the front door.

Steps

For a formal effect, use matching containers and planting schemes that have an upright habit, such as tulips or boxwood balls.

For an informal look, use trailing plants including nasturtiums, ivy-leaved pelargonium, and *Erigeron karvinskianus* (commonly called Mexican fleabane). A combination of herbs such as thyme, sage, rosemary, and marjoram is not only aromatic but particularly appropriate grown near the kitchen. Placing containers at the sides of the steps, or at the top and bottom of the flight, not only softens hard edges but also draws attention to the different levels.

Above: Step up to spring
These wide brick steps are softened with spring plantings of *Tulipa* 'Lilac Perfection', forget-me-nots (*Myosotis* spp.), and narcissus.

Below: Standing to attention
Bay trees in terra-cotta containers make for a balanced, formal entrance.

Right: Boxing match
The boxwood balls in terra-cotta containers on the steps give a sense of occasion while hiding hard edges. Note that the heavy square containers fit perfectly on each step, making them secure and passable.

TIPS ON ENTRANCES

- Avoid too many small pots, which can look messy, are high maintenance, and may be easy to trip over.
- You might need to secure an attractive, expensive container against theft. You could cement it into the ground or run a chain through the drainage hole and secure it to the wall or an immovable object.
- Secure a trellis on either side of your door, as well as above it, as a frame to train climbers around the doorway to superb effect. However, the planting must be well maintained and well trained throughout the year.

Low maintenance

Do you long for beautiful containers in your yard but know realistically you don't have the time to look after them? Well, there's no reason a low-maintenance container garden cannot look just as good as one that's fussed over on a daily basis.

PLANT LIST

Alpine
Alpine poppy
Saxifrage
Sedum
Sempervivum

Architectural
Agapanthus
Agave
Aloe striatula
Beschorneria yuccoides
   'Quicksilver'
Phormium
Puya alpestris

Easy-flowering plants
(All have a long
   flowering season)
Achillea
Anthemis
Dianthus
Lavender
Nicotiana
Petunia
Viola

Easy plants for shade
Euphorbias
Fatsia
Ferns

To achieve a low-maintenance container garden, simply concentrate on careful planning to avoid the later challenge of constant gardening. Go for shrubs that are year-round performers and, once established, need only an occasional pruning, watering, or feeding.

Here's a selection of easy-to-maintain container plants:

• Evergreen shrubs such as Japanese aucuba are highly tolerant, and a good female variety will reward you with bright red berries in winter.

• Mexican orange blossom (*Choisya ternata*) does well in most situations, from hot, sunny sites to partial shade. Moreover, for your minimal efforts, you'll be rewarded with fragrant white flowers in the spring (though it is not winter-hardy in all areas).

• Architectural plants such as *Fatsia japonica* and the succulent, yuccalike *Beschorneria yuccoides* are extremely tolerant (although, depending on where you live, they may need to be brought inside for the winter).

• A boxwood ball makes a stylish statement that needs little attention. Plant it in a contemporary container for instant impact the easy way.

• A specimen tree in an attractive container with year-round interest such as a crabapple will take up very little time but continue to perform for most of the year.

• Most alpine plants will grow happily in containers, and are a favorite choice for shallow sinks and stone troughs. They require little feeding but do need free-draining potting mix mixed with extra grit.

Design ideas
Once established, sempervivums need little watering. Petunias continue to flower throughout the summer with virtually no deadheading. Large evergreen plants need only occasional but thorough watering.

sempervivums

petunias

fatsia, ferns, & phormium

PLANTING

HINTS AND TIPS

• Use a soil-based potting medium, and incorporate a slow-release organic fertilizer.

• After planting, mulch well with bark chips or pebbles to conserve moisture and discourage weeds.

• Water well for the first season, giving a thorough soaking when needed rather than a little dribble every day.

• Once the roots have been established, the plants can manage very well on their own, with just an occasional watering in very hot, dry weather.

• Invest in an irrigation system to keep your plants watered without you ever filling a watering can again. These systems also save water, which makes them an environmentally friendly option.

• If even this is too much for you, just splurge on a beautiful container, and forget about the plant.

TOP 5 easy-care plants

1 Hardy geraniums

The new hybrids of the hardy geraniums will flower from late spring to fall. Cultivars like *Geranium* 'Ann Folkard', *G.* 'Okey Dokey', and *G.* 'Purple Pillow' are all reliable bloomers.

2 "Wave" petunias

Easy-to-grow "wave" petunias are extremely colorful and vigorous, with a fabulous display of flowers from spring to late summer.

3 Daylilies

The new daylily cultivars come in an enormous array of colors and form, and with careful choice, you can have varieties that will give you continuous bloom from early to late summer.

4 Grasses

The grasses miscanthus and feather grass (*Nassella* a.k.a. *Stipa tenuissima*) look great all year round and only need cutting back in spring.

5 Sempervivums

Sempervivums thrive on neglect and multiply readily. The star-shaped flowers are mostly shades of pink or red, and there are literally thousands of cultivars to choose from.

Above: **Potted petunias**
Petunias are relatively inexpensive, easy to grow, and low maintenance. Shown here in a rustic urn, they also work in hanging baskets, window boxes, landscaping, and combination planters.

Above: **Calm and cool**
An unusual ceramic container is planted with succulents and epitomizes the calm that minimal and low-maintenance planting can achieve.

Right: **Neat shapes**
Many of us live in built-up areas where fossil fuel emissions are high, and noise and light pollution make conditions for gardening immensely tough going. This is where grasses in containers can bring a more natural feel to the backyard or balcony while requiring minimal maintenance.

Attracting wildlife

With the urban and suburban sprawl and intensive agriculture encroaching farther into the countryside, more wildlife seek refuge in our backyards. To a butterfly trying to negotiate a polluted inner-city area, your window box will be an oasis of food and shelter. Welcome wildlife as allies that help us maintain a healthy environment.

BELOW: **Butterfly-friendly plant** Nectar-filled flowers, and early- and late-flowering plants will attract butterflies. Marigold is a good bet for luring these eye-catching creatures.

TOP TREES FOR ATTRACTING WILDLIFE

Fruit trees
Hawthorn
Holly
Juniper
Magnolia
Mountain ash
River birch
Witch hazel

TOP 10 WILDLIFE-FRIENDLY PLANTS FOR BIRDS

Black-eyed Susan
Cardinal flower
Cosmos
Elderberry
Globe thistle
Joe-pye weed
Purple coneflower
Sunflower
Verbascum
Viburnum

ABOVE: **Aphid alert** Lady beetles are highly efficient aphid controllers and should be encouraged to visit your containers. Lady beetles themselves are food for butterflies—even more reason for encouraging them.

The food chain

All animals and insects are part of the important food chain—interdependent on each other as a source of food. When we encourage them into our gardens, they become the gardener's friend rather than foe. The diversity of plants is one of the most important factors in providing shelter, food, and water for wildlife. In return we are rewarded with a living garden instead of a sterile showpiece.

Shelter

Climbers such as honeysuckle and clematis are not only a rich source of food but also provide shelter for overwintering insects and nesting places for small birds. They can also offer refuge from predators. Carefully chosen native trees attract all forms of wildlife, particularly birds and insects, by giving shelter and sometimes flowers and fruit. Even the piles of leaves in the fall will offer insects and beetles precious shelter during the winter.

RIGHT: **Welcome home**
Thrift is ideal in a rockery or alpine container. This plant is visited by bumble bees for its pollen and nectar.

BELOW: **Toad in a hole**
A toad seeks shade from the midday sun in abandoned terra-cotta pots. Don't be too quick to tidy up unused containers.

Soft fruit bushes

A container-based hedge of native trees and shrubs such as blueberries, hawthorn, dogwood, and viburnums offers a valuable source of food and shelter. Fruiting hedges can be left uncut until the birds have eaten the berries. Do not cut back until mid or late summer in case there are birds nesting. The next best thing is to grow native climbers such as Virginia creeper, honeysuckle, and trumpet vine. Do not trim back too closely, as small birds like to hide in the vines on wintry nights. Try growing at least one prickly shrub to provide birds with a safe haven from predators.

TOP 10 WILDLIFE-FRIENDLY FLOWERS FOR BEES

Agastache
Aubrieta
Candytuft
French marigold
Hebe
Lavender
Marjoram
Michaelmas daisy
Red valerian
Sedum

GO GREEN

DUSK DELIGHT

Planting night-scented species such as evening primrose or a tobacco plant (*Nicotiana sylvestris*) will lure moths with their starry flowers at dusk—even the giant hawk moths.

TOP NECTAR-RICH
SPRING FLOWERS

Aubrieta
Crocus
Dianthus
Forget-me-not
Grape hyacinth
Heather
Hyacinth
Primrose
Viola
Wallflower

TOP NECTAR-RICH
SUMMER FLOWERS

Aromatic herbs
Buddleia
Butterfly weed
Catmint
Evening primrose
Nicotiana sylvestris
Heliotrope
Honeysuckle
Verbena
Zinnia

Attracting birds

Flowers and nectar plants that attract insects will also attract birds. Leave flowers and grasses to seed after flowering, especially those that are still standing when fall comes. They give fantastic structure throughout winter and provide a place for spiders to weave their webs. Cut back these plants in late winter/early spring. Shrubs with berries, such as elderberry and cotoneaster, are attractive to most birds, especially thrushes and blackbirds.

Avoiding pesticides

Do not use chemicals in the garden—especially when it comes to controlling insects, which are an important source of food for other wildlife. Companion planting, growing different species of plants together for their mutual benefit, offers an effective alternative. Not only does this look attractive, but it can also help control pests and diseases without harming the wildlife. Here are some potentially useful combinations:
• Marigolds and tomatoes; garlic and roses: Both combinations ward off aphids.
• Nasturtiums and cabbages: Caterpillars prefer nasturtiums and so will hopefully leave the cabbages alone.
• Carrots and leeks or onions: The strong scent keeps the carrot fly away.

Water

A key attraction for wildlife is a source of water. A wooden half barrel or an old sink filled with water and planted with aquatic plants, combined with pots of nectar-rich flowers, fruiting shrubs, and seed-producing grasses and flowers, will attract numerous insects, birds, and amphibians.

To make your own pond in a pot, place a small pile of stones in the container so that a few stick up above the water line. This will act as a safe place for any animal that has fallen into the container. (For more on ponds in a pot, see page 123.) Make sure that some of the water is covered by nearby plants to create a safe and sheltered area. A small piece of wood floating on the surface will act as a landing platform for thirsty insects. Place a wooden plank up to the sides of the water to attract frogs and newts, which in turn will eat slugs and snails. If you want a wildlife friendly pond, don't keep fish.

GO GREEN

WILDFLOWER MEADOW

A mixture of grass and flower seeds which you can buy in early fall from a garden center will give you a meadow in spring. Simply choose your favorite short annuals, mix the seed, and plant the container—even a window box will suffice.

Place the container among other foliage that will encourage wildlife to a more natural and sheltered environment.

Make sure you plant oxygenating aquatic plants to prevent the water from going stagnant.

An old butler's sink is a perfect containerized pond—provided you fill in the plug hole. You may need an extra sealant to ensure it is watertight.

THIS PAGE: **Don't throw out the bathtub** What could be more appropriate for a recycled water container than an old bathtub?

Wildlife in pots

HINTS AND TIPS

- To attract wildlife, it's best that your containers aren't kept too tidy. Leave dead branches and fallen leaves to provide food and shelter.
- Place your containers in groups or rows to create a wildlife "corridor."
- Insects and birds are attracted to abundant plantings that can provide shelter as well as food. Try to group your containers together or near other plantings or, in the case of a balcony or roof terrace, in a sheltered position near a wall.
- A wide variety of diverse plants in your containers will be attractive to wildlife.
- Even if you have just one window box, carefully choose your plants so that it can still provide a valuable refuge of food and shelter for an array of insects, butterflies, and moths.
- Wallflowers, yarrows (*Achillea*), and sedums will provide animals with a valuable source of food through the long months of winter.
- Fragrant flowers not only make gardens a sensory delight for our friends and us, but also attract butterflies and moths.
- When choosing varieties of nectar-rich flowers, go for those with single rather than double flowers, as they will contain more nectar.
- Although regular deadheading promotes longer flowering, leave a few to develop into seeds to provide food for the birds.
- To extend the diversity of your containers, grow a pot of nettles beloved by lady beetles, hoverflies, and butterflies.
- Sow a wildflower meadow in a large container or window box.
- Try not to be too thorough when weeding, and allow wild flowers to grow among your cultivated container plants.

RIGHT: **Diversity**
Keep your plantings diverse and group together to create a mini eco-system.

RECIPE FOR: A WILDLIFE FRIENDLY HANGING BASKET

You will need a 16-inch hanging basket for this early summer living bird table.

1 French lavender
(*Lavandula stoechas*)

2 Alpine strawberry
(*Fragaria vesca* 'Semperflorens') × 5

3 Sweet alyssum
(*Lobularia maritima*) × 5

4 Candytuft
(*Iberis sempervirens*) × 2

5 Silver variegated ivy
(*Hedera helix* 'Glacier')

6 Creeping thyme (*Thymus serpyllum*) × 2

7 Dish of water

8 Bird feeder of nuts

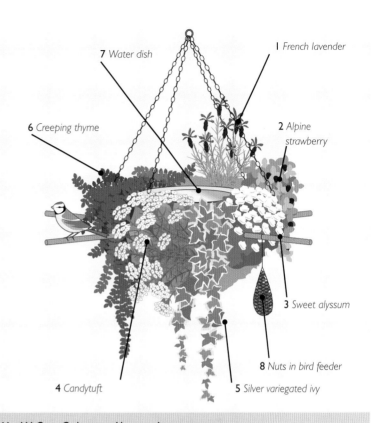

7 *Water dish*

1 *French lavender*

6 *Creeping thyme*

2 *Alpine strawberry*

3 *Sweet alyssum*

8 *Nuts in bird feeder*

4 *Candytuft*

5 *Silver variegated ivy*

At-a-glance selecting wildlife friendly plants

Plant type	Possible plants	Attracts
Flowering aromatic herbs	Cilantro, lavender, catnip, chives, rosemary, thyme, parsley, mint	Butterflies and beneficial insects
Annuals	Calendula, phlox, petunia, zinnia, cosmos, lobelia, salvia, sunflowers	Butterflies, beneficial insects, and birds
Shrubs	Buddleia, juniper, cedar, American elderberry, winterberry holly, cotoneaster, pyracantha	Birds and butterflies
Tall plants	Shasta daisy, bachelor's button, iris, aster, bergamot, goldenrod, foxgloves, mullein, nicotiana	Butterflies, moths, and beneficial insects
Shade or semishade-tolerant plants	Honeysuckle, Solomon's seal, Jacob's ladder	Butterflies, moths, and pollinators
Trailing plants	Fuchsia, morning glory, lobelia	Bees, butterflies, and hummingbirds
Perennials	Achillea, delphinium, sedum, wild strawberry	Hummingbirds, butterflies

SEASONAL PLANTING

There is no closed season for containers: In any given month, they can be filled for colorful or structural year-round interest. They bring to our attention all the best in flowers and plants that otherwise might be lost or neglected in the hurly-burly of the herbaceous border. Containers can be showy, throughout the year, with permanent plantings underplanted with seasonal bulbs. If you are clever, this on-going drama can be staged so that while one plant "exits stage right," another makes its way into the limelight.

Spring planting ideas

The bulbs you planted in fall should now be making a welcome appearance. If you haven't planted any, don't panic, as the garden centers will be filled with a colorful variety of ready-grown spring flowers and bulbs.

PLANT COMBINATIONS FOR SPRING

Dark purple, yellow, and indigo
• *Dark purple tulips with primrose yellow wallflowers and indigo-blue forget-me-nots*

Green and blues
• *Variegated ivy with prostrate rosemary, blue hyacinth, blue ipheion, and blue grape hyacinth*

Orange and acid green
• *Orange tulips and acid-green euphorbia*

White and green
• *Weeping pussy willow combined with white crocus and small-leaved variegated ivies*

Yellow, blue, and white
• *Yellow tulips, blue grape hyacinths, white anemone, and white bellis*

Yellow and mauve
• *Yellow cowslips with pale yellow and mauve violas*

To avoid leaving the pots looking bare over the winter (see page 82), try planting some herbaceous perennials, such as hellebores, low-growing grasses, or colorful red twig dogwood (*Cornus* spp.) stems, for the bulbs to grow up through.

If you want the bulbs to grow unaccompanied, cover the potting soil with a thick, luxurious layer of moss so your containers will look more attractive and complete. If you are in a cold zone, you'll need to protect the container with row cover fabric or other insulating material to prevent the damage of freezing and thawing; otherwise, bring them into a greenhouse or cold frame or under cover.

Snowdrops, crocuses, and miniature daffodils will be among the first to arrive, standing up well to the cold late winter or early spring weather. A wide range of colorful cyclamens, pansies, and primroses will be available as winter comes to an end. They can contribute color until spring takes over.

As the spring flowers fade, take out the spent bulbs and replant them in the garden. Fill the gaps with fresh plants or summer-flowering bulbs, such as lilies for fragrance or dahlias for color.

Early spring is the best time to plant permanent specimens, such as trees and shrubs. Most summer-flowering bulbs and tubers can be planted later in spring, when the frosts are over and the soil has warmed up. Late spring is also the time to start on your summer-flowering containers and hanging baskets.

ABOVE: **Springtime style**
This spring setting of *Tulipa* 'Black Parrot' underplanted with white violas in an oak barrel planter makes a stunning combination. Plant the tulips close together to give extra support.

Signs of spring

Description: At only 6 inches high and with deep yellow flowers, *Narcissus* 'Tête-à-tête' is deservedly one of the most popular dwarf daffodils for containers.

Bloom time: It's one of the earliest daffodils to arrive in spring and a perfect complement to the more delicate early flowering bulbs such as crocus.

Container type: Use any small container with good drainage.

Planting: Plant daffodil and crocus bulbs in fall. Primroses can then be added in late winter to early spring. However, all these plants can generally be bought in pots and planted together in early spring. Apply liquid organic fertilizer in early spring when the bulbs are beginning to emerge.

Planting medium: Use a multipurpose or soilless potting medium to which a slow release fertilizer has been added.

Position: Place in the sun, and when flowering is over, replant in the garden.

Quantity

5 × Daffodil 'Tête-à-tête'

5 × Crocus

6 × Primrose

Orange zest

Description: Tulips have to be among the most gorgeous of all the spring bulbs and are particularly easy to grow in containers. *Tulipa* 'Prinses Irene' is an outstanding tulip, 12–14 inches tall with orange petals subtly streaked with purple, red, and green. Pale yellow wallflowers provide a classic underplanting.

Bloom time: It flowers in midspring and looks wonderful with pale yellow, acid green, and indigo blue.

Container type: A large wide-rimmed container would be particularly suitable.

Planting: To set off the gorgeous orange of the tulips, try interplanting with indigo-blue Forget-me-nots or dwarf dark blue cornflowers. Buy the tulip bulbs and wallflowers in late fall. Forget-me-nots are best bought fresh in the spring as they can be prone to mildew.

Planting medium: Use a soil-based potting medium with added slow-release fertilizer. When the tulip leaves emerge in early spring apply a liquid fertilizer. Repeat when the tulips begin to bloom.

Position: Sunny and sheltered.

Quantity

24 × *Tulipa* 'Prinses Irene'

8 × Dwarf cornflowers or Forget-me-nots

12 × Wallflowers, dwarf pale yellow

Delightful daisies

Description: This *Bellis perennis* is a double form of daisy.

Bloom time: *Bellis* is spring flowering, whereas the white bacopa plant will continue to flower throughout the season until early frosts.

Container type: A smaller low-level container is suitable.

Planting: Plant *Bellis perennis* in the early spring; add white bacopa to the display in April.

Planting medium: Plant in a soil-based planting mix to which a slow-release fertilizer has been added.

Companions: Spring-flowering bulbs such as tulips, primroses, and grape hyacinths are perfect companions.

Position: Place in a sunny position.

Quantity

2 × *Bellis perennis*

4 × Bacopa, white

Little angels and little devils

Description: This grouping of *Helleborus* 'Deep purple', *Narcissus* 'Tête-à-tête', and *Acorus gramineus* 'Ogon' can remain as a permanent planting. To retain a good display of narcissus, remove the bulbs after flowering and replant with new ones in fall.

Bloom time: This container will look best in early spring.

Container type: This grouping is suitable for any container but should have depth. Here it is planted in a Victorian-style chimney pot.

Planting: Plant in mid fall. These plants are generally extremely tolerant of most sites and soils.

Planting medium: Plant in a soil-based planting mix, and keep well watered while ensuring adequate drainage. Apply fertilizer in the early spring.

Companions: The deep purple hellebores look good with *Pulmonaria* 'Sissinghurst White' and *Heuchera* 'Chocolate Ruffles'.

Position: This container would be suitable for either a sunny or shady spot.

Quantity

6 × Daffodil 'Tête-à-tête'

1 × *Helleborus*, deep purple

2 × *Acorus gramineus* 'Ogon'

Synchronized blooming

Description: *Anemone blanda* with emerging tulips.

Bloom time: This display will come together in midspring.

Container type: Suitable for wide-mouth containers; here, it is in a terra-cotta flowerpot.

Planting: Plant the bulbs in late fall.

Planting medium: Plant in a soil-based planting mix with added fertilizer.

Companions: Try to get a midspring tulip for a synchronized blooming. A late-flowering narcissus, such as the delicate *Narcissus* 'Thalia', would also look particularly attractive.

Position: Place in light shade.

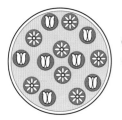

Quantity
❋ 7 × *Anemone blanda*

🌷 7 × Tulips

Spring Planting

Hints and tips
- Remember there are early and late-flowering varieties of the same flower or bulb—tulips and daffodils, for example. When you are combining them with other spring-flowering plants, make sure they will bloom at the same time.
- To deter wild animals and cats from damaging your containers, stick prunings from a prickly holly or rose into the soil.

Other spring plants
- Azaleas
- Camellia
- Corydalis
- Cowslips
- Crocus
- *Cyclamen coum*
- Grape hyacinth (*Muscari armeniacum*)
- Pansy
- Primula
- Snowdrops (*Galanthus nivalis*)

Go Green

Discover your sunniest and most sheltered spot in springtime, and then place a container planted up with either *Erysimum* wallflowers, primroses, or violets so that insects have an early food source as they emerge in spring.

Summer planting ideas

The secret of a successful summer container is choosing a combination of plants that not only complement one another in color and form but continue to flower throughout the summer months. Cultivars of the same species can vary enormously in their longevity, so it's always wise to do a little research, lest a tired plant spoil an otherwise vigorous display.

PLANT COMBINATIONS FOR SUMMER

Pastels
- Isotoma axillaris, Helichrysum petiolare 'Limelight', and Petunia 'Prism Sunshine'

Blue, white, and pink
- Lilium 'Arena', lobelia, and pelargonium

Fiery colors
- *Nasturtiums and cordyline*

Mauves
- *Lavender and* Verbena bonariensis

White, pink, and magenta
- *White* Argyranthemum foeniculaceum, *pink Marguerite daisies, licorice plant, and magenta-colored trailing petunias*

Pale pinks and purple
- Pelargonium 'Lady Plymouth', *licorice plant, and heliotropes*

Purple and mauve
- *Giant alliums and lavender*

Green and orange
- *Agave and California poppy*

Purple, orange, and scarlet
- *Purple leaved cabbages, French marigolds, and scarlet nasturtiums*

Beige and purple
- Nassella (a.k.a. Stipa) tenuissima *and dark purple iris*

Red and lime green
- *Red canna, ivy-leaved pelargoniums,* Nicotiana 'Lime Green'

Hardier, more permanent plants should be planted in spring to give them time to get established. For tender seasonal plants, wait until late May.

Summer is also the time to enjoy the versatility of containers. Annuals are the popular choice, but shrubs, climbers, perennials, and summer-flowering bulbs should not be overlooked.

Even if you only have a small, concrete backyard, you can bring nature to your doorstep by growing a wildflower meadow in a container or a window box.

A wide variety of summer bulbs are ideal for containers, such as gladioli, alstroemeria, and *Galtonia candicans* (often called summer hyacinth). The huge range of lilies includes the showy trumpet-flowered varieties, notably, the very fragrant regal lily, *Lilium regale*.

When planting containers in early summer, be aware of how much each plant will grow both above and below ground. Make sure there is enough space for developing roots, foliage, and flowers. Containers can dry out quickly in the summer heat, so before embarking on an ambitious array of container displays, make sure someone will be able to water them at least once a day (see also low maintenance, pages 60-61) if you're planning to be away.

Summer containers are also excellent for growing herbs and vegetables.

BELOW: **Regal rose**
Rosa 'Anne Boleyn', named after one of the six wives of King Henry VIII, is a lovely, repeat-flowering, compact rose with warm pink blooms. It is the perfect choice of rose for a container.

Vibrant display

Description: The pale pink marguerite daisy cultivar 'Summer Melody' and spectacular *Pericallis* 'Senetti Magenta Bicolor' make a vibrant summer combination. Argyranthemums, otherwise known as marguerites, are free-flowering tender perennials that are the mainstay of many summer containers. There are more than 80 types available in a variety of colors and form.

Bloom time: With regular deadheading, these flowers will continue to bloom throughout summer and into fall. Cut back any yellowing marguerite foliage to new young shoots.

Container type: Try to plant in a deep container to accommodate roots.

Planting: *Argyranthemum frutescens* and 'Senetti' should be planted in late spring.

Planting medium: Use a soil-based potting mix, and incorporate an organic water-retaining gel. Three weeks after planting, feed with a weak fertilizer solution, and continue every 2 to 3 weeks.

Companions: Gray-leaved *Helichrysum petiolare*, verbena, and *Isotoma axillaris* are suitable companions.

Position: Place the container in a sunny spot.

Quantity

 1 × *Pericallis* 'Senetti Magenta Bicolor'

1 × *Pericallis* 'Senetti'

 1 × *Argyranthemum* 'Summer Melody'

Cool and collected

Description: The star of this summer display is the wonderfully rewarding lavender blue scabious. Flowers shaped like pincushions held by tall delicate stems will bloom throughout the summer from June to September and as an added bonus are highly attractive to butterflies and bees. The other plants are harmoniously and closely linked on the color wheel with soft purple and blue flowers set off by the contrasting pale yellow of the argyranthemum and slight acid yellow edging of the pelargonium leaves.

Bloom time: With regular deadheading, these flowers will continue to bloom well into the fall.

Container type: A deep and tall container will alow the plants to trail over the edges and also contain a sufficient amount of soil to support a continuous summer display. This galvanized metal container is particualry harmonious with the blue and mauve pastel flowers.

Planting: Plant in late spring or early summer when the risk of frosts is finally over. Water regularly and feed every 2 to 3 weeks with an organic fertilizer.

Planting medium: Use a soil-based potting mix with a slow-release fertilizer.

Companions: Trailing petunias and purple heliotropes.

Position: Place in a sunny spot.

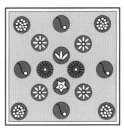

Quantity

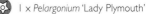 1 × Argyranthemum, primrose yellow

1 × *Pelargonium* 'Lady Plymouth'

4 × Brachycome, blue

2 × Scabious

4 × Helichrysum, silver

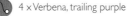 4 × Verbena, trailing purple

Firework display

Description: The grass 'Pony Tails' paired with *Erigeron karvinskianus* provides maximum effect for minimum effort. The display will not only do well in an exposed site but also provides a wildlife haven.

Bloom time: Cut both the erigeron and the grass back in spring when new shoots start emerging for an explosive display throughout summer and into early fall.

Container type: Large 'Ali Baba' style terra-cotta.

Planting: Plant both 'Pony Tails' and erigeron in fall or early spring.

Planting medium: Plant this combination in a soil-based mix to which slow-release fertilizer and sand or perlite have been added for extra drainage. You may also include organic water-storing gels to the planting soil for a consistent supply of moisture.

Companions: *Phormium tenax* and *Allium sphaerocephalon* are good companions.

Position: Place in full sun.

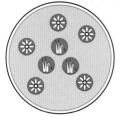

Quantity
 1–3 × *Nassella* (a.k.a. *Stipa*) *tenuissima* 'Pony Tails'

✳ 5 × *Erigeron karvinskianus*

GO GREEN

Leave the grass stems over winter—not only are they beautiful, but they're also sources of food for seed-eating birds. In summer, erigeron attracts both bees and butterflies.

SUMMER GROWING

HINTS AND TIPS

- Mix water-storing gels in the potting soil to help keep a continuity of moisture during the hot weather.
- To promote a long flowering season, deadhead fading flowers and fertilize on a regular basis.
- Instead of mixing perennials and annuals in the same pot, plant them up individually and then move them around for different container groupings.

Bold and beautiful

Description: What can be more cheerful than a window box full of colorful trailing pelargoniums? This mix includes 'Decora Red', 'Happy Face Mex', 'L'elegante', and scented pelargonium 'Attar of Roses'.

Bloom time: This window box will bloom throughout the summer. Deadhead on a regular basis, and remove any damaged or diseased leaves.

Container type: Use a window box. If it's heavy, fix in position before planting.

Planting: This should be done in late spring, when the frosts are finally over.

Planting medium: Use a multipurpose planting mix, and apply a liquid fertilizer every 2 weeks or incorporate slow-release fertilizer into the mix.

Companions: Lime green tobacco plants would look stunning interplanted with the pelargoniums.

Position: Place in full sun. *Note:* Window boxes can get very dry in hot or windy weather so check twice a day to see if you need to water.

Quantity

2 × 'Decora Red'

3 × 'Happy Face Mex'

1 × 'L'Elegante'

1 × 'Attar of Roses'

Go Green

- Verbena is a great plant for attracting butterflies, so you can watch them smother the flowers in search of nectar during the flowering season.
- When planning your wildlife garden, keep in mind that while butterflies need nectar, their larvae require plant foliage.

Summer Planting

Hints and tips

- Save money by taking cuttings in late summer from the current season's growth of your shrubs and herbaceous perennials.
- If space is tight, plant some of your favorite perennials in separate pots, and then group the containers together.
- Use miniature varieties of common herbaceous flowering plants, such as hollyhocks and delphiniums.

Other summer plants

- *Argyranthemum* 'Jamaica Primrose'
- Bidens
- Lavender
- *Lilium* 'Arena'
- Lobelia
- Nasturtiums
- *Rosa* 'Anne Boleyn'
- *Salvia elegans*
- Trailing verbena

Fall planting ideas

By the end of summer, most plants that were potted in spring start to look rather bedraggled and sad. However, fall is the time for harvesting fruit and berries and the season when trees and shrubs steal the show with glorious fall color. So why not have one last splash of spectacular color before winter sets in?

PLANT
COMBINATIONS
FOR FALL

Green and gold
• Heuchera *'Obsidian'*, Pennisetum orientale, *and* Carex *'Evergold'*

Green, red, and orange
• Skimmia japonica *'Rubella'*, Carex testacea, *and* Leucothoe *'Scarletta'*

Pink, green, and purple
• Erica gracilis, Gaultheria *(a.k.a Pernettya)* mucronata *and* Heuchera *'Plum Pudding'*

Pink, gold, and green
• *Carex, euphorbia, and Erica (heather)*

Purple, silver, and black
• Heuchera *'Silver Scrolls'*, alumroot (Heuchera americana), *and* Ophiopogon planiscapus *'Nigrescens'*

RIGHT: **Hot dog**
These potted dogwood shrubs provide glorious fall reds.

The *Acer palmatum* 'Dissectum Atropurpureum' is probably one of the finest trees, not only for its compact size and fine texture, but also for its fall color. Other good cultivars are A. 'Garnet' and A. 'Red Pygmy'.

Colorful fall berries and fruit also provide a feast for wildlife. Cotoneaster and rowan (*Sorbus* spp.) have bright red berries, and the crabapple that was covered in blossoms in spring will now have red and yellow fruits. *Malus* 'Red Sentinel' is especially recommended for containers.

Many climbers, classically Virginia creeper and crimson glory vine (*Vitis coignetiae*), also have wonderful fall color, as do a variety of bulbs, including *Cyclamen hederifolium* and fall crocus (*Colchicum* spp.). Dahlias are absolutely glorious. The shorter-growing varieties are more suitable for smaller containers such as window boxes. The larger have to be well staked and pinched back to encourage bushier plants. Probably the most popular of all is 'Bishop of Llandaff', with its bronze foliage and scarlet flowers.

Grasses are low-maintenance and reliable container plants for fall. Some grasses, such as fountain grass, will produce long-lasting brushlike flowers in the later summer that will persist through the winter months, until they are cut back in spring to make way for new growth.

LEFT: **Fall pink**
An arresting combination features early fall pinks with *Nerine* 'Stephanie', the darker pink *Nerine undulata*, and the white, trumpet-shaped flowers of *Hosta plantaginea* 'Grandiflora'. Nerines should be placed in a sheltered position, preferably next to a sunny wall.

A step in fall

Description: Grasses have to be one of the easiest and most trouble-free plants to grow in a container.

Bloom time: Heucheras have year-round interest throwing up masses of spikes of tiny pink flowers in summer months and through into fall. The grasses will grow attractive feathery plumes during late summer. The saxifrage will bloom in late spring.

Container type: Glazed ceramic container.

Planting: Plant in early fall. Keep the soil moist throughout winter but do not overwater. If the foliage starts to look scruffy and unattractive cut back in late winter just before the new seasons growth. Also, why not mulch any exposed soil with favorite stones and pebbles picked up while on vacation?

Planting medium: Soil-based potting medium. All these plants prefer moist soil.

Companions: Grow spring bulbs through the grass such as tall white, pink, and purple tulips.

Position: Sun or semishade. These plants don't like to bake in the midday sun.

Quantity

4 x *Heuchera* 'Plum Pudding'

1 x *Carex stricta*

1 x *Carex brunnea* 'Variegata'

1 x *Carex buchananii*

2 x *Saxifraga* 'Southside Seedling'

Oriental splendor

Description: *Acer palmatum* 'Dissectum Atropurpureum' has finely divided leaves and a broad rounded shape that's reddish purple in summer, turning to vivid orange-red in fall.

Bloom time: It's particularly great for color in fall.

Container type: It looks good in a large, glazed, oriental-style container.

Planting: Plant in fall or spring for best results.

Planting medium: Use a soil-based potting mix with slow-release fertilizer.

Position: Semishade is best, although full sun can be tolerated.

Quantity

1 x *Acer palmatum* 'Dissectum Atropurpureum'

Drought-tolerant display

Description: A container with *Sedum* 'Autumn Joy', *S.* 'Matrona' (purple leaves), *S. telephium ruprechtii*, and *S.* 'Ruby Glow' (trailing). *Aloe vera* is shown with *Aeonium arboreum* in a terra-cotta pot. Bees and butterflies will find the sedums irresistible.

Bloom time: They'll bloom in fall.

Container type: Terra-cotta is ideal (plastic may be too water-retentive).

Planting: Plant in spring for a good summer display that will come into its own when it flowers in early fall.

Planting medium: Plant in a soil-based mix with plenty of sand.

Position: This display likes hot, dry sites.

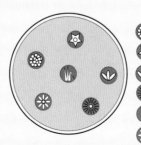

Quantity

1 x *Sedum* 'Autumn Joy'

1 x *Sedum* 'Matrona'

1 x *Sedum telephium ruprechtii*

1 x *Sedum* 'Ruby Glow'

1 x *Aloe vera*

1 x *Aeonium arboreum*

Amazing grace

Description: A group of containers holds pheasant's tail grass (*Stipa arundinacea*), *Carex* 'Cappuccino' (a recent form of *C. tenuiculmis*, superior to most other brown-foliaged grasses), and *Festuca glauca* 'Elijah blue'. These graceful grasses form a dense tuft of fine foliage.

Bloom time: The summer color continues to look great throughout fall and into winter. 'Cappuccino' has wonderful orangey brown fall coloring.

Container type: Terra-cotta works well.

Planting: Grasses are easy to grow. Plant in fall or spring.

Planting medium: Plant in a soil-based mix incorporating a slow-release fertilizer. Keep moist but well drained.

Position: Place in sun or partial shade.

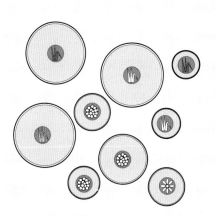

Quantity

 2 × *Stipa arundinacea*

 1 × *Carex* 'Cappuccino'

 2 × *Festuca glauca* 'Elijah Blue'

 1 × *Sempervivum*

 3 × *Sedum*

FALL PLANTING

HINTS AND TIPS

- Lilies are best planted in fall and kept in a cool, frost-free spot over winter. They can also be planted anytime through to spring, but the flowers will not be as spectacular.
- To encourage the brightest-colored dogwood stems, cut all the shoots back to a few buds from the base in late winter.
- There are over 2,000 horticultural varieties of dahlias, so it's best to research a little before you grow them in your pots.

OTHER FALL PLANTS

- *Ceratostigma willmottianum*
- *Colchicum*
- *Cotoneaster* 'Cornubia'
- *Cyclamen hederifolium*
- Dahlias
- Dogwood
- Michaelmas daisies
- Nerines
- Pyracantha

Winter planting ideas

It would be easy to assume that winter containers are somehow not as rewarding as those planted for spring or summer. But in fact they offer an instant eye-catching effect in an otherwise monochromatic and chilly season. There is a wide variety to choose from including winter-flowering shrubs, early spring-flowering bulbs, evergreens, and winter-flowering annuals.

PLANT
COMBINATIONS
FOR WINTER

Green, gold, and cream
• Skimmia × confusa *'Kew Green'*, Acorus *gramineus 'Ogon', and* Leucothoe *'Rainbow'*

Bronze, red, and green
• Carex comans, Skimmia *japonica, and trailing ivy*

Black, dark purple, and a dusting of silver
• Ophiopogon *planiscapus 'Nigrescens' and* Heuchera *'Plum Pudding'*

Green and pink
• *Boxwood, trailing ivy, and cyclamen*

Winter containers can lend color and interest when the rest of the garden may look drab. Moreover, because the effect is instant, it does away with some of the uncertainty of how the container will eventually look. The plants are not going to grow half as much as those in spring and summer containers, so you can literally plant them for the finished effect.

September is the best time to start planting winter containers. The end of the growing season allows the plants to become established before the winter months. When planting a winter container, plants can be placed closer together than in spring or summer as very little growth takes place during winter months. When planting a winter container, plan ahead by underplanting with spring bulbs.

Bulb strategies

To prolong the display, select different types that can be planted in two or three levels at different depths that flower at different times (see diagram on page 114). For example, plant tulip bulbs at about 6 to 8 inches, and above them, plant smaller bulbs, such as early flowering crocus, at 2 to 4 inches deep. You could also plant large allium bulbs below the tulips for a dramatic display of flowers in summer.

The general rule for planting bulbs is to place them at a depth of three times their diameter. Although you can keep bulbs in containers for several years, their performance will deteriorate progressively. Therefore, it's better to restock every year. After flowering, the bulbs can be lifted and stored or replanted into the garden.

RIGHT: **Light metal**
Metal pots give a well-weathered feel to these *Cyclamen coum.*

WINTER PLANTING

HINTS AND TIPS
• Containers should be frost-proof if you plan to leave them out all winter.
• Alternatively, wrap them in a protective material to shield them from the cold.
• Always check once a week to see if they need watering.
• Never water in freezing weather.
• Wait until spring to apply fertilizer.
• If planning a long-term planting, use a loam or soil-based planting mix. If it is purely seasonal planting, use a multipurpose soilless mix.

Winter fire

Description: The red stems of bloodtwig dogwood, *Cornus sanguinea* 'Midwinter Fire', and the black leaves of *Ophiopogon planiscapus* 'Nigrescens' are cooled by the pure white flowers of snowdrops.

Bloom time: Although this dogwood produces small, creamy white flowers in early summer, its starring role is in fall, when the glorious flame-colored stems are revealed.

Container type: Any type is fine, as long as it's reasonably deep and frost-proof.

Planting: This container should be planted in fall. Cut the dogwood stems back to 2 to 3 inches from the ground in spring.

Planting medium: Use a soil-based potting mix with a slow-release fertilizer.

Position: Tolerant of sun and semishade, this arrangement can also be maintained as a permanent planting.

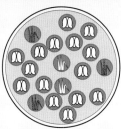

Quantity

 2 × Bloodtwig dogwood, *Cornus sanguinea* 'Midwinter Fire'

 3 × *Ophiopogon planiscapus* 'Nigrescens'

 15 × *Galanthus* 'Sam Arnott'

Green and gold

Description: This display incorporates *Helleborus argutifolius*, *Euonymus japonicus* 'Ovatus Aureus', hybrid primroses, *Erica carnea* cultivars, and *Ophiopogon planiscapus* 'Nigrescens'.

Bloom time: The hellebore is a striking structural plant with light green cup-shaped flowers that bloom from January to March. After flowering, the primroses can be planted out into the garden and the rest, if desired, maintained as permanent planting.

Container type: Stone is ideal. Make sure it's reasonably deep and frost-proof.

Planting: In mid fall, plant all but the primroses, which should be planted as soon as they appear in garden nurseries. The hellebores will come into flower in late winter or early spring.

Planting medium: Use a soil-based potting mix with a slow-release fertilizer.

Companions: The architectural foliage of the hellebores is evergreen and continues to look good long after the flowers have faded.

Position: This container is suitable for both sun and shade.

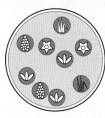

Quantity

 2 × *Helleborus argutifolius*

1 × *Euonymus japonicus*

3 × Primroses

 2 × *Erica carnea*

 1 × *Ophiopogon planiscapus* 'Nigrescens'

Seasonal berries

Description: Skimmia is displayed with *Euonymus* 'Emerald 'n' Gold', Tiarella (also known as foamflower), and small-leaved variegated ivy. Skimmias are neat, dome-shaped evergreen shrubs. The more vigorous male plants have white, slightly fragrant spring flowers, and the females have beautiful glossy red berries in winter. Their red and green coloring makes them the perfect seasonal plant for the winter container.

Bloom time: This runs from midwinter to early spring.

Container type: Any type is fine, as long as it's reasonably deep and frost-proof.

Planting: Plant this container combination in mid fall. It is fully hardy to zone 7.

Planting medium: Choose a potting soil made for acid-loving plants, and plant in mid fall. Add a slow-release fertilizer.

Companions: To get bright red berries from the female skimmias, plant one male plant in with the females.

Position: This container can be in the sun during winter and spring, but move it to a shady spot in summer.

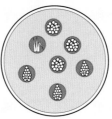

Quantity

3 × *Skimmia* spp. (two female and one male)

1 × *Euonymus* 'Emerald 'n' Gold'

3 × *Tiarella*

Winter basket

Description: A wicker hanging basket holds ivy, skimmia, and winter pansies.

Bloom time: Every winter, pansies can be relied on to bring a colorful palette to an otherwise foliage-dominated container. The pansies bloom all through winter, halted only by heavy frosts and snowfalls. The flower buds lay dormant during these very cold spells but will bloom when warmer weather comes around.

Container type: Wicker hanging basket.

Planting: Plant the combination in the fall to give it time to get established before the first frost normally arrives.

Planting medium: Plant in a general-purpose soilless mix with slow-release fertilizer.

Position: Place in semishade.

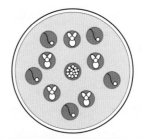

Quantity

5 × Ivy

5 × Pansies

1 × Skimmia

Textured display

Description: If your winter climate is relatively mild, the standard bay tree will make an attractive yet formal centerpiece in this winter container display. (If you suffer from colder winters, there are a variety of hardier evergreens that can be bought as standards such as holly or *Viburnum tinus*.) The good news is they are easy to grow in a container as they like to be pot-bound. They can be moved to a cool room if frost threatens.

Bloom time: Late winter to spring.

Container type: Frost-proof terra-cotta.

Planting: Plant in fall.

Planting medium: Keep the potting medium moist. Start to feed in spring, increasing to at least every two weeks during the growing season in summer. Prune in late spring or late summer to retain shape.

Companions: In spring it can be underplanted with a new selection of plants (herbs look particularly good), or else replant the euphorbia in the garden leaving in the saxifrage, which will reward you with a mass of glorious white flowers on tall delicate stalks in spring and throughout summer.

Position: Sheltered.

Quantity

1 × Standard bay

2 × *Skimmia japonica* spp. *reevesiana*

3 × Saxifrage

2 × *Euphorbia* × *martini*

WINTER PLANTING

HINTS AND TIPS

• To add color to a container, incorporate the fall-flowering cyclamen, *C. hederifolium*. From late winter onward, these can be replaced by early flowering *Cyclamen coum*.

• If you are planting bulbs in an exposed spot, use smaller or dwarf varieties; otherwise, the bulbs can suffer from wind damage.

• Although you can plant snowdrops as dry bulbs in fall, they will probably do better if planted after flowering or "in leaf" in early spring.

• For permanent planting, use a soil-based potting mix, and top-dress with fresh potting medium every year.

• Do not overfeed hanging baskets. You may have to move them to a sheltered spot if the winter is particularly severe.

OTHER WINTER PLANTS

• Conifers
• *Cyclamen coum*
• Dwarf iris (*Iris reticulata*)
• *Daphne odorata*
• Early snowdrop (*Galanthus* spp.)
• *Erica carnea*
• Hellebores
• Ornamental cabbages
• Winter flowering pansy (*Viola* × *wittrockiana*)
• Winter aconite (*Eranthis hyemalis*)

THE KITCHEN GARDEN

Regardless of size and space, you can grow a variety of fruit and vegetables in containers and hanging baskets that will look attractive, taste good, and be far more economical than pricey store-bought produce. You will also have the added benefit of knowing that your plants were grown without harmful pesticides. Try to choose not only your favorite vegetables, herbs, and fruit but also those that look pretty. Having fruit and vegetables so easily accessible in containers by the kitchen is also an excellent way to encourage children to eat healthfully, and to get interested in gardening, by being rewarded with delicious things to eat.

The container herb garden

Herbs are probably the most rewarding of all plants to be grown in containers. Regardless of where you live and how big or small your gardening space is, what could be nicer than having an abundant supply of fresh herbs by your kitchen door? As well as tasting and looking great, they are also very easy to grow.

PLANT LIST

French
Basil
Lavender
Rosemary
Tarragon
Thyme

Indian
Basil
Bay
Chile
Cilantro
Curry leaf
Fennel

Italian
Basil
Oregano
Parsley
Rosemary
Sage

Mexican
Basil
Bay
Cilantro
Chile
Tarragon

Throughout history, herbs have been valued for their medicinal and culinary properties as well as their fragrance and beauty. Herb gardens are also abundant with pollen and nectar, making them havens for foraging bees and butterflies. As far back as the first medieval kitchen gardens, herbs have been grown in pots as well as raised beds, and containers offer an easy and organic way to grow herbs. The extra height of containers makes it easier to gently crush the leaves in your hands, releasing their aromatic oils.

The meditative nature of herbs makes them ideal plants for unusual containers—

tin buckets, colanders, and old watering cans. Most herbs like a sunny position, although some, such as mint, chives, and parsley, also do well in semi-shade. Some such as cilantro and basil are annuals and need to be sown each year. Other herbs including tarragon, fennel, and mint are perennials, while others such as rosemary and thyme are shrubs.

Although herbs can be placed with other ornamental plants, they generally look best grouped together. Herbs thrive on regular clipping, which keeps them compact and bushy.

Go Green

A dense planting of thyme can give valuable cover for many insects, as well as a rich source of nectar for honeybees.

BELOW: **Thyme on your hands** Pots of thyme bring a fresh aromatic appeal to an otherwise drab flight of steps.

Top 12 herbs

FOR CONTAINERS

1. Basil
2. Bay
3. Cilantro
4. Dill
5. Thyme
6. Rosemary
7. Chives
8. Parsley
9. Mint
10. Sage
11. Oregano
12. Marjoram

(See Plant Directory starting on page 136 for details)

LEFT: **Fragrant seat**
Medieval apothecary's garden with wicker screen, thyme seat, boxwood balls in pots, foxgloves, and crushed shell mulch. This is a modern take on the classic medieval turf bench. A favorite feature of this period, it was a wooden or brick seat-shaped container filled with earth and then planted with grass or sweet smelling herbs, for sitting on.

BELOW: **Strawberry planter**
A terra-cotta strawberry planter can work really well for herbs. The trailing herbs are better suited for the side pockets, whereas herbs with a more upright habit are better planted in the top.

When planting herbs, add a mulch of gravel to prevent the surrounding area from drying out. Mint should be planted in its own pot because it can be aggressive.

Some herbs are known more for their flowers than their foliage. The vibrant orange petals of calendula can be used to flavor food or give a spicy, colorful accent to a salad. Nasturtiums also have brilliant red, orange, and yellow flowers that, along with the leaves, have a peppery taste.

Plant your herbs in a soil-based planting mix to which sand or grit has been added for extra drainage, along with a slow-release fertilizer for long-lasting nutrients. Do not allow the pots to dry out. Deadhead flowers to get the optimum quality and quantity of leaves for cooking or drying. Cut back the perennials in fall, and bring any tender herbs into a cool room or greenhouse. Mulch with gravel, and water sparingly.

Herb planting

HINTS AND TIPS

- Mint, basil, and cilantro—unlike most other herbs—prefer a moist soil.
- Never use a herb for medicinal properties without first consulting a medical professional.
- In case they do not survive the winter, take cuttings from the slightly tender rosemary, lavender, and sage for new plants next year.
- Herbs can also be grown in window boxes and hanging baskets, but make sure the eventual size of the plant is suitable for the container.
- Consider growing herbs used together, such as Indian or Italian, in the same pot.
- If the roots begin to grow out of the container in spring, repot the herbs. Alternatively, remove the top inch or two of potting mix and refresh with new. Add a slow-release fertilizer into the soil, and water well.
- Parsley, garlic, mint, and chives all grow well in shady spots.

The container vegetable garden

Growing your own vegetables satisfies on many levels: environmentally, spiritually, and for that good old-fashioned pleasure of picking food packed full of flavor and nutrients, untouched by pesticides. You save money, too.

SHADE-TOLERANT VEGETABLES

(shade for half a day)
Beets
Kale
Lettuce—"Little Gem'"
Radish
Spinach

VEGETABLE COMBINATIONS

- *Mixed baby lettuce leaf, radish, and scallion*
- *Tomatoes, zucchini, and eggplant*
- *Nasturtiums and zucchini, or baby tomatoes, in a hanging basket*
- *Tomatoes, onions, garlic, and basil*

VEGETABLES TO GROW AGAINST A WALL

- *Sweet peppers (Capsicum)*
- *French beans (Phaseolus vulgaris)*
- *Tomatoes in growbags disguised in wooden troughs*

Mention growing vegetables, and chances are you'll conjure up images of digging, weeding, and watering and be all too easily put off by the thought of hard work. Or you may reckon your concreted backyard is too small to sustain a vegetable patch. But you can grow vegetables in just a window box. With containers, it's possible to grow organic vegetables whatever your situation or soil type. Without a doubt, a container is more convenient and even easier than a vegetable patch, while still providing the satisfaction of working hand-in-hand with nature.

Vegetable checklist
- *Which ones do you like to eat?*
- *Do you want them to look as good as they taste?*
- *Do you want to store vegetables or eat them straight from the garden?*
- *Will you be away from home for any amount of time, and for how long and when?*
- *Do you have friends who might look after your plants in return for some vegetables?*

LEFT:
Veg hedge
Tomatoes grown in faux metal troughs by a trellis on the edge of a patio provide both shelter and nourishment—a winning combination. The trellis, as well as acting as a support for the tomatoes, also provides a useful screen. Be warned, however, that this is a high maintenance affair.

Top **12** vegetables

FOR CONTAINERS

1. Salad greens
2. Tomatoes
3. Eggplant
4. Peppers
5. Swiss chard
6. Zucchini
7. Dwarf beans
8. Cucumbers
9. Garlic
10. Radish
11. Potatoes
12. Arugula

(See Plant Directory starting on page 136 for details)

RIGHT: **Lettuce display**
Who said you can't grow vegetables in a hanging basket? This display of salad vegetables in a woven wooden basket is both eye-catching and easily accessible.

BELOW: **If you can't lose it, use it**
Carrots in an old, watertank lined with plastic. Carrots need a deep container so this improvised and recycled tank makes the perfect planter.

GO GREEN

- Grow fennel or dill nearby to attract hoverflies, whose larvae eat aphids.
- Interplant vegetables with marigolds, onion, and garlic not only to look attractive but also to deter pests.
- Look for disease-resistant varieties so you can avoid using pesticides.
- Consider growing edible podded peas. They're delicious but quite pricey in the stores, plus growing your own means no resources will be used to transport them.

Sowing and growing

HINTS AND TIPS

- Most vegetables can be raised from seed; however, many can also be bought as young plants in the spring.
- In warmer zones, you can sow early vegetables such as spring cabbage, spinach, lettuce, and fava beans in early fall so they're well established by early spring.
- Some seeds including lettuce, broccoli, or tomatoes can be started indoors and transplanted into the containers as young plants.
- Some vegetables such as lettuce or carrots can be sown on a periodic basis for a succession of crops throughout the season. They can be sown directly into containers in spring.
- Sow or plant vegetable varieties that mature quickly and are best picked fresh.
- Choose varieties for taste rather than size. Bigger is not always better when it comes to flavor.
- Grow a selection of lettuces for a variety of colors and shapes.
- Do not plant too closely, as they will become overcrowded as they grow.
- Grow flowers with your climbing vegetables, such as sweet peas through runner beans.
- Try to grow vegetables that are picked when young and tender for a succession of crops, such as radish, baby carrots, and scallions.
- If you're working with limited space, grow only a few plants—preferably, those you love to eat but cannot easily buy in the supermarket.
- Plant basil in a growbag under your tomato plants.
- Do not grow vegetables, especially leafy varieties, near busy roads or very polluted areas because the leaves can absorb toxins in the atmosphere.

ABOVE: **Jewel in the pot**
Chard growing from a glazed pot makes a striking showpiece using a functional container.

Exposure

Most vegetables don't like growing in the shade, so choose a sunny, sheltered spot—in front of a south-facing wall would be ideal. The plants should get at least 6 hours of sun a day. Faster-growing vegetables such as spinach prefer some shade, especially later in summer. Make sure, however, that they're in a good position for catching the rain; that is, not under an overhanging roof or tree.

Containers for vegetables

You can grow vegetables in just about anything—from cleaned-out trash cans to truck tires. There are also purpose-made containers available, including potato and strawberry barrels. Use a deep black bucket with holes drilled in the base to grow leeks, carrots, and even asparagus. You'll get much better results by growing several plants in one large container than by growing each plant separately in lots of smaller pots.

Growing vegetables in bags of potting soil is another option, but these can be difficult to water and do not allow for effective root development. A variety of devices for watering, feeding, and support make growbags more efficient. Place an insulating layer of polystyrene (often called Styrofoam) or similar material under your growbag to protect it from temperature fluctuations if it is lying on concrete. For maximum benefit, choose smaller-growing crops.

Plastic containers hold water better than terra-cotta ones do. If you prefer the natural look of terra-cotta, you can line your pot with plastic (but don't forget to make drainage holes before filling with potting soil).

Remember, the larger and deeper your container, the more success you'll have with your vegetables. The minimum depth should be 9 inches.

Once planted, containers can be placed in a porch, greenhouse, or cold frame to get a head start on the rest of the garden. Group containers together for easy watering.

TIPS FOR PLANTING

Drainage
Make sure there's really good drainage from your containers—even though vegetables need consistent and thorough watering, they hate being waterlogged.

Planting medium
As with all containers, never use soil straight from the ground; it may introduce pests and diseases. Use a good soil-based planting mix with added slow-release organic fertilizer. All vegetables need a lot of water and a good supply of nutrients. Give your plants an extra feed with a seaweed-extract fertilizer.

Root crops in containers
Root crops such as potatoes and parsnips need more soil than most vegetables. Potatoes and sweet potatoes can be grown in large pots (at least 12 inches across and 12 inches deep). You can also use plastic crates or even a large plastic bag, but don't forget to put drainage holes in the bottom. If container space is limited, plant dwarf cultivars, or try small rooted varieties such as baby beets, carrots, or turnips. Bush varieties of zucchini and squash are also more compact than trailing varieties. It's best not to grow vegetables with a long growing season, such as Brussels sprouts and cauliflower in containers.

Intercropping
If your space is limited, try planting small, fast-growing crops such as lettuces and radishes next to slower-growing ones such as carrots and broccoli. The latter will fill the space left when the fast growers are harvested.

Growing tip
For an instant display or effect, purchase plants as seedlings rather than sowing direct into the soil.

Top-up tip
Only grow pumpkins if you are prepared to do an extra amount of watering. They are greedy feeders.

BELOW: **Well ordered veg**
Vegetables and ornamental plants in metal containers on a town roof garden include French beans, beets, kale, and bay trees.

The container fruit garden

Throughout history, fruit has been grown in containers for ornamental display as well as for self-sufficiency—and there's no reason you can't have your own orchard or grow fruit in pots with only a paved courtyard, a tiny yard, or even a balcony.

FRUIT
    COMBINATIONS

- *Peach underplanted with strawberries*

- *Standard red currant or black currant underplanted with nasturtiums*

- *Grow lemons, figs, and pomegranates as the Ancient Romans did*

- *Strawberries in a strawberry jar especially for children*

Although fruit in pots generally require more attention than that grown in the garden, the pleasure derived from picking and eating what that you've grown yourself can't be overstated. The size of a fruit tree normally is determined by grafting the cultivar (variety) onto what is called a rootstock—but a container will also restrict the growth and size of the tree. Some say a more vigorous rootstock can be a better choice because it will grow into a more resilient tree, although some fruits such as figs benefit by having their roots restricted, encouraging the plant to put its energy into making fruit instead of foliage.

Fruit tree size

Tree size is determined by the rootstock on which it is grown, which may be dwarf or half standard. A vigorous variety of tree is a better choice for cordons, fans, and espaliers and is generally more resilient. Dwarf trees make sense for pots, however, some garden experts believe there's no need to consider rootstock when planting in a container, which naturally restricts the growth of a vigorous tree.

Being small and containerized means that fruit trees can be maintained and protected in areas that might be too cold naturally. It's easier to wrap a smaller fruit tree with horticultural fabric or move it in or out of cover.

Position

Apples, pears, nectarines, and peaches do well in a sunny spot, preferably in the shelter of a west- or south-facing wall.

Because pears come into flower early, they are most at risk of frost damage. If your tree does succumb to frost, move it into the shade until it has fully thawed. Plums and cherries prefer full sun but will tolerate a small amount of shade—particularly the Morello cherry, which can be grown in light shade. Currants and gooseberries are also relatively tolerant of shade.

Hardy fruit trees can be left outside in winter, but less hardy varieties should be brought under cover.

Pollination

Many cultivars of fruit trees, such as apples and pears, are not satisfactorily self-fertile and therefore may need to be grown with a cultivar with similar flowering times. Check when buying that you have compatible fruit trees.

Containers for fruit trees

If you are growing a fruit tree that needs to be moved, it's probably best to grow it in a light plastic container. For those that will remain in the same place, a frost-proof clay pot will be aesthetically more pleasing as well as more stable. Choose a pot that's no more than about 3 inches larger than the tree's root ball. As the tree grows, the size of the container can then be increased.

GO GREEN

Aphids love nasturtiums, so plant some in or near your containers to attract beneficials that prey on them.

Go Green

• You may pay more for organically grown fruit but knowing that your pot produce is pesticide-free makes it worth the extra cost.

• Plum trees benefit from nitrogen in the soil, so try planting clover under your plum trees to give them an extra fix.

Top 10 fruit

FOR CONTAINERS

1. Apple: cross-pollinate; prune as pyramid or bush

2. Pear: cross-pollinate; prune as pyramid or bush

3. Cherry: some self-fertile; train as pyramid

4. Plum: most self-fertile; train as pyramid

5. Peach and nectarine: self-fertile

6. Fig: prune as a bush on a short stem

7. Blueberry: needs well-drained acid soil mix

8. Red, white currant, gooseberry: look best as standard; convenient to pick

9. Grape vine: looks good trained as standard

10. Strawberry: plant in late summer; crop for 1 year only; good for hanging baskets and window boxes

   (see Plant Directory starting on page 136 for details)

ABOVE: **Pear tree**
Pyrus 'Vereinsdechant', a pear tree in a white ceramic container stands beside a basket of its fruit. The container's confining space means you should go for dwarf fruit tree varieties. They will require constant watering and feeding.

RIGHT: **Rhubarb, rhubarb, rhubarb**
Rhubarb can be grown in containers successfully, so long as the pot is large enough—like this sturdy example shown here—to accommodate a season's growth. This attractive container plant is ideal for a deck, patio, or balcony. The stalks may be delicious to eat but beware, rhubarb leaves are toxic.

FRUIT TREE

HINTS AND TIPS

- More tender fruits such as apricots and citrus may benefit from being moved in and out of a greenhouse or conservatory when cold or frosty weather threatens.
- If you do not have access to cover and you live in a frost-prone area, choose late-flowering varieties, or else be willing to wrap your plants with horticultural fabric to protect them in cold weather.
- If space is restricted, why not train fruit trees in the form of fans, espaliers, or cordons against a wall or fence? Even a balcony can accommodate a row of fruit with horizontally trained side branches grown in containers.
- If you're planning to have quite a few small fruit trees, try to choose cultivars that will produce fruit throughout the season rather than all at once. Bear in mind that early ripening varieties of apples and pears don't store as well as those that mature at the end of the season.
- If your fruit tree is next to a wall, turn the pot around once every 2 weeks or so.

GO GREEN

Blueberries are highly popular as "superfoods" because they are high in antioxidants. They like an acidic soil, so feel free to recycle your used coffee grounds into the pot from time to time, to help create a good growing environment.

Potting medium

Use a rich soil-based potting mix. Apply a nitrogen-rich fertilizer when the fruits start to swell. Also add nitrogen-rich fertilizer toward the end of the summer. In spring, renew the top of the pot with 2 inches of potting mix.

Maintenance

1 Every other winter, take the plant out of the pot.
2 Gently remove old soil from around the roots, and cut away any nonfibrous woody roots.
3 Repot into a larger container with new potting soil.
4 Water regularly. In summer, this could be up to two or three times a day.
5 Ensure adequate drainage, and do not forget to place your container on risers if it's on a hard surface.

LEFT: **Training tree**
This 'Regali Delkistar' apple tree is being trained as a fan so that the two opposite shoots grow from the main stem. The special metal frame allows for a freestanding container.

Soft fruit

Hints and tips

- Strawberries grow well in a variety of containers—single pot, hanging baskets, and strawberry planters.
- Raspberries, black currants, gooseberries, and rhubarb grow naturally at the woodland edge and will tolerate some shade. However, they fare better in a sunny spot.
- Blueberries are becoming increasingly popular for growing in containers, not only for their flavor, but also for their health benefits.
- The more sun your fruit gets, the sweeter and riper it will be.
- To tell if your fruit is ripe, gently twist it; if it comes away easily, it's ready for eating.

Top: **Strawberry jam**
These 'Gorella' strawberries are grown in old terra-cotta pots. Strawberries are easy to grow; one problem you may encounter is slugs.

Right: **Gooseberry fool**
Gooseberry 'Invicta' in a large terra-cotta pot sits on a decked patio along with thyme and marjoram.

The aromatic container garden

Aromatic plants have been documented for their culinary and medicinal properties at least since Ancient Egyptian times. Their pungent and evocative aroma can lift the spirits and bring us closer to nature. By crushing the leaves in our hands, we release aromatic oils that have soothed and nourished people for centuries.

AROMATIC PLANTS SUITABLE FOR CONTAINER GARDENS

Basil (Ocimum basilicum)
Calendula (Calendula officinalis)
Dill (Anethum graveolens)
Mint (Mentha *spp.*)
Rosemary (Rosmarinus officinalis)
Sage (Salvia officinalis)
Santolina (Santolina chamaecyparissus)

AROMATIC PLANTS FOR MAKING TEA

Chamomile (Calms the nervous system, promotes restful sleep)
Lemon balm (Aids relaxation, improves sleep)
Peppermint (Relieves digestive disturbances)
Thyme (A general tonic)

(All these tea herbs thrive in full sun)

RIGHT: **Care-free containers** *Lavender (Lavandula* spp.*) looks striking in these large pots, which help get the fragrance to nose level and help you relax with minimum effort.*

Aromatic plantings

We tend to think of aromatic plants only as herbs, but in fact they include many perennials, trees, and shrubs. Although some are not particularly showy, many aromatic plants have beautiful flowers and foliage. For those with limited space, they add a Zen-like quality to the garden for healing and contemplation, while the nectar-filled flowers attract bees and butterflies. Trees with aromatic properties include eucalyptus (which requires pruning to control its size), juniper, and bay. Lavender is probably the most beautiful and satisfying of all aromatic plants. Originating from the Mediterranean area, lavender was used by the Romans to perfume linens and bathing water. Scented geraniums are superb container plants tolerant of hot temperatures. Favored by the Victorians for their aromatic foliage, they come in a wide variety of scents, including peppermint, sandalwood, cinnamon, and nutmeg. Try growing a lemon-scented geranium on your patio—it is said to ward off mosquitoes in summer.

Ideal position

Place pots of aromatic plants along pathways, doorways, or patios where they can be lightly brushed or touched, releasing their scent.

GO GREEN

Planting aromatic plants and herbs among other containers may help protect your plants against animal pests.

5 PLANTING IDEAS FOR AROMATICS

TEAPOT TOWER

Taking tea on the patio? This stunning three-pot aromatic arrangement provides you with a relaxing brew, no shopping required. You will need three round terra-cotta pots—the largest at the bottom—say, 14 to 16 inches across, the middle 3 to 4 inches smaller, and the top container another 3 to 4 inches smaller. The best time to snip off a few leaves for tea is just after the rain or dew has dried and before it gets too hot. This is when the oils in the leaves are at their strongest and most flavorful.

1 Put 2 to 3 inches of gravel in each pot.
2 Place a 3-foot cane in the center hole of the largest pot, and then fill it with potting soil to 1 inch from the brim.
3 Slide the middle pot down the cane until it rests on the bottom pot. Then fill that pot with soil.
4 Plant the top pot (which you have not yet placed) with your focal plant—lavender is an ideal choice.
5 Cut the cane now so it's tall enough to secure the top pot, and place the planted top pot onto the soil of the middle pot. Take care not to disturb the roots.
6 Now plant the middle pot: Choose tea plants that are not so tall, such as chamomile, lemongrass, and thyme.
7 Put rosemary, spearmint, peppermint, and lemon balm around the edge of the bottom pot.
8 Plant close together avoiding any gaps. Water well.
9 Feed with a seaweed based fertilizer every 2 weeks in summer.

HERBAL PLEASURES

HINTS AND TIPS

• Save lavender clippings and throw them into your fireplace in winter to perfume your house.
• Throw bay and rosemary onto your barbecue to flavor outdoor cooking.

1 To attract beneficial insects

Fennel and nasturtium

Fennel is best grown in a container at least 12 inches deep and approximately 15 inches wide. Plant three per pot plus nasturtium seeds in a light potting soil with good drainage. Fertilize about once a month, and water throughout the summer months. Once winter arrives, cut it back for the fennel to grow again the next year.

3 An aromatic silver garden

Curry plant (Helichrysum italicum), Artemisia *'Silver mound'*, *and santolina*

Grow this grouping of highly aromatic plants for the pretty yellow flowers and pale silver leaves, which will glow and shimmer into the fading light of a warm summer night. Plant these in free-draining soil and keep them in a sunny position.

ABOVE: **Double duty**
Lemon verbena (*Aloysia triphylla*) leaves are tasty in tea and also as a scent for a potpourri.

2 To attract bees, butterflies, and moths

Lavender, pink valerian, catmint, and Achillea *'Moonshine'*

These four aromatic perennials have superb complementary colors. Although their roots will happily tolerate a restricted area, the plants can grow fairly large, so it's important to choose a large container.

4 Authentic aromatics to spice up your curries

Cilantro (Coriandrum sativum), *lemongrass, chiles, Thai basil, and caraway*

If you savor the aromatic flavors of Indian and Thai curries, plant a selection of Southeast Asian aromatics in a container, using chile pepper as the central plant. All are easy to grow and maintain in a sunny spot—handy for your kitchen door.

5 To create a potpourri

Scented geraniums

Of all the container plants, scented geraniums are among of the most rewarding. Not only do they have elegant aromatic foliage and pretty flowers, they're also extremely easy to grow. Choose plants from a wide variety of colors, textures, and scents, most of which will grow happily in the same container. However, make sure they are equally vigorous; otherwise, smaller plants can be easily swamped by more robust ones. Plant in a free-draining container mix and keep in a sunny or semishade position.

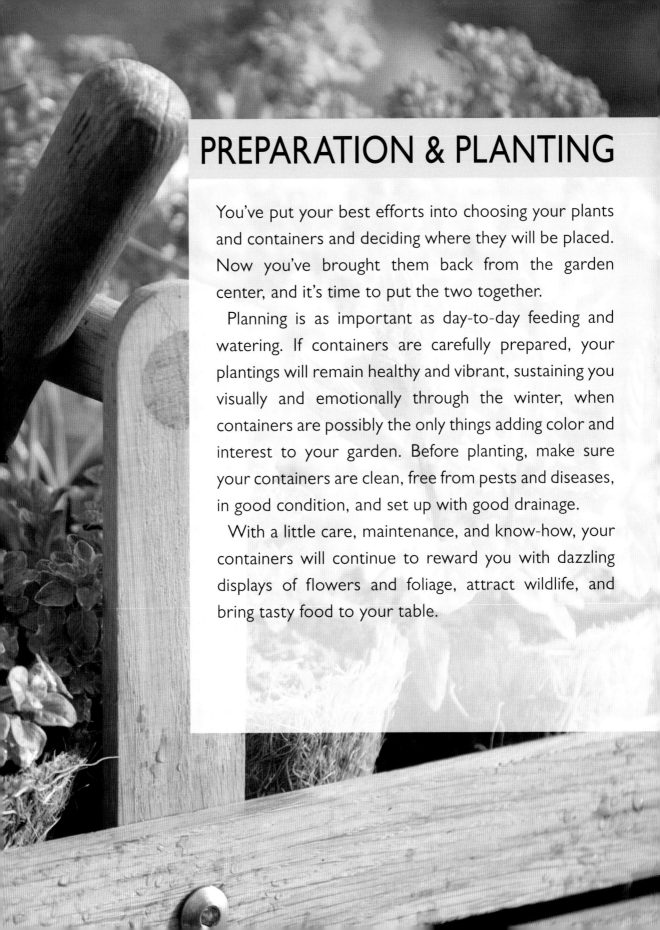

PREPARATION & PLANTING

You've put your best efforts into choosing your plants and containers and deciding where they will be placed. Now you've brought them back from the garden center, and it's time to put the two together.

Planning is as important as day-to-day feeding and watering. If containers are carefully prepared, your plantings will remain healthy and vibrant, sustaining you visually and emotionally through the winter, when containers are possibly the only things adding color and interest to your garden. Before planting, make sure your containers are clean, free from pests and diseases, in good condition, and set up with good drainage.

With a little care, maintenance, and know-how, your containers will continue to reward you with dazzling displays of flowers and foliage, attract wildlife, and bring tasty food to your table.

Types of containers

"Anything goes" to make a successful container provided it can hold enough potting soil for plants to grow healthy roots and it has drainage holes so that excess water can escape. So the good news is that any object will do—from a tin pail to a rustic wooden wheelbarrow to a geometric graphite "designer" planter.

8 POINTS TO CONSIDER

LEFT: **Pot-pourri**
The enormous variety of containers available at many garden stores can sometimes seem overwhelming with all their designs and materials—and at times can seem overpriced. However, once you give your planting method and intended location some thought, your options will narrow and your decision will become easier. Here is just one corner display of a large garden center—showing glazed and unglazed terra-cotta pots and troughs.

RIGHT: **Oak and stone**
This modular planter combines decorative stone with solid oak legs. Once set in place (here with a cordyline), you wouldn't really want to move it again, it's that heavy.

1 Environment

A container is an artificial environment few plants would instinctively choose for their growth. Therefore, it's important to choose one that will match as closely as possible the natural environment in which a particular plant will thrive.

Plants can be very sensitive to extreme temperatures, both heat and cold. Certain containers that are black, metal, or—worse—black metal, can absorb and conduct heat that will "cook" the plant roots if placed in a sunny spot.

If a plant is located in a hot area, use a thick stone or timber container, or cascading plants to shade the sides and keep the soil temperature consistent. Painting containers white or a pale, cool color also helps hold the temperature down.

LEFT: **Egg-cup shape**
This large terra-cotta pot is excellent for a block planting of tall tulips.

RIGHT: **Lead-lite**
A faux metal trough is a good choice for window ledges and balconies where the container needs to be light.

when choosing containers

2 Size

Generally, the larger the container the better. This allows for:
• Generous root growth and plantings
• Stability
• Less plant maintenance
• A wide range of aesthetic choices

3 Style

The style of the container should be sympathetic to its location. For example, is the location formal, informal, contemporary, or rustic?

BELOW: **Nice 'n'neat**
An attractive hardy begonia sits neatly in a terra-cotta pot—perfect for semishade. The white flowers bloom from late summer till frost. Likes regular watering.

4 Harmony

Consider the hard landscaping materials already in the house and garden. Do stone, wood, brick, metals, or other materials predominate?

5 Space

What space do you have available? Is it on a floor, roof terrace, or windowsill? Are you intending to plant just flowers, or trees, or herbs? These considerations will determine the size and shape of your container.

6 Strength and weight

If your choice is a large container in a permanent setting on ground level, it's best to go for weight and strength. The weight will add stability, and you need a container strong enough to withstand the elements, such as frost and general wear and tear. It's worth paying extra now to get the container that is most aesthetically pleasing and will weather the best over the years.

On the other hand, if the planting will be moved around or placed on a roof terrace or balcony, some large but extremely light containers can be used without adding too much of a burden to supporting structures. Conversely, smaller pots can be made with heavier materials to give them more stability.

7 Durability

The durability of containers can be affected by many factors, such as:
• Rain
• Root growth
• Contraction and expansion of both container and potting soil due to extremes of temperature
• General wear and tear

For more permanent plantings, make sure your containers, particularly terra-cotta, have been appropriately treated for weathering, or else protect or shelter them during the winter months. With terra-cotta, it's best to select pots with straight or tapered sides. Potting soil freezes, thaws, and expands, and narrow-necked pots are liable to crack from the pressure.

8 Safety

If growing vegetables, choose a container made from inert materials or that has not been treated with hazardous chemicals—that is, anything that will react with the soil, fertilizers, or water. If you are unsure, stick with untreated wooden tubs or barrels, or those that have been treated with natural wood preservatives.

Some metal containers have sharp corners and are prone to rust. It's best to leave them out of a narrow garden or one used by children or the elderly.

Wood

Natural and harmonious

As an organic material, wood is naturally harmonious with most plants and settings. Two classic containers, the elegant Versailles box and the rustic half barrel, are examples of the visual versatility of wood. This natural insulator is frost-resistant and will help protect against extremes of temperature. Unlike terra-cotta, wood is good for water retention and therefore will not dry out so quickly. We do not recommend the new types of pressure-treated lumber for their use with food plants. They have not been available long, and their safety has not been proven.

ABOVE RIGHT: **Classic to rustic wood**
From the formal Versailles box to the rustic beer or rum barrel, wooden containers are truly organic and attractive—but they need oil or a preservative to extend their life.

Small tall boy planter

Rustic wavy line tub

Varnished oak barrel

Versailles bo

Small patio tub

Large quarter barrel

Two-bar trough

Half barrel

Small patio planter

Fruit and veg box

Good-looking lumber

HINTS AND TIPS

• Don't place the container directly on the ground—especially where it is damp.
• Place mini supports, or even old bricks or stone beneath your container to prolong its life and help with drainage.
• Unless treated, softwood containers will quickly rot, so it's best to buy those that have been made from cedar, which is naturally rot-resistant.

• For added protection, apply a wood stain that contains a natural preservative or rub with linseed oil both inside and out.
• Use a plastic or metal liner to lengthen the life of your container.
• Make sure that any hardwood container you make or buy has come from a renewable source.
• Update a wooden container with a fresh coat of paint or stain (although it still needs regular maintenance).

Stone

Textural and long-lasting

There is an enormous range of true stone containers, in colors that vary depending on the region where they were sourced. The texture will vary from rough-hewn to highly polished. Stone is inherently heavy, both visually and physically, making it suitable only for ground-floor planting. However, it lends weight to any planting composition, and because it is so durable, it's perfect for a permanent planting. Stone is also virtually maintenance free, and it's one of the few materials that is positively enhanced by weathering and with age. There's also an enormous range of reconstituted "stone" pots, from traditional shapes such as urns to contemporary clean-cut styles, which are far cheaper and lighter.

Naturally durable

HINTS AND TIPS

• When placing stone containers against other hard stone landscaping materials, make sure they complement each other. For example, highly polished marble will look extremely uncomfortable on a rustic stone surface.
• To speed up a weathered look, paint yogurt or spray liquid fertilizer onto your pot to encourage the growth of lichen and algae. Stone offers the added advantage of being durable, strong, and nonporous and therefore plants are more resistant to drying out.

Tall tapered granite planter

Stone urn on pedestal

Modern fluted planter

Bow trough

Low tapered slate planter

Terra-cotta

Popular and versatile

Throughout history and into the modern day, terra-cotta, or "baked earth" clay, has been the most popular and widely used material for plant containers. It's highly versatile and ranges dramatically in size, shape, and price. It looks good in a variety of spaces and situations and complements most planting schemes. Glazed varieties are also popular.

Hand-thrown containers come in a wide range of colors: from pale ochers to deep, rich, earthy reds, depending on the region the pot has come from. The great thing about terra-cotta is that these lovely colors only improve with age as algae grow on the salts and nutrients that leach out through the porous surface.

Mass-produced terra-cotta pots may be much cheaper, but they lack the decorative elements and subtle colors of the pricier handmade varieties.

If you are going to leave your terra-cotta pots out over winter, make sure they are frost-resistant.

ABOVE: **Glazed**
This large "misty blue" glazed terra-cotta provides a highly attactive color to brighten up a back yard.

Handthrown Ali Baba jar pot

Lattice trough with pot feet

Cylinder with lemon motif

Egg pot stem on clay saucer

Handthrown jar

Florentine tree planter

Strawberry planter

Window box

Hand-thrown Cretan pot

Clay pots (not frost-resistant)

Cube, small long tom, egg pot selection

ABOVE: **Visually versatile terra-cotta**
A selection of terra-cotta including strawberry planter window boxes, plain pots, and troughs. Variations in color come from different clays and firing temperatures.

Large frost-proof sandstone

Sandstone cube

LEFT: **Stone, naturally**
Durable, extremely heavy, and quick to take on a weathered look.

Marble stone trough

Heavy bowl

Clay care

HINTS AND TIPS

- Always soak your pot in water before planting. Terra-cotta pots are more porous than other containers and tend to dry out quickly. On the plus side, they do not become waterlogged and allow air to get to the plant roots.
- Glazed terra-cotta pots are more impervious to water and easier to maintain, but the glaze can be damaged by frost. To help protect planted pots, line the inside of the container (apart from the drainage holes) with a thick layer of plastic sheeting to prevent it from absorbing extra water in winter.
- Terra-cotta pots can be fairly brittle and easily broken. Buy those that are frost-proof; otherwise, bring them indoors during winter.
- If you intend to have permanent plantings in terra-cotta, avoid plants with tough, fleshy roots such as agapanthus, as they can break through.
- Store empty terra-cotta pots upside down or on their sides in a dry area during the winter.

Metal and faux metal

Tough and stylish

Once considered dated, metal containers are back in style. Metal can now be treated using various techniques such as galvanizing, polishing, and painting to create a wide range of finishes, including matte, polished, and colored, in an up-to-date, contemporary style.

Tough and frost-proof, metal containers are very easy to maintain and require no more than a wipe-down with each new planting. However, most oxidize with exposure to the elements and will eventually loose their patina; if handled roughly, they can be easily scratched or dented.

As nice as it would be to own a traditional metal container, faux, or fake, metal pots, especially faux lead, are very popular—being nontoxic, much lighter, rust-proof, and generally cheaper than the real thing. They are made with polymers, plastics, resins, and fiberglass but look highly authentic.

Galvanized is good for a contemporary urban look. Shiny to start with, these planters will eventually dull over time.

Zinc does not dull or show watermarks. It's lightweight, too. It will begin to rust but only if exposed over a long time to extreme weather.

Stainless steel can be used outside as well as inside. It will not rust but can corrode due to chemicals such as fertilizer in the potting soil. Use a plastic liner to help protect the container from corrosion.

Scalloped half-cut metal planter

Framed imitation lead cube

Metal urn and plinth

Faux lead trough

Zinc weathered pots

Weathered metal urns with and without handles

ABOVE: **Heavy metal and metal "lite"**
A selection of galvanized, color-powdered, polished, and faux metal containers. The real ones come in steel, zinc, copper, and aluminum.

Steel, zinc, and aluminum

HINTS AND TIPS

- If your container will rust, causing staining on the surface it is standing on, make sure it is on a drip tray to collect excess water, or ensure that the water can drain easily away from the pot.
- Avoid very hot and sunny positions; metal containers can conduct heat to the roots and cause them to scorch.

Synthetic

Strong and lightweight

It's easy to dismiss synthetic containers as inferior copies of the more desirable "real thing." Yet plastics, resins, fiberglass, and other synthetic materials offer the designer an opportunity to create beautiful and innovative containers that would be otherwise unachievable and too expensive.

Synthetic containers have the advantage of being lightweight (good news for balconies and roof terraces) while also adding strength and stability, conserving moisture, and being frost-proof and affordable. Many faux copies of more traditional materials, especially lead and stone, can be exceptionally convincing.

A very handy container for growing vegetables is a tough, collapsible polyethylene growbag. It is reusable and will fold away when the growing season is over.

ABOVE: **Grow bag grow**
A clever, practical, and reusable container comes in the shape of this sturdy garden growbag.

Alternative materials

HINTS AND TIPS

- Cheap synthetic pots can be planted and inserted in more expensive decorative containers, protecting them from wear and tear.
- Note that concrete and limestone containers can leach lime into the soil, creating an alkaline environment.

Conical pot

Improvise

Creative and fun

Plants can grow in anything that holds water; is durable, weatherproof, and free of contaminants; and has drainage holes and sufficient depth for the roots, depending on the plant. If you take these factors into account, then places like thrift stores, flea markets, garage sales, and hardware stores become invaluable. Have fun and improvise with containers. Why not harmonize the plant with the container: Grow an olive tree in an old wholesale decorative olive oil tin? Or plant herbs and vegetables in old kitchenware? Or ginger in a large oriental-style tea caddy?

Faux lead Moroccan cylinder

Do-it-yourself containers

HINTS AND TIPS

- Here are a handful of possibilities to try: baking pans with pretty labels; old wheelbarrows; old zinc tubs; metal mop buckets; wooden baskets; chimney pots; glazed terra-cotta drainage pipes; hollowed-out tree trunks; rubber boots; large seashells and even old rowing boats. Work on the old adage, if you can't lose it, use it.
- It's not a good idea to use rubber tires as containers, especially for growing vegetables, as they can leach toxic chemicals that contaminate both the soil and the plants.
- If you want a giant recycled olive oil or other produce tin, try asking at your local delicatessen stores or restaurant for unwanted items.

ABOVE: **Recycling recycled**
A two-tier planter of hostas helps to deter slugs and snails and is made from discarded stainless steel washing machine drums supported by bamboo poles.

At-a-glance container suitability

Material	Durability	Frost resistance	Water retention	Stability	Easy care
Wood	■ ■ ■	■ ■ ■ ■ ■	■ ■ ■ ■ ■	■ ■ ■ ■	■ ■ ■
Stone	■ ■ ■ ■ ■	■ ■ ■ ■ ■	■ ■	■ ■ ■ ■ ■	■ ■ ■ ■ ■
Clay	■ ■ ■ ■	■ ■ ■ ■	■ ■ ■ ■	■ ■ ■	■ ■ ■ ■
Metal	■ ■ ■ ■	■ ■ ■ ■	■	■ ■ ■ ■	■ ■ ■ ■
Synthetic	■ ■ ■ ■ ■	■ ■ ■ ■ ■	■	■ ■	■ ■ ■ ■ ■

Tools, tips, and tricks

Although there is an enormous amount of gardening equipment at most garden centers, when it comes to planting containers, very little is needed. Much depends on the size of your plants, how many you have, and where you want to plant them. Equally relevant is how much storage space you have at home. If your containers amount to a couple of window boxes, then you'll only need a long-spouted watering can, hand pruners or snippers, gloves, and a trowel.

Tools and toolcare

HINTS AND TIPS

- Keep all of your container-gardening tools in one place. A large canvas bag is especially useful because it can hold everything and is easy to carry. You may want to keep sunscreen and a hat in it, too.
- When buying equipment, go for quality. Your tools will last longer and work better.
- Always clean your equipment after use. Ideally, wipe down each piece with an oily rag, and lubricate moving parts with oil.
- It's very easy to lose equipment when gardening, so try painting a bright stripe on a handle, or entwine it with a strong, colorful hair band so you can easily locate and identify each tool.
- For staking, make sure you have the items below:

Plastic ties

Scissors

Labels

Garden wire

Garden twine

Split and bamboo canes for support

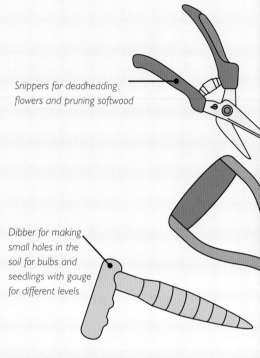

Snippers for deadheading flowers and pruning softwood

Dibber for making small holes in the soil for bulbs and seedlings with gauge for different levels

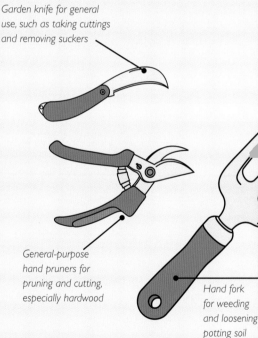

Garden knife for general use, such as taking cuttings and removing suckers

General-purpose hand pruners for pruning and cutting, especially hardwood

Hand fork for weeding and loosening potting soil

Essential tools

One of the big pluses of container gardening is that it doesn't require an arsenal of tools, unlike mainstream gardening. Visit a good garden store and compare like with like for size, lightness, gripability, and potential durability. Plastic tools weigh less but are not so tough. Wooden-handled with metal tips are the traditional tools but require regular cleaning, oiling, and scraping clean. Don't get carried away, and keep what you need to a minimum. Keep safety latches on and sharp tools out of reach of children.

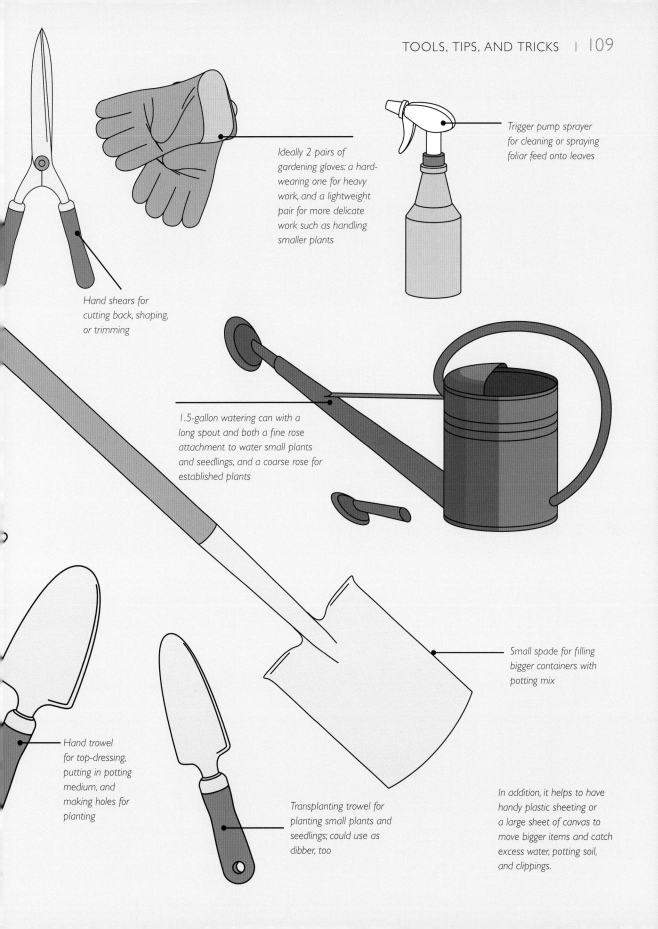

Ideally 2 pairs of gardening gloves: a hard-wearing one for heavy work, and a lightweight pair for more delicate work such as handling smaller plants

Trigger pump sprayer for cleaning or spraying foliar feed onto leaves

Hand shears for cutting back, shaping, or trimming

1.5-gallon watering can with a long spout and both a fine rose attachment to water small plants and seedlings, and a coarse rose for established plants

Small spade for filling bigger containers with potting mix

Hand trowel for top-dressing, putting in potting medium, and making holes for planting

Transplanting trowel for planting small plants and seedlings; could use as dibber, too

In addition, it helps to have handy plastic sheeting or a large sheet of canvas to move bigger items and catch excess water, potting soil, and clippings.

Potting mix

Before planting up your container, make sure you have the right growing medium—that is, potting mix—for your specific plant or display. This will ensure your plants have the best start in life and stay in tip-top condition.

Soil-based mix

Soil-based mix (sometimes also called loam-based mix) contains high-quality soil as its main ingredient and has several benefits. This type of soil is normally broken down into standard noncommercial formulations.

Germinating mix is suitable for sowing seeds and growing seedlings. Use a different mix for alpines, which you can get at specialty nurseries or mail-order suppliers.

Standard potting soil contains more fertilizer than germinating mix does. This is the most versatile of the soil formulations and suitable for a wide range of plants.

POTTING MIX TIPS

- Most potting soils will benefit from the addition of an organic slow-release fertilizer.
- Vermiculite or perlite can be added to help retain water while allowing for good drainage.
- Woodland plants will particularly benefit from using leaf mold as a peat substitute.

ADVANTAGES

- Free draining
- Good structure
- Good aeration
- Dries out slowly
- Less likely to become waterlogged
- Heavy; gives stability, especially to larger, more mature plantings

CAUTIONS

- Because it becomes heavy once water is added to it, it is not really suitable for hanging baskets, window boxes, balconies, or terraces, especially where large containers are concerned.

Soilless (or loamless) mix

A potting mix that contains no soil is generally known as a multipurpose mix. Its main ingredient is peat or a peat substitute. Try to avoid peat-based mixes because the extraction of peat is environmentally damaging. Instead, use those made with peat substitutes, such as coir, which have a variety of benefits.

ADVANTAGES

- Easy and clean to use
- Economical
- Lightweight
- Great for balconies, roof gardens, and for hanging baskets

CAUTIONS

- Once dry, it's very hard to get it to reabsorb water, so incorporate compost or natural water-retaining gels for a constant supply of moisture.
- Can become waterlogged

Loam
This is sterilized garden soil. It is high in nutrients, has good moisture retention, aeration, and drainage.

Gravel
Add it to compost to improve drainage and aeration. There are various grades available.

Sand
There are coarse and fine varieties that will help you achieve more open and finer textured mixes.

Potting mix
Combinations of ingredients (i.e. loam, natural fertilzer, sand, perlite, vermiculite) making up whatever is suitable for your planting.

- Plants that have been growing in soilless mix may not transplant into the garden too well.
- It's low in nutrients; always incorporate a slow-release organic fertilizer.

Multipurpose potting soil

If you are uncertain which growing medium to use, there are some excellent multipurpose commercial products specifically mixed to combine the best of both types. Always choose good-quality mix that hasn't been lying around the garden center too long.

Ericaceous potting soil

Some plants, such as *Skimmia japonica*, heather, and magnolia, prefer an acid soil. This is when you need a soil mix formulated for acid-loving plants.

Coir
An environmentally-friendly peat substitute, which is good at retaining moisture but low in nutrients; requires frequent feeding.

Go Green

TRULY ORGANIC

To make life easier for yourself there are plenty of commercial organic potting mixes for sale in garden centers. Such products may have "OMRI Listed" on their label. (OMRI is the Organic Materials Review Institute.) Such certification will mean it's okay for organic container gardening. Alternatively, you can make your own.

MAKE YOUR OWN SOIL MIX

Mixing your own soil is fun and ensures that your planting gets exactly what it requires rather than a general versatile mix. Never use soil directly from the garden unless it has been sterilized, as it may contain diseases and pests. This also applies to homemade mixes. Never use contaminated soil, especially in vegetable containers.

HOMEMADE SOIL-BASED MIX

This basic recipe can be adapted to suit a particular plant or planting. For extra drainage, for example, increase the amount of sand or grit. Add small amounts of wood ash for extra alkalinity; add fine bark, coffee grounds, or decomposed pine needles to increase acidity.

- 1 part sterile rich loam
- 1 part sterile potting mix or peat substitute
- 1 part grit or coarse sand
- 1 tablespoon ground limestone (for approximately 1 gallon mixture)
- 1 tablespoon bonemeal

"COOKING"

To sterilize garden soil, moisten and spread it approximately 3 inches thick on a baking tray and place in the oven at 180° to 200°F until the soil temperature maintains a temperature of 180°F (no higher) for about 30 minutes. Or put it in a roasting bag, place it in a microwave, and cook at full power for 1 minute per pound.

Preparing pots for planting

Nothing is worse than taking all the time, effort, and expense of potting up a really beautiful container of plants—particularly a permanent one—only to have the container disintegrate or collapse. With careful preparation, you can prolong the life of both your container and your plants.

GENERAL CONTAINER CARE

- *Unless wooden containers are placed on blocks that allow free circulation of air, they will rot very quickly. Any untreated wood should be treated with a horticulturally safe preservative or outdoor oil-based paint.*
- *Most metal containers will eventually rust (with the exception of aluminum), so it's wise to insert a plastic liner to prolong their life.*
- *Whenever possible, keep containers under shelter during the cold winter months—particularly terra-cotta because, unless it's frost-proof, it's liable to crack.*
- *Cracks and chips in most types of containers can be filled with an adhesive sealant. This will prevent the damage from spreading as well as keeping out the water and so help prevent frost damage.*

Drainage

Every container must have adequate drainage holes in its base so that any surplus water can escape. Otherwise, the potting soil will become waterlogged, and the plants will eventually die. Most containers come ready-made with drainage holes. However, for those that don't or for items such as tin pails or half barrels, it's a fairly easy matter to make them yourself using a small drill at a slow speed (so as not to crack the container). Before you drill, cover the area with masking tape to avoid splintering. If you are drilling into metal, place a block of wood for support under the area you are about to drill. Always protect your eyes with safety goggles.

Drip trays

Drip trays are useful where excess water escaping from the container may cause staining, excessive algae growth, or dampness. Fill the tray with either small stones or gravel so that the pot is not standing in the water. If your container is raised on runners or blocks, it is possible to slide a shallow tray underneath the pot's base. Use drip trays with metal containers that are beginning to rust to avoid staining decking or stone paving.

Moving containers

In most cases, it's better to plant your container in its final position. However, if you need to move it elsewhere, first let the container dry out a little so it's lighter. For smaller containers, bags of soil mix, and plants, use a wheelbarrow instead of making endless trips back and forth. For larger containers with a circular base, try rolling them carefully. Otherwise, use a trolley with rollers or a short plank laid over circular pipes or poles that can be rolled. Some containers come with built-in wheels for ease of movement. These are particularly useful for roof gardens and terraces.

To avoid back injuries, invest in a porter's trolley or moving dolly. Nowadays, they come in lighter aluminum and are retractable so they don't take up too much space when not in use. Take care when moving large, earth-filled planters. Adopt the safe lifting technique: Always keep your back straight and legs bent.

Cleaning

HINTS AND TIPS

If you want to reuse a pot, first clean it to prevent the spread of pests and diseases. If your container, particularly a terra-cotta one, has acquired a delightful patina with age, leave the outside alone and just clean the inside.

1 If the pot is excessively dirty, soak it in water overnight. This applies in particular to porous pots that may have accumulated harmful salts.
2 The next day, scrub the pot with a mild detergent using a stiff brush or, if that's too abrasive, a soft sponge or cloth.
3 Rinse with clean water.
4 If the cleaning seems like more work than it's worth, just insert a plastic liner into the pot before adding any potting soil. Don't forget to put drainage holes in your liner as well.

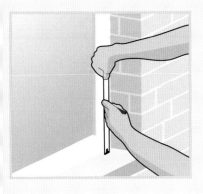
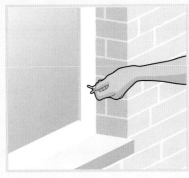

Securing containers

GROUND LEVEL

- All containers must be well secured because if they fall over, they could cause damage not just to the pot and plant but also possibly to a passerby.
- Large containers should be placed on a level and, if possible, graveled base.
- Do not place containers directly onto the earth because this can give easy access to pests and diseases.
- Smaller pots should be grouped together for extra support.

ROOF TERRACES AND BALCONIES

- All containers on roof terraces and balconies should be kept as light as possible; therefore, it is imperative that all containers are well secured—especially taller plantings that can catch the wind.

- Use containers with wide, preferably square bases. Place them close to walls or where they will be protected from the wind.

WINDOW BOXES

- Whether or not you can rest window boxes on the sill, always secure them with steel brackets. For safety, screw them onto the sill or window frame.
- Chains can also be attached to the bottom end of the window box and secured at an upward angle to the wall.
- If your windowsill slopes downward, place two wedges under the window box to make it horizontal, before you secure it.
- Try to maintain as much space as is practical around the window box to allow for air circulation.

ABOVE: **Window boxes**
A fully planted window box will be very heavy but still subject to wind turbulence on a windowsill. To secure it firmly, use heavy-duty metal brackets, wedges, or fixing plates or hooks. Large or heavy window boxes should be secured prior to planting.

HANGING BASKETS

It's essential that any hanging basket bracket is secure and strong enough to support a fully planted and watered hanging basket.

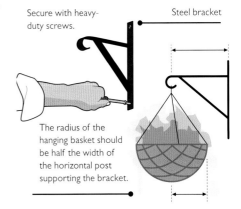

Secure with heavy-duty screws.

Steel bracket

The radius of the hanging basket should be half the width of the horizontal post supporting the bracket.

ABOVE: **Hanging baskets**
The usual form of support is a steel or wrought-iron bracket. Make sure that the length of the bracket is longer than half the diameter of the hanging basket so the plants have room to grow out without being crammed against the wall.

LEFT: **Brush strokes**
Use a stiff bristle brush and a mild detergent to clean the exterior of the container.

How to plant a container

Having carefully considered your choice of container, types of plants, and potting mix, you now have the key ingredients and are ready to plant.

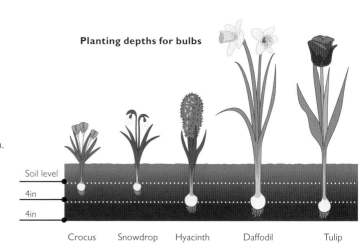

Planting depths for bulbs

Soil level

4in

4in

Crocus   Snowdrop   Hyacinth   Daffodil   Tulip

Pre-planting

Inspect the pot and make sure it has sufficient holes for drainage in the bottom. If you are using a terra-cotta pot, soak it first so that it doesn't draw out moisture from the soil mix. Make sure that all the plants have been well watered before planting.

10 SIMPLE STEPS:

1 Place a layer of gravel or broken crocks at the bottom of the container to prevent the drainage holes from clogging and the soil from leaching out.

2 Fill the container three-quarters full with potting soil.

4 Place the pots on the ground, keeping them in the same arrangement.

3 Place plants still in their pots on top of the surface and arrange until satisfied with the design.

PLANTING BULBS

When choosing bulbs, select the largest available for successful flowering. The general rule is to plant bulbs at two or three times their own depth and as close as 1 inch apart. Some bulbs—for instance, stem rooting lilies such as *Lilium regale*—should be planted at least 6 to 8 inches deep. Bulbs can be left in containers to continue to flower year after year. However, the quality of the blooms can be compromised, so it's best to replace and plant new bulbs every year.

To achieve continuous spring flowering, it is quite possible to plant in layers, starting with tulips at the bottom at depths up to about 12 inches deep, followed by a layer of potting soil, and then a layer of narcissus or daffodil bulbs. Crocuses or other small bulbs or corms such as *Anemone blanda* can be planted on another layer of soil approximately 2 to 3 inches from the surface.

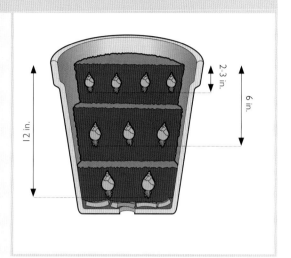

for container planting

5 Carefully tip your central plant (generally the tallest one) out of its pot, and plant it in the center of the container.

6 Continue to plant, starting with the next tallest and gradually working your way down to the smallest plants. Always remove the pots the plants were purchased in.

7 Add extra potting soil until the level of the soil is about 1 inch from the top of the rim.

8 With both hands, gently firm in the plants. Avoid excessive pushing.

9 Stand back and check to see if you are satisfied with the design. If not, carefully reposition the plants. If it will help the overall design, tilt them so their flowers and foliage face outward.

10 Water the container thoroughly with a fine hose.

Trees in containers

Trees in containers not only give an instant sense of permanence and maturity to a garden, they also provide year-round interest and drama.

ABOVE: **Beautiful bay**
Bay trees thrive in containers, making them ideal for the patio. [?] them every fall, and administer a liquid feed throughout summer

TOP TEN TREES FOR CONTAINERS

Japanese maple (Acer palmatum)
Juniper (Juniperus communis 'Compressa')
Tree fern (Dicksonia antarctica)
Holly (Ilex)
Yew (Taxus baccata)
Lemon (Citrus limon)
Olive (Olea europaea)
Kilmarnock willow (Salix caprea 'Kilmarnock')
Bay tree (Laurus nobilis)
Weeping pear (Pyrus salicifolia)

WHEN TO PLANT

Trees for containers come in three categories: container-grown, bare-rooted or root-balled (where the roots and surrounding soil are wrapped in a material such as burlap). For best results buy and plant all three types when dormant, i.e. in late fall, or early spring. Container-grown trees, however, can be planted almost any time of the year.

When choosing a container, first make sure that it has a wide base and is made of a heavy material for extra stability such as frost-resistant terra-cotta. It should also be about twice the width and depth of the roots so that it will allow them enough room to develop. Because of the limited root space, most trees will need regular watering and feeding. Make sure to wet the medium to the full depth of the container especially during hot dry weather. Apart from dwarf fruit trees, it is best not to buy trees that have been staked as they will be unable to stand up on their own. Avoid large, fast-growing trees as they can become unstable. However, trees such as willows (*Salix* spp.) and eucalyptus are tolerant of coppicing. Use a loam-based potting medium to give added weight and stability. Then add a slow release fertilizer. You'll need-lime-free medium for trees that require acidic soil.

Maintenance

Feed in midspring and then every two weeks throughout the summer months. In early spring remove the top 1 inch of old medium and replace it with new. Re-pot every three to five years preferably into a new container, which should be about 2 inches wider.

GO GREEN

- Hawthorn, willow, and birch support many beneficial insects.
- Fruit on apple trees are a valuable source of food for birds in fall and winter.
- Include trees that produce berries for birds to feed on.
- Evergreens provide shelter for birds in winter.

Trees to attract wildlife and birds:
- Crabapples (*Malus* spp.)
- Holly (*Ilex opaca*)
- River birch (*Betula nigra*)
- Yew (*Taxus baccata*)
- Mountain ash (*Sorbus americana*)

6 SIMPLE STEPS: for planting a tree

1 Water the tree in its original container. Scrub your new pot and then soak it in clean water. Place pieces of broken pots over the drainage hole. If possible place it in its final position before planting, as it will become too heavy to move later on.

2 Fill about one-third of the pot with a loam-based potting medium (you'll also need to add a slow-release fertilizer).

3 Hold the tree sideways and gently ease out the root ball keeping it intact. If the roots are tightly wound round the root ball, tease a few out before planting.

4 Place the tree in the new pot and continue to add potting medium until it is planted at the same depth as it was previously. Firm down the roots and cover with more medium until it reaches the soil line on the stem.

5 Make sure that the tree is upright and if needed add more medium firming it around the roots. The finished layer of soil should be at least 1 inch below the rim of the pot. This allows for watering.

6 Thoroughly water the tree and apply a mulch of bark chips or similar material to help conserve moisture. Do not move until the pot has fully drained (or your back will suffer!)

Hanging baskets

Hanging baskets need no longer be a cliché mix of trailing summer annuals. Today they come in all shapes and sizes—as well as a variety of materials—and contain plants as diverse as lettuces, tomatoes, herbs, clematis, and ferns. Choose the largest basket that can be attached securely to your wall—it will be easier to look after and less prone to drying out.

TIPS FOR HANGING BASKETS

- *To help retain water, line the inside of your natural liner with a recyclable plastic sheet.*
- *To promote continual flowering throughout the summer, deadhead any old or faded flowers on a regular basis.*
- *Choose plants that have been grown in individual pots, as their root balls will be easier to manage.*
- *Feed flowers and tomatoes once a week with a high-potash organic liquid fertilizer.*
- *Feed herbs once every 2 weeks with a general-purpose organic liquid fertilizer.*
- *If you have a large hanging basket, try placing a small plastic bottle pricked with holes within. Pour water into the open neck of the bottle to facilitate easier watering and a better distribution of moisture.*

Potting soil for a basket

A soil-based potting mix is the ideal medium for hanging baskets. It needs to retain water without waterlogging and should be extremely fertile—both qualities are essential in an environment where plants will compete for food.

There are two disadvantages to soil-based versus multipurpose potting mix: It's heavier and not as clean to handle. In some cases, therefore, it's advisable to use the lighter soilless mix, but it will have to be regularly fertilized and must never be allowed to dry out. This type of potting mix will need watering at least twice a day in hot weather, otherwise water once a day—even when it rains.

ABOVE: **Silver moon**
Clematis 'Silver Moon' is a compact clematis, perfect for an unusual but stunning planting in a hanging basket. Place in a semishade position.

ABOVE: **Two halves together**
Be experimental: Try planting two hanging baskets with *Sempervivum* joined together to form a finished ball as seen here.

10 SIMPLE STEPS: for planting hanging baskets

1 Place the hanging basket on an empty bucket and line it with an environmentally friendly material such as a coir liner.

2 Half fill the lined basket with potting medium mixed with a slow-release fertilizer. Do not firm down. If you intend to have trailing plants, make small holes in the sides of the liner using scissors or, if necessary, a utility knife.

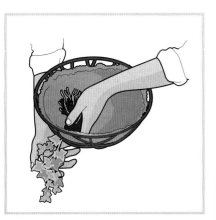

3 With both hands, carefully pull the roots of the trailing plant through the hole or cut in the liner.

4 As each layer of plants is added, cover the roots with potting mix and firm in gently.

5 Add another layer of potting mix until the basket is nearly three-quarters full.

6 For the top layer of planting, place your tallest and largest plant in the middle of the basket. Again firm in gently.

7 Add the remaining plants, giving careful consideration to an aesthetic and balanced display. It's fine to overplant the hanging basket as long as the root balls aren't squashed together.

8 When planting is finished, gently firm the soil before adding the final layer of potting mix, which should come to just below the rim of the container.

9 Water the basket thoroughly but carefully, using a watering can with a fine rose.

10 Allow to stand for at least 10 minutes so that the excess water can drain out before the basket hangs in its final position.

GO GREEN

HINTS AND TIPS

- Make sure your moss or other lining has been farmed from a renewable source.
- Do not strip from local woods—this can be extremely damaging to the natural environment.
- Mock moss, which is made from coir or wool, is also available but will not hold water as effectively as sphagnum moss does.
- An alternative liner could be phormium leaves, fern fronds, or even an old woolly sweater.

Window boxes

Window boxes makes great use of ledges—especially where there is little or no garden space—for growing flowers, herbs, and vegetables. They look equally good on or by a wall, or on a balcony edge that plants can trail over, creating color and interest.

TIPS FOR WINDOW BOXES

- *Too much color in a window box can be overpowering, so include a good foliage plant such as a scented geranium or Helichrysum petiolare in your planting.*
- *Although plastic window boxes are cheap, they tend to buckle and bulge under the weight of the potting soil. Fiberglass or wood is stronger and will last longer, although wood will need regular maintenance.*
- *If you do use a wooden container, line it with a plastic sheet to prevent it from rotting.*

- *Pot feet are tailormade for window boxes and troughs. One fits at each corner, raising the pot above the windowsills, ensuring good air circulation and preventing waterlogging or sill damage.*

Window boxes are classically rectangular to match a standard sill, but they come in a wide range of materials, such as plastic, wood, metal, and terra-cotta. Try to find one that not only complements your style of house but matches as near as possible the length of the windowsill. The bigger the better, too (as long as it fits), so it will be easier to maintain.

10 SIMPLE STEPS:

1 Clean the window box with warm water and mild detergent.

2 Place broken crocks or a layer of gravel over the drainage holes.

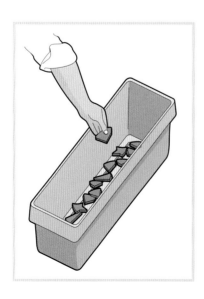

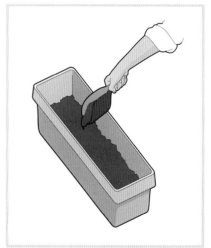

3 Half fill the window box with potting mix appropriate for your plants—soil-based for permanent planting, multipurpose or soilless for seasonal planting.

RIGHT: **Seashore planting**
A driftwood style balcony window box with a selection of seaside planting that can stand up to exposed, windy conditions including armeria, sempervivum, saxifraga and *Veronica teucrium*.

LEFT: **Neat symmetry**
A profusion of white Marguerite daisy (*Argyranthemum frutescens*) show off from this terra-cotta window box.

For planting a window box

4 Arrange your plants—still in their pots—into the pattern you want. Place the taller ones at the back of the box and the smaller and trailing plants at the front and sides. Remember that window box displays usually look best with a degree of symmetry.

5 Remove the plants and place them on the ground in the same positions they were in the window box.

6 Tip the largest plant out of its pot, gently tease the roots out, and place it in its intended position. Using extra potting mix, firm the plant so that it is in its correct depth and position.

7 Continue to plant from side to side, starting with the largest plants. Firm in gently.

8 When the planting is finished, add extra potting mix until, when firmed in, it is just below the rim of the window box (about 1 inch).

9 Water carefully but thoroughly, and then allow the window box to drain before placing it in its final position.

10 Don't forget to water, feed, and deadhead on a regular basis to get the best possible display from your window box. Use an organic high-potash fertilizer at least once a week.

Watering

The most important thing to consider when watering your containers is not so much "how" but "when." Just because your plants are wilting doesn't mean that they need watering. Bad drainage due to a blocked drainage hole or over-vigorous taproot could be causing waterlogging.

ABOVE: **Potted pond**
A blue glazed ceramic pot planted with *Ranunculus aquatilis, Oenanthe fistulosa, Nasturtium officinale, Gratiola officinalis, Preslia cervina* and *Glyceria aquatica variegata*

When to water

During the growing season and especially in high summer, you may need to water once or twice a day. In fall and winter, keep watering to a minimum, but never let the potting mix completely dry out. Test the soil for watering by pushing your finger into the soil.

• If it is wet and clammy, it could be waterlogged.
• If it is crumbly and dry at least an inch below the surface, it needs watering.

Take a clue from the weather as well. If it is hot, dry, and windy, it is far more likely that your containers will need watering than if it is cool and damp. However, it doesn't mean that your soil is moist enough just because it's rained.

How to water

It is important to give your pots a thorough soaking so that the potting mix is fully saturated and the water will drain out of the bottom. A light sprinkling on top will do more harm than good because it will cause the roots to turn toward the surface rather than grow deep into the pot.

Drip irrigation

Drip systems deliver water to containers at a measured rate. You can buy them individually to place in a single pot or as a set attached to many pots via tubing from a faucet (*see illustration below*) or rain barrel. Because the soil can more easily absorb water delivered at a slow and steady rate and there is no excess water draining out of the bottom, they are efficient systems that waste little water. Drip irrigation systems can be bought at most garden stores and are quite easy to assemble. Install a timer to regulate when and how much water is dispensed.

In some locations, the law may require you to fit a backflow-prevention valve to avoid any possible contamination of water supplies. The downsides of drip irrigation systems are that they are basically ugly and not easy to hide, and your containers have to be positioned in reach of their tubing.

BELOW: **Triple drip**
Simple but effective irrigation via tubing attached to an outside faucet.

A water-based container

To have a truly wildlife-friendly backyard, you need to incorporate a water-based feature. All you need is an old sink or water tank, a bucket, a barrel, anything in fact that will hold water and doesn't leach chemicals. Containers such as terra-cotta will need a liner or several layers of yacht varnish inside, wooden barrels will need to be soaked, but whatever you use plug up any drainage holes with cork or sealant.

To give your plant a head start, include mud or slime from a nearby pond, as it will contain microscopic pond life and nutrients. You will also need oxygenating water plants such as aquatic moss and water starwort. Place your pond with other containers to give protection to wildlife visitors. To create a "pond in a pot" see page opposite.

Mulch

Mulch is a protective layer covering the top of the potting mix. It can be organic, such as bark chips, or inorganic, such as pebbles. Mulch is excellent not only at conserving water by reducing evaporation but also at discouraging weeds and soil erosion, particularly during watering. It also comes in decorative forms, including polished stone, glass chips, and seashells.

5 SIMPLE STEPS: pond in a pot

1 Make sure your intended container is watertight. Place it in its intended position before filling. It should have access to full sun.

2 Cover the base with a good layer of gravel and fill with water until it is two-thirds full.

3 Pot up aquatic plants in individual mesh baskets with garden soil or an aquatic potting medium. Put a layer of gravel on top.

4 Carefully place pots into the water to the appropriate depth. Marginal plants (i.e. shallow water plants) should be placed with their soil line just below the surface; deep water plants can be placed 12 inches down.

5 Sit plants on bricks or half-bricks to adjust depth. Add floating plants, such as *Azolla caroliniana* or submerged oxygenators such as *Eleocharis acicularis*. To maintain the pond, protect from heavy frosts and don't add fish.

Watering worries

HINTS AND TIPS

- Ali Baba-shaped pots with narrow necks are less likely to dry out than those with wide rims.
- It makes environmental sense to collect rainwater for free rather than pay for the tap water we so desperately need to conserve. Invest in a rain barrel or any sort of container that can collect water from your gutters and downspouts.
- Some "lime-hating" (or "acid-loving") plants such as orchids or azaleas prefer rainwater, especially if you live in a hard-water area.
- If you're worried about the chlorine in tap water, let it stand in the sun for a few days.
- If a pot has been neglected and the plants have wilted, stand the pot in water in the shade for about half an hour. Then take it out and let it drain. If the plant hasn't recovered by the next day, it is beyond help.
- If your potting mix dries out, it will shrink away from the sides of the container, causing the water to flow down the sides rather than soak the soil. If this happens, poke holes in the soil with a cane and then pour the water over the holes. If that doesn't work, pour a tiny drop of dish soap into a large watering can, fill it with water, and water the plants with the mixture (liquid soap increases the water's effectiveness in clinging to dry soil).
- Some water-retaining gels on the market claim to be organic, biodegradable, and safe to use when growing vegetables. They're useful for moisture-loving plants as well as hanging baskets. Don't use more than the manufacturer's recommended amount, or you'll end up with something looking like a jellyfish, which will push the potting mix out of the container.

Feeding

In a natural environment, plants are sustained not only by photosynthesis—the process by which they acquire food through their leaves—but also by the absorption of water and nutrients through their roots. Containers, by definition, restrict root run and limit the amount of potting mix. So feeding is vital.

- *Always feed bulbs after flowering; they need to store nutrients in order to successfully flower the following year.*
- *Roses need more frequent feeding than most other trees or shrubs and respond well to regular foliar feeds.*
- *Perennials benefit from high-nitrogen feed in the spring to promote good foliage growth. Switch to a high-potassium feed in the early summer to promote flowering.*
- *Alpines prefer to grow in a low-fertility environment, so feed these sparingly.*
- *Dilute your tomato fertilizer in warm water, rather than cold, to stimulate root growth. Also perfect for those Halloween pumpkins.*
- *For all foliage vegetables, such as lettuce, feed with a high-nitrogen fertilizer.*
- *It is essential to carefully follow the manufacturer's recommended dosage, otherwise damage can be done to both plants and soil.*

Nature obligingly provides water and nutrients through a natural process of growth and decay. However, plants growing in a container are confined and consequently rely on us, their growers, for their food.

Fertilizers

In the restricted space of a container, any nutrients in the potting soil quickly get used up. Fertilizer provides the plants with a steady supply of food. There are two types of fertilizer.

ORGANIC FERTILIZERS

These are derived from either animal or plant substances. Good organic fertilizers are blood, fish, and bone, which contain the three major minerals.
- Nitrogen for general leaf growth

- Phosphorus for root development
- Potassium for flower and fruit growth

Despite the fact that organic fertilizers are highly efficient, many people do not like handling or dealing with animal by-products.

SYNTHETIC FERTILIZERS

Man-made fertilizers contain the three main compounds—nitrogen, phosphorus, and potassium. Although they can provide the plants with a quick boost of nutrients, especially during the growing season, they can quickly leach out of the soil resulting in a less nutritionally rich and diverse feed than the natural alternative.

Dry or liquid?

There are two ways to deliver fertilizer to the plant: One is through the soil using dry, slow-releasing, granule-type products; the other is to use a liquid feed that provides a quick boost. The truly organic approach is to feed the soil that then feeds the plant. It's preferable to have a well-structured soil containing an adequate supply of nutrients to give a steady rate of growth, but there are times in container gardening when an instant nutritional hit is desirable.

LEFT: **Tomato top-up**
Tomato fertilizers are high in potassium, and they're excellent not only for tomatoes but for all fruiting vegetables and flowers.

HOW TO USE SOLUBLE OR LIQUID FEED

1 Pour it into a watering can before filling with water.
2 Mix thoroughly with a clean stick.
3 Always follow the manufacturer's instructions.
4 Use the feed every 2 weeks during the growing season.

Foliar feeds

Foliar feeds are for spraying on plant leaves—ideally, on a cloudy day. They can help with specific problems such as iron deficiency in azaleas. In general, however, they act more like a tonic and do not have any long-term value.

• Mix as above before evenly spraying the leaves.
• Do not spray in the midday or full sun, which will scorch the leaves.

Organic liquid feed

Organic liquid fertilizers can be purchased or homemade. Commercial products include liquid manures, fish emulsion, rock phosphate, and plant extracts. The recipe below is particularly beneficial for high-performing seasonal flowering and fruiting plants. Don't overdo it though, or you'll get excessive leafy growth that's vulnerable to cold weather and bugs.

HOMEMADE RECIPE

1 Soak 2 pounds of nettle leaves in 2 gallons of water.
2 Leave for 2 weeks with some sort of covering.
3 Mix 1 part nettle mixture to 10 parts water for use. Use young nettles, cut in spring for the best nutritional hit.

Dry foods

There are various forms of dry organic and inorganic fertilizers. They can be mixed in with the potting soil or sprinkled on top during the growing season to refresh permanent plantings in large pots.

1 Slow-release granules take 2 to 3 weeks to release fertilizer into the soil, thereby providing a steady supply of nutrients to the plants.
2 Slow-release pellets can be pushed into the surface of the potting soil after planting.
3 Organic fertilizer is best mixed in with the potting soil or dug into its surface.

ABOVE: **Flower power**
Adding slow-release fertilizer to the potting medium in a hanging basket.

Slow-release granules

Slow-release pellets

Organic fertilizer

Inorganic top dressing

At-a-glance feeding chart

Plant	Feeding requirements	Feeding action
Perennials	Fast growing	High-nitrogen feed in spring for growth; potassium-rich feed for flowers; every 14–21 days
Alpines	Slow growing and low fertility	Light, if any, annual dressing
Annuals and bedding	High performance and hungry	Generous feed at planting; liquid feed weekly
Vegetables and fruit	Greedy feeders	Nitrogen feed to start; potassium fertilizer for fruiting

GO GREEN

SEAWEED EXTRACT

Seaweed is an organic plant-growth stimulant and a good choice of liquid feed. Use in the early stages, or later on as a foliage spray to discourage sap-feeding insects. It's also helpful for greening up leaves and increasing root growth. You can buy seaweed as a liquid kelp extract, dried kelp meal, or blend. It can be purchased in tea-bag form that you brew as a concentrate or dilute as a foliar spray.

Pruning, training, and support

Container plants such as trees and shrubs generally require minimal pruning because growth is more limited in containers than it would be in the garden. It is normally a matter of keeping them tidy, in good health, and in an attractive shape.

BASIC PRUNING
PRINCIPLES

1 Always use a sharp pair of pruning shears.
2 Cut stems back to healthy tissue or wood.
3 Make a diagonal cut just above (technically, ⅛ inch) an outward-facing bud and a straight cut above opposite-facing buds.

Prune directly across if the buds are placed on opposite sides.

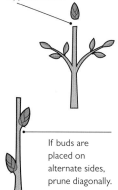

If buds are placed on alternate sides, prune diagonally.

4 If the main or leading bud is cut, the secondary buds farther down will be encouraged to develop. Flower stems will yield two smaller flowers as opposed to one large one.
5 Cut out any dead, diseased, straggly, or overcrowded shoots.

Why prune?
- To remove unwanted growth
- To control size
- To open out or tighten plant growth
- To increase flowering and fruiting
- To create attractive shapes
- To improve circulation of air and access to light
- To remove any dead or diseased parts

When to prune
Follow these guidelines:
- Deciduous trees can be pruned in either summer or winter—never in spring or fall.
- Conifers can be pruned in either spring or summer.
- Spring flowering shrubs should be pruned soon after flowering.
- Prune summer flowering or fruiting shrubs after flowering or fruiting or in late winter or early spring.

Climbers
Climbers grown in containers generally need more pruning than those grown in the open garden; this is because their smaller and more contained root systems cannot feed or support an enormous amount of top growth.

Some climbers are obligingly self-supporting and are best grown in a permanent position against a wall or house. Others need appropriate support, depending on their habit or situation. If you are growing a climber up a wall, make sure there is adequate support, such as a trellis, or horizontal wires fixed onto the brickwork for the plant to grow up. Allow a gap of at least 2 inches so that the air can circulate around the plant.

Support systems, such as a tepee of bamboo canes, can be fixed into the container so that the climber can grow without a wall. The container, however,

Plant support systems

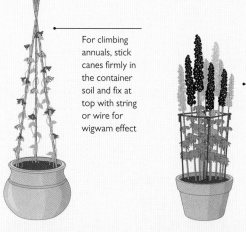

For climbing annuals, stick canes firmly in the container soil and fix at top with string or wire for wigwam effect

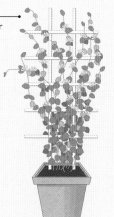

A mini trellis is ideal for twining climbers.

Many tall, soft stemmed plants such as delphiniums require support such as wire frames. Twigs can provide a more natural-looking support than linked wire stakes.

LEFT: **Training into shape**
Use two old pairs of hanging baskets wired together to form a frame for a climbing plant to be trained over.

RIGHT: **Clipping shears**
Use clipping shears for a smooth topiaried cut on any ball-shaped boxwood.

will need to be heavy and deep so it can safely support the plant and structure. Young growth will need to be gently secured and guided against the support. Before long, stems will grip on by either twining or by tendrils.

Check that the ties are secure but not too tight. Recheck every so often as the plant grows.

When it comes to pruning climbers, treat them much the same as you would shrubs, except that you have to tie in the new growth to some kind of support. Deciduous climbers can be pruned from late fall to early spring, whereas evergreens are best pruned in spring.

When pruning, cut out any damaged or diseased stems at the base. Cut back stems by about one third, as well as weak and twiggy ones. Climbers that flower on the current season's growth should be pruned in winter or early spring. Those that flower on the previous season's growth are best pruned after flowering.

Staking

Some of the taller plants that you grow will need some assistance, not only to keep them looking good, but also to protect them from wind damage and passersby. To stake a plant, place a single stake near the central plant stem to provide support to which the drooping parts of the plant can then be tied. Then place three canes at the outer edges of the container and create a support with string tied between the canes.

• Bamboo canes are probably the most commonly used and economical means of staking. They can be used singly or arranged into tepees.
• The height of the support should be two-thirds that of the mature plant.
• L-shaped metal stakes linked together are easy to use and can be reused year after year.
• A free and natural support is a multistemmed branch stuck into the pot. Try to use two or three so that their branches intertwine.
• A trellis is the perfect support for any twining climber.

At-a-glance pruning container shrubs

Type of shrub	Pruning tool	What to do	When	Why
Large-leafed evergreens (e.g., choisya, camellia)	Hand pruners	Remove older wood, shape and trim	Late winter, early spring	To shape and encourage new growth for flowering next year
Small-leaved evergreens (e.g., boxwood, yew)	Pruners/shears	Trim to keep from looking straggly; clip after flowering	Late spring and late summer or after flowering has finished	Ideal for training into formal and neat shapes, such as topiary
Spring and early flowering plants and shrubs (e.g., forsythia, lilac)	Hand pruners	Cut back old flowering shoots to young nonflowering growth; cut out diseased and spindly growth	As soon as flowering is over	To encourage new growth for flowering next year and to shape
Summer flowering shrubs (e.g. abelia, clethra, rose)	Hand pruners	Prune old stems after flowering to main framework	Mid spring, after frosts, before new season's growth has started	To produce flowering shoots; to cut out dead and diseased growth

Long-term care

Well-planted containers demand attention and will often take center stage over and above anything else in the garden. Therefore, it is important that they always look their best. This requires not only regular watering and feeding, but also general care and maintenance.

TIPS FOR REPOTTING

- If your plant has been grown in an Ali Baba-style jar and is proving impossible to get out, first soak the plant thoroughly. Then, with a high-pressure watering gun, hose directly into the pot to wash the soil away from the roots. The plant can then be pulled out easily.
- Some plants, such as *agapanthus*, flower better with their roots restricted. So don't pot them again unless absolutely necessary—for example, if the pot looks damaged.
- When deadheading roses, let some of the flowers develop into rose hips to provide food for overwintering wildlife. Also allow some seedheads to stay on grasses and perennials as this not only adds structure to your winter garden but also attracts foraging birds in the winter months.

Grooming

Any plants that have been overwintered will probably look a bit straggly by the time spring comes. Remove any diseased or frost-damaged leaves; they will be prone to infections that will plague your display later in the year.

Pinching back straggly stems or untidy foliage will also encourage denser and more attractive regrowth. Careful grooming of your display may have to be done throughout the season if you are to maintain a healthy, well-balanced, and attractive display.

If for any reason a plant does die, carefully remove it without disturbing the other plants' roots. Replant with a replacement after removing as much of the old potting mix as possible and replacing with new.

Deadheading

Removing deadheads and faded flowers will not only make your display look more attractive, it will also encourage the production of more flowers rather than seed or fruit.

Deadheading can be done between finger and thumb or with a pair of scissors or hand pruners, depending on flower type. Clusters of flowers such as Marguerite daisies (*Argyranthemum*) and lobelias will benefit if you shear off all the faded flowers at once. You will be rewarded with a second flowering later on in the season.

If you intend to keep your bulbs in place for next year, remove the faded flower head and stalk. This helps the plant store its energy instead of putting it all into seed production.

Winter protection

Overwintering tender perennials can be expensive, both in terms of heating and hard work. However, stem cuttings can be taken from the soft growth of perennials or shrubs such as fuchsias and pelargoniums in the spring and early summer. Semiripe cuttings from the shoots of woody plants, such as lavenders and boxwoods, may be taken in the fall. Hardwood cuttings are taken while trees or shrubs, such as gooseberry or dogwood, are dormant in late winter. Nevertheless, buying new stock in the spring can be a more practical option.

Conserving large pots

Large pots with permanent plantings, such as trees and shrubs, are worth conserving despite being vulnerable to the alternate freeze-and-thaw of winter weather, which causes their roots to be particularly at risk. Ideally, the more tender deciduous trees and shrubs should be moved into a frost-free and unheated place of shelter such as a garden shed, summerhouse, or greenhouse. These plants will have a better chance of survival if they are kept almost dry throughout the winter months.

If the containers are too large to be moved inside, they are best wrapped with some kind of insulating material such as burlap. Evergreen branches or bags filled with straw are another insulating option. These will help protect the container and roots from frost damage. The plants may also need extra protection: Mulch well and wrap with horticultural fabric. Make sure that snow does not accumulate on plant leaves because this can cause branches to break off.

Grouping pots

Where the location is vulnerable or restricted, such as on a balcony or roof terrace, it is not always possible to move pots inside. Instead, group the pots together in the most sheltered area, placing the hardier or larger ones on the outside to help protect the smaller ones in the middle.

Another option is to put the tallest and sturdiest plant in the center and then drape the top with horticultural fabric to create a tent effect. Secure at the bottom against wind and snow.

Spring strategies

As the weather warms up during spring, the overwintered plants can be hardened off by bringing them outdoors and uncovering them. Be warned, though: Hot, sunny days can often be followed by surprisingly cold and frosty nights, so be well armed with enough horticultural fabric to do a quick dash out into the garden to cover up your tender plants.

Keeping your eye or ear tuned to the weather forecast for frost warnings can save not only your plants but also your sanity!

ABOVE: **Boxed in**
Why not use a wooden box lined with bubble wrap to protect a group of smaller containers against frost in winter? Don't be in a hurry to remove the dead leaves as they give added protection, not just to the plants, but also to insects and invertebrates seeking winter shelter.

RIGHT: **Wrapping up**
Wrap pots in fleece, burlap, or bags filled with straw to help protect against frost.

Repotting

Depending on its rate of growth, a container-grown shrub or tree will need to be repotted every 3 to 4 years once it is mature. The new container should be about one size up from the old one. Any larger and the plant will put all its energy into root and leaf development rather than flowers.

The best time to repot is in the spring, when the plant is just beginning to grow again after the dormant winter months.

RIGHT: **Top-dressing**
For a permanent planting such as a bay tree, top-dressing is a way of supplying fresh potting medium.

6 SIMPLE STEPS: for repotting

1 To remove the plant from its container, give it a good soaking and leave to drain.

2 Gently ease the plant out of the old container and tease out the roots.

3 Before replanting, cut back any nonfibrous roots by about a half. The plant can then be repotted, if desired, into the same container. This method works well for plants that like to have restricted root growth or minimal root disturbance.

4 Place the plant in a new container that is already a third full of fresh potting mix.

5 Make sure that the plant is at its original depth, then continue to fill the container with fresh potting mix.

6 Firm down and water well, using a fine hose nozzle.

Top-dressing

If the plant is to remain in its original container, it's possible to top-dress it by removing as much of the top layer of potting mix as possible and replacing it with fresh soil-based potting mix (ericaceous, if applicable) to which slow-release organic fertilizer granules have been added. Water thoroughly. Top-dressing should be done every year in the spring.

Going on vacation

Unless you have obliging next-door neighbors who are prepared to come in day in and day out, whatever the weather, to water your lovingly planted containers, you may find yourself making an agonizing choice between your plants or your summer vacation. However, there are ways around it.

• An automated drip irrigation system is the second best alternative. Otherwise, pay a local gardener, whose work may have slackened off during the summer, to care for your plants while you are away.

• Failing this, arrange the plants close together in a shady part of the garden, water well, and cover with shade netting to slow the rate of water loss due to evaporation.

• Another alternative is to bury the pots in the ground so that the surface of the pot is level with that of the soil. When the potting mix dries out, it will then absorb water from the soil.

ABOVE: **Shady break**
A group of containers are grouped in the shade in preparation for a vacation.

RIGHT: **Protected toms**
Burying the pot in the earth will help conserve water from evaporation. This cherry tomato plant is protected in a sunken terra-cotta pot.

Seasonal care YEAR PLANNER

Mid winter

CHECK
- Check that winter protective fabric insulation is still intact.
- Check to see that winter containers need watering, especially those in sheltered positions.

Keep hand trowels and forks clean and oiled.

- Check that containers continue to be well insulated against the frost.

REMEMBER
- Remember that it's better to keep the potting mix on the drier side as this concentrates the sap and protects the plant from freezing.
- Continue to deadhead any winter-flowering plants such as pansies.
- Shape and prune trees grown in containers.

DO NOT
- Do not water if frost is forecast.

Late winter

CHECK
- Continue to check containers to see if they need watering.

PREPARE
- Divide snowdrops after flowering. They can be replanted in the garden.
- Onions and parsley can now be sown indoors for later planting.

PRUNE
- Prune damage from your evergreens and winter-flowering shrubs.
- Summer flowering climbers and shrubs will also need pruning.
- Prune deciduous trees including fruit trees.

REMEMBER
- Top-dress any permanent plantings of shrubs or trees.
- If you have a greenhouse, buy young plants so you can grow them under cover.

If you have a greenhouse, buy young plants in late winter for a head start in the summer.

Early spring

CHECK
- Check for pests and diseases.

PREPARE
- Prepare and clean your containers for summer displays.
- Top-dress any permanent plantings.

PRUNE
- Cut back seed heads to allow room for new growth.
- Deadhead faded flowers on early-blooming bulbs.
- Spring prune roses but not during frost.

PLANT
- Plant summer-flowering bulbs in containers.
- Plant roses in containers.

Time to prune the roses.

- Plant up containers with your choice of plants including trees, climbers, shrubs, and perennials.
- Plant early potatoes.
- Sow salad crops and other early vegetables, including spinach and peas.

WATER
- Water containers and feed regularly with a high-potash fertilizer.

Mid spring

CHECK
- Buy summer bedding plants from garden nurseries. Check to see when they get their major deliveries so that you can get the pick of the crop and a wide choice of plants before they sell out.
- As the plants grow, pot up, and increasingly harden off outside.
- Take cuttings from tender perennials.

PLANT
- Plant an alpine garden. Remember that they like good drainage and a low fertility soil.
- Plant and sow herbs in pots.
- Continue to sow salad and vegetable seeds.
- Bulbs that are removed before the foliage has died can be replanted temporarily in a shallow trench. When the foliage has turned yellow and died, lift, dry, and store the bulbs in a cool and dry place.
- Keep the bulbs carefully labeled, otherwise you'll have no idea what type they are by the time you replant them in fall.

PRUNE
- Deadhead any faded spring flowering bulbs and remove any leaves or stalks that have been damaged by the frost.
- Prune lavender.

REMEMBER
- Tie in any young shoots on climbers.
- Remove spring planting and, if desired, replant into the garden.

Watch out for snails and slugs.

Late spring

FEED
- Feed and water your containers regularly.

CLEAR
- Finish clearing spring bedding from all of your containers.

PRUNE
- Prune and tidy evergreens.
- Prune flowering shrubs after they bloom.
- Take softwood cuttings from new young growth of shrubs, such as lavender and fuchsia, and tender perennials such as pelargonium and argyranthemums.
- Deadhead spent flowers, including spring-flowering bulbs.

SUPPORT
- Stake any tall stemmed plants such as Lilium regale.
- Secure new grown stems on climbers to supports to avoid wind damage.

PLANT
- Toward the end of May, plant up summer displays while checking the weather forecast for any late frosts that will kill or damage the more tender plants.
- Plant containers and hanging baskets, but only if you can keep them in a frost-free environment, such as a greenhouse or summer house.
- Continue to sow vegetable seeds in outdoor containers.
- Early crops such as 'cut-and-come-again' salad leaves can be harvested.

REMEMBER
- Once the frosts are over, tender perennials and shrubs can be brought outside.
- As long as night frost is not forecasted, strengthen plants by leaving them out of doors for longer periods each day.
- Carefully inspect both new and established plants and their potting mixes for pests and diseases.
- To prepare for fall, plant containers with late-flowering plants such as agapanthus and dahlias.

Early summer

CHECK
- Containers and hanging baskets can now be placed out of doors.
- Despite the fact that it's officially summer, the odd frost may still appear. Keep listening to the weather forecast and have burlap on hand just in case.
- Continue to inspect for pests and diseases. Treat accordingly.
- Continue to train and tie in climbing plants.
- Continue to stake tall perennials.

WATER
- If you have a vacation planned, ask a neighbor to water your containers, or install a drip irrigation system.
- Make sure your containers are regularly watered. This could be done twice a day.

HARVEST
- Continue to harvest your container crops.

PLANT
- If you haven't done so already, plant containers, troughs, and hanging baskets with tender perennials and annuals.
- Plant out young vegetable plants such as peppers, brassicas, and cucumbers.
- Sow or plant sweet corn, pumpkins, squashes, cucumbers, and zucchinis.
- Plant tomatoes, in your sunniest spot.
- Continue to sow salad seeds every 2 to 3 weeks for a continual supply of fresh leaves over the summer.

PRUNE
- Deadhead regularly to prolong the flowering period.

Last chance to pot up those hanging baskets

Seasonal care YEAR PLANNER *(continued)*

Mid summer

Keep up that watering.

PRUNE
- Continue to deadhead faded flowers.
- Groom plants regularly and pinch out any straggly growth.

REMEMBER
- July is a particularly bad month for pests and diseases, so keep an eye out.

LEARN
- Your containers will now be in full flower. Enjoy the successes and learn from your mistakes. If you don't like a certain flower or flower combination this year, you won't like it next year either.

WATER
- Water regularly, at least once a day.
- Feed with a high-potash fertilizer to promote flower growth.

CUTTINGS
- Take cuttings from shrubs, such as hydrangeas.

HARVEST
- Harvest vegetables. Don't let them become too mature, as most taste better when young.
- Herbs can be picked and dried.
- Spring-flowering bulbs can now be dried, labeled, and stored for the fall.

PLANT
- Plant fall-flowering bulbs, such as nerines and fall-flowering crocuses, for a colorful fall container.

Late summer

WATER
- Continue to water well. Neglected plants are more susceptible to pests and diseases such as mildew.

CUTTINGS
- Continue to take cuttings from shrubs and tender perennials.

PRUNE
- Continue to groom and deadhead plants.

REMEMBER
- Leave a few flowers to develop into seedheads to provide food for wildlife.

FEED
- Continue to feed at least once a week with high-potash fertilizer.

HARVEST
- Continue to harvest crops.

Enjoy the rewards of all your hard work.

Early fall

PRUNE
- Continue to groom plants by deadheading and cutting back any straggly growth.

WATER
- Continue to water and feed summer annuals as required.

REMEMBER
- Permanent plantings with trees and shrubs should no longer be fed.

CLEAR
- Clear out any summer annuals that are past their prime and clean out containers. Leave containers that house plants with seedheads, such as sedums, as these provide food for birds.

PLANT
- Plant up spring containers with spring flowers and bulbs. Overwinter in a frost-free but cool environment.
- Plant fall containers with plants such as grasses, brunnera, and red twig dogwood for an instant effect.
- Tender perennials should be moved to a greenhouse or summer house.
- Continue to harvest fruit and vegetables.

Blackberries can be grown in large containers.

Mid fall

CUTTINGS
- *Hardwood cuttings can be taken from deciduous shrubs.*

PLANT
- *Plant tulip bulbs later in the month.*
- *Continue to plant spring flowering bulbs.*
- *Plant lily bulbs.*
- *Continue to plant spring containers.*

Plant up your spring bulbs.

Late fall

CHECK
- *Check containers for watering. Keep on the dry side.*

PLANT
- *Plant bare-rooted shrubs and trees.*
- *Continue to plant tulip bulbs and alliums.*

PROTECT
- *Protect containers that are to remain outdoors by wrapping them in burlap or another insulating material.*

CLEAN
- *Clean and disinfect empty pots and unused stakes.*

Early winter

WATER
- *Water plants sparingly.*

CLEAR
- *Clear snow from trees and shrubs.*

PLANT
- *Continue to plant lily bulbs.*
- *Leaf through catalogs and books to plan container displays for next year.*
- *Plant up winter containers and hanging baskets for color and seasonal interest.*

PRUNE
- *Continue to groom permanent planting in containers.*

Pests and Diseases

Containerized plants are as susceptible to pests and diseases as any others. The same preventive and control strategies apply, too, but fortunately, are easier to achieve in a containerized garden. Approaches such as those outlined below will protect your potted plants all through the year—simply adapt traditional techniques for the outside garden to your container-grown plants.

SPRING: Early pests include insects such as aphids. In a container garden, it's easy to place small-flowered plants such as sweet alyssum (*Lobularia maritima*) in nearby pots to feed aphid parasites and predators. It's also easy to move a severely infested plant away from the others and give it a special spray of insecticidal soap if necessary. Early in the year, insects such as leaf hoppers and winged aphids are likely to fly into an area looking for summer homes for themselves and their young. As they feed, they often transmit viral diseases. These might not show up until midsummer, but they've been present since spring—a couple of weeks under the cover of insect barrier material will help prevent these problems.

MIDSUMMER: This time of year often brings a few weeks when flying pests such as Japanese beetles and striped cucumber beetles are particularly bad. Covering an outside garden with insect barrier cloth to protect it can be a huge task, and expensive, too, when you account for the cost of the cloth. But when they threaten container plants, it's relatively simple, and much less expensive, to cover only the susceptible species.

MID- TO LATE SUMMER: Fungal diseases are likely to attack in mid- to late summer when the humidity in the garden increases. You can prevent them by increasing air circulation around the plants—just move the pots farther apart in a container garden.

PLANT DIRECTORY

Most plants grow well in containers. You may be surprised, in fact, to see garden favorites listed here. It may be that a container-size cultivar is available, or that the plant fares well when the spread of its roots is restricted. But as a general rule, as long as you keep the soil mix at the correct moisture and nutrient level for a particular plant, your container will reward you with a lavish display.

Understanding the symbols

Each entry in the plant directory has a label that gives essential information about the plant. This helps you plan the best location for each plant and prepare for special needs.

HARDINESS ZONE

The hardiness zone indicates whether a plant will survive your winters but remember to insulate the pots to keep roots from freezing. Turn to page 186 for the zone map, which will tell you which temperature zone you are in.

ZONE
8-10

REPOTTING

In years: Frequency is only an estimate. If your plants begin to look too big for their pots, repot right away.

1-2

WATERING

How frequently you need to water depends on the temperature. Always check pots in the summer months to see if soil has dried out.

Low moisture
Generally requires water only every 2–3 days if the pot size is adequate.

Medium moisture
Generally requires water every 1–2 days if the pot size is adequate.

High moisture
Generally requires water at least once, sometimes twice a day, even in an adequately sized pot.

PLANT TYPE

This shows if a properly cared-for plant will live or die over winter or during the following season.

Annuals live for only one year. Many plants grown as annuals are actually perennials in frost-free climates and have a hardiness zone rating. True annuals don't have a hardiness zone rating.

Biennials live for two years. Most form a rosette of leaves in the first year and send up a flower stalk before dying in their second year. They do have a hardiness zone rating.

Perennials live for three or more years. All perennials have a hardiness zone rating.

Evergreen plants retain their leaves year-round. Remember: Some plants are evergreen only in frost-free zones.

Perennials

Perennials are plants that live for three or more years, although many live longer than that. In the container garden, these plants offer continuity; rather than having to plant every single pot you own every year, perennials allow you to leave some in place, year after year. Like your perennial trees and shrubs, they will soon come to form the basic architecture of your garden, and you'll find yourself planning a design around them.

Many perennial plants require what is called a chilling period in order to break dormancy in spring and resume growth and flowering. To provide this, you'll have to keep the plant in an environment where temperatures average about 40°F for a period of weeks. Few homes have a room this cool, so if you live in a cold-weather climate, you may want to place these plants in a frost-free garage or shed. Temperatures can certainly go lower than 40°F, but some plants die if their roots freeze solid, so insulate the pots (see page 129), to prevent damage over winter months.

Anemone blanda
Grecian windflower

Windflowers bloom early enough to be a signal of spring. They get their name because of the way the daisylike blooms wave in the wind above the deeply lobed, dark green, almost fernlike leaves.
Size: 4 to 9 inches tall, 4 to 6 inches wide
Bloom: In midspring, windflowers bloom in shades from white to pink, violet, blue, and purple. Flowers of many cultivars have a prominent yellow center surrounded by petals that are white toward the center and then a vivid rose, blue, or purple.

Exposure: Full sun to partial shade
Soil mix: Well drained, moderately fertile, with a pH of 6 to 7
Companion plants: In separate but adjacent pots, pair windflowers with late spring bulbs such as tulips and daffodils. If you have a large container filled with tulips, they make a good underplanting, too.
Options: Soak the corms for 12 hours before planting them in midfall. If they should come up before the winter sets in, mulch them thoroughly. North of Zone 5, plant them in early spring for summer bloom, and lift the corms before the ground freezes in late fall. Store them in cool, dark, dry conditions and

This pot of brilliant red begonias demands a prominent position where it's easy to admire.

plant them again the following spring. Be aware that all parts of this plant are poisonous; don't grow it if your children are likely to eat it.

Begonia spp.
Begonias

The more than 1,300 species of begonias include plants for almost every situation. Choose the small annual wax begonias for bronze or red-green foliage and flowers that last all summer, tuberous begonias for luxurious leaves and breathtakingly beautiful blooms, or Rex begonias for showstopping, multicolored foliage.
Size: Varies from 8 inches to 3 feet tall, 10 to 18 inches wide
Bloom: Varies; some species bloom in winter, some in spring, and some in the summer months. Colors include everything but blue and purple.
Exposure: Full sun to partial shade
Soil mix: Well drained, moderately fertile, with a pH of 6 to 7
Companion plants: Wax begonias make good underplantings for tall, vividly colored flowering plants. A group of Rex begonias, each grown in its own pot, makes a gorgeous display that lasts the whole season, and tuberous begonias are so showy that they look best alone.
Options: Experiment with the many types of begonias to learn which work best in your environment. Some, such as the cane-stemmed begonias (B. aconitifolia, B. albo-picta), make wonderful houseplants all through the year, whether in bloom or not. Rex begonias (B. rex) also persist all through the year when in a moderately lit spot in the house and give a luxurious look to any room they grace. Semperflorens begonias (B. schmidtiana, B. cucullata var. hookeri), also known as wax begonias, can play a strong role in the summer container garden because they stay in bloom so long.

Their foliage is also decorative on its own. Tuberous begonias (*B.* x *tuberhybrida*) go dormant for the winter, so lift their tubers and store in dark, dry conditions, at about 45° to 50°F, through the winter. Plant them again in early spring, and take their pots outside for a lavish display once the weather has settled. Winter-flowering species (*B.* x *cheimantha* and *B.* x *hiemalis*) do well in heated homes as long as temperatures stay below 70°F because they thrive in low-humidity environments. Their leaves are lovely enough to showcase when they aren't blooming, so they make a good contribution to the container garden.

Canna

Canna lily

These tender perennials add a tropical look to a container garden. Their leaves are almost banana-like but are more varied in coloration. Some cannas are variegated, others are striped, and many are pure green. No matter their color, these plants are erect and draw the eye even when the plant is not in bloom.

Size: Varies from 2 to 6 feet tall, 1½ to 2 feet wide

Bloom: In summer, showy blooms in hot colors—red, orange, yellow, and pink—shine through the foliage.

Exposure: Full sun

Soil mix: Fertile, moist soil with a pH of 5.5 to 6.8. Fertilize every 2 weeks during the summer, cutting back in mid fall.

Companion plants: These plants are showy enough to be the focal point in an arrangement of pots. The delicate look of perennial statice (*Limonium* spp.) makes a nice contrast to the boldness of cannas.

Options: Favorite cultivars include 'Lucifer', a 2-foot tall plant that produces bright red flowers with yellow margins. 'The President' is another red cultivar but is taller. 'Bengal Tiger' has green and yellow variegated foliage and orange blooms, while 'Stuttgart' has orange flowers and green and white variegated leaves.

Plant the rhizomes 4 to 5 inches deep, after all danger of spring frosts, or start them indoors. Maintain a constant supply of moisture, but don't let the pots stay wet while the plants are young. Once plants are mature, they thrive in moist conditions—do not let their soil dry out.

Cut off spent blooms right away and the plant will send up additional flower stalks. You can also cut the blooms for bouquets; the flowers will last well for up to a week. Some people grow the plants for foliage to cut; remember that the plant needs about five leaves to produce and store a sufficient nutrient supply to see it through winter and beginning of the following season.

Cyclamen spp.

Cyclamens

Of the 19 species of cyclamens, two types are commonly used in container gardens: the so-called florist's cyclamen, or *C. persicum*, and the hardy cyclamen, or *C. coum*. Both are extraordinarily showy,

with decorative leaves and soft-looking blooms. From a distance they remind one of a group of hovering butterflies.

Size: *C. persicum*, 8 to 10 inches tall, 6 to 8 inches wide; *C. coum*, 3 to 6 inches tall, 4 to 6 inches wide

Bloom: In winter or early spring, depending on species and location, white, pink, or purple blooms form. *C. persicum* is generally used as a houseplant, where it will bloom in late December into early February; *C. coum* will bloom in early spring if it's spent the winter outdoors.

Exposure: Partial shade or filtered light

Soil mix: Well drained, moderate fertility, humusy, with a pH of 6 to 7

Companion plants: Plant either alone or use as an underplanting in a pot with a tropical climber.

Options: *C. coum* grows well from seed. Sow the seed on a layer of vermiculite and mist it into niches. Cover the pot with light-excluding material. Seeds germinate in 1 to 2 months. Good cultivars of *C. coum* include 'Shell Pink' and 'Rose Pink'. They look quite similar, although 'Rose Pink' blooms tend to be darker than those of 'Shell Pink'.

If leaves begin to drop, suspect that the environment is too warm. Move to an area that maintains daytime temperatures of 65 to 68°F and nighttime temperatures of 45 to 58°F. If temperatures exceed 68°F for long, the plant will begin to go dormant.

All parts of the plant are somewhat poisonous, so do not eat them. If your skin is very sensitive, you may react to touching the tubers, too.

Erigeron karvinskianus

Fleabane, Mexican daisy

Fleabane daisy does double duty in a container garden. First, it is decorative in its own right, with a cloud of small, white, daisylike blooms. Second, it attracts the tiny beneficial wasps that feed on aphids and other soft-bodied pests. It also attracts bees and butterflies.

Large as they are, cannas (seen in the large pot) thrive in pots, as do the bougainvillea (smaller pot) that echo their color.

Size: Varies from 8 to 12 inches tall, 18 to 24 inches wide

Bloom: This plant has an exceptionally long bloom time for a perennial; under good circumstances, it will continue to bloom for the majority of the year.

Exposure: Full sun

Soil mix: Well drained, moderate fertility, with a wide pH tolerance.

Companion plants: Move containers to sit next to plants suffering from aphid attacks so that the beneficial wasps can parasitize the aphids.

Options: This plant is often used as a groundcover. In the container garden, you can use it at the front of a grouping. or alternatively to add a cheerful note to a collection of bright annuals.

E. karvinskianus 'Profusion' is one of the most common, and also one of the best, cultivars. It lives up to its name, producing a profusion of blooms.

Other Erigeron species are also good additions to the container garden. Try growing E. aureus 'Charity' for pink, 'Azurfee' for lavender-blue, or 'Canary' for yellow blooms. E. pulchellus cultivars include 'Quakeress', which has light, blush pink blooms, 'Serenity' with semidouble purple flowers, and 'Rotes Meer' with semidouble dark red flowers.

Deadheading prolongs the bloom time, but you can simply cut the entire plant back and it will regrow and rebloom quickly.

Helleborus x hybridus

Lenten rose

Many people believe that these are among the most beautiful of all flowers and count it a true blessing that they are also among the earliest to bloom. However, the leaves, stems, and roots of these plants are poisonous, and people with extremely sensitive skin have been known to have a mild allergic reaction to them when dividing them or planting bare-root seedlings.

Size: Varies from 12 to 18 inches tall, 12 to 18 inches wide

Bloom: In very early spring, lovely pink, white, green, coral, magenta, spotted, or streaked blooms appear.

Exposure: Filtered light to moderate shade

Soil mix: Well drained, fertile, high humus content, with a pH of 6.8 to 7.5

Companion plants: Scatter pots of hellebore among the pots of spring bulbs.

Options: There are hundreds of good cultivars of hellebores, and you're sure to develop your own favorites. But as an introduction to the wonderful world of Lenten roses, look for H. x ballardiae and other "Ballard" cultivars, including 'Peggy Ballard', a reddish pink and purple-pink cultivar, and 'Philip Ballard', with dark blue-black blooms.

Iris spp.

Irises

At last count, over 300 species of irises had been identified. Briefly, they fall into several groups. Among those that grow from rhizomes, there are bearded forms—these are the irises you see most frequently in gardens—and beardless forms, including the Siberian, Japanese, and Louisiana groups. Those grown from bulbs include reticulata, juno, and xiphium irises. Bearded irises grow well in deep containers. They thrive when planted in midsummer through early fall. Ensure the soil is well drained and remember to leave the top one-third of the rhizome above the surface.

Size: Varies; 6 to 36 inches tall, 12 to 24 inches wide

Bloom: From early spring, when reticulata irises bloom, to midsummer, when the last of the Japanese and bearded irises bloom

Exposure: Full sun to filtered light

Soil mix: Well drained, fertile, with a pH of 6 to 6.8

Companion plants: Pair reticulata irises with snowdrops and crocuses—they bloom at roughly the same time and are close enough in size to be complementary to each other. Note that taller irises need pots to themselves.

Options: You can find cultivars in just about every imaginable color combination, so take your time researching to find the plants that will best complement your home and the other plants in your container garden. Siberian irises (I. sibirica) are among the easiest irises to grow. Plant their rhizomes 1 to 3 inches below the soil surface, and don't divide them until the plants look truly crowded in the container. Their only requirement that is sometimes challenging in a container is a steady supply of moisture. But if you pot them in a humusy mix and water them every morning, they will perform beautifully. Their 3 to 4-inch-long blooms appear in early summer, and the thin, elegant, upright leaves persist for the whole season. Look for 'Caesar's Brother', a deep purple bloom with a yellow-and-white blaze and black veining on the falls; 'Lavender Bounty', with lavender-pink falls and light pink standards; and 'Butter and Sugar' white standards with soft yellow falls.

Iris reticulata is known as a dwarf iris because it grows only 6 to 8 inches tall. It needs moisture early in the season, when it is blooming and then manufacturing sugars to store for the following year, but it requires relatively dry soil from midsummer through winter.

Group plants such as this Iris histrioides 'George' for a stunning display in a pot and, in this case, an intense fragrance.

n fall, plant these bulbs 3 to 4 inches deep at a spacing of 3 to 4 inches for the best display.

Many reticulata cultivars have a light fragrance; search for these if this matters to you. 'Cantab' is such a cultivar; it also has a lovely sky blue bloom with yellow blotch, and 'Purple Gem' is a deep purple color with a white blotch.

Isotoma fluviatilis

Blue star creeper

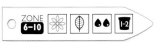

This native of Australia has been classified, at one time or another, as *Laurentia fluviatilis*, *Pratia pedunculata*, and *Lobelia pedunculata*, so if you can't find it under one name, try another. It's often used in the garden between stepping-stones because it is so sturdy that it can take a certain amount of foot traffic—it is also short. In the container garden, you can use it in a hanging basket.

Size: Varies from 2 to 6 inches tall, 10 to 12 inches wide

Bloom: In midspring, light blue, star-shaped flowers form.

Exposure: Tolerates a wide range, from partial shade to full sun

Soil mix: Well drained, moderately fertile, with a pH of 5.5 to 7

Companion plants: This plant makes a good companion to pots of bulbs.

Options: Plants bloom until fall, making them an ideal plant for semishady areas. In warm climates where they overwinter well, the plants are evergreen. Where they are marginal, the tops may die back.

Primula spp.

Primula, primroses

The genus *Primula* contains 425 species and numerous cultivars. They can be roughly divided into five main groups: Auricula, Candelabra, Acaulis, Polyanthus, and Juliana. Cultivars in all groups are suitable for

container culture, but Polyanthus primroses are those most commonly found for sale.

Size: Varies from 8 to 10 inches tall, 6 to 10 inches wide

Bloom: In early spring, flowers in shades of blue, orange, pink, red, white, and yellow appear on the top of stems that hold them above the dark green foliage.

Exposure: Partial shade to filtered light in most regions; full sun in cool areas

Soil mix: Fertile, moist soil, with a pH of 5 to 6.5

Companion plants: Primulas make wonderful companions to early spring bulbs. Plant them in separate containers so you can remove the bulb pots to a less visible place once they have finished blooming.

Options: The Polyanthus group of primroses is evergreen in most environments. Their leaves look something like flattened romaine lettuce leaves, although they form a rosette just above the soil surface. The one thing their blooms have in common is a bright yellow center. Gold-laced primulas are one of the showiest types. Their petals are such a dark red that they look black, and the golden center and picoteed edge make them dramatic in any setting. Pacific Giants Mixed are also popular. Their flowers are large—hence the name—and also vividly colored.

Rosa spp.

Roses

Roses can be easy or challenging, depending on the type of rose and the environment in which it is growing. They are notorious for disease problems in humid climates and attract pests from far and wide. Nonetheless, they are well worth growing. Even if you have to take some extra time with them, the blooms are likely to make you feel that every moment spent on them is repaid a hundredfold.

Roses vary in size from patio to rambling roses. Choose cultivars, such as this *Rosa* 'Ballerina' that has masses of blooms to make lavish displays in your pots.

Size: Varies from 1 to 2 feet, to more than 10 feet tall for climbers

Bloom: From midspring to midsummer, depending on cultivar

Exposure: Full sun

Soil mix: Well drained, fertile, with a pH of 6.5 to 6.8. Fertilize every 2 to 4 weeks during the growing season with a well-balanced, complete material.

Companion plants: Roses need a pot to themselves but can be placed near other plants that bloom in midseason.

Options: The following cultivars are good container plants. 'The Fairy' is a Polyantha rose, meaning that it is a small shrub that grows 2 to 3 feet tall and wide. The blooms are lightly fragrant and a soft pink. It blooms from midspring throughout the season. Aside from maintenance pruning, you won't have to do much to keep it looking good.

'New Dawn' is a climbing rose that will reach 10 feet if its pot is large enough to keep the roots vigorously growing. It's classified as a modern climber and blooms on year-old wood, so it shouldn't be pruned until after it blooms, which it does almost continuously from early to late summer! The double flowers are scented and a pale, pearly pink. This rose can tolerate a bit of shade but, like all roses, it grows better with at least 6 hours a day of sun.

'Zephirine Drouhin' is an old-fashioned bourbon rose that is easily trained as a climber. The amazing number of deep pink, double, fragrant blooms is truly impressive—the foliage is completely covered when it blooms. Position it where it gets good air circulation because it is susceptible to fungal diseases, including black spot. 'Danse du Feu' is also a climber, but it's a modern rose, so its disease resistance is better. It has lovely brick red blooms and very dark green foliage.

You may have come across the name Knock Out™ Rose. The shrub roses are not only beautiful, but they are also resistant to black spot, the bane of growers in humid climates, as well as being drought-tolerant and unattractive to most pests, including Japanese beetles, leafhoppers, and rose midges. It can grow well with only 4 hours of sunshine a day and blooms for a long time, even without deadheading. Its red blooms change from clear red in cool weather to a bluer red in hot weather. The foliage has purple undertones and changes to a more burgundy color in fall.

Sempervivum spp.

Hen and chicks, Houseleeks

These charming little plants can provide year-round interest in the right location. Some have what looks like a covering of spiderwebs on their leaves, some are a brick red color, and some are green with red edging on their leaves. Left to their own devices, they form a community— hence their name—of dome-shaped, succulent plants. Consider placing them in a rounded pot to make the most of their rounded forms.

Size: 3 to 4 inches tall, 4 to 6 inches wide
Bloom: In summer, yellow, red, or purple flowers rise above the rosette of leaves.
Exposure: Full sun
Soil mix: Extremely well drained, moderate to low fertility, with a pH of 6 to 7

Companion plants: These plants do not make good pot mates with most other plants because they are so quick to throw offsets all around themselves. There is an exception to this caution: Grow several different Sempervivum species and cultivars in the same tub to create a stunning display.
Options: *S. tectorum* 'Pacific Hawk' is a brick red cultivar that forms rosettes about 2 inches wide at maturity. It makes a wonderful pot mate to any of the green or red-tinged cultivars. The cultivar 'Commander Hay' is also red and forms larger rosettes that are up to 4 inches across. *S. arachnoideum* is sometimes known as the Cobweb houseleek because it is liberally coated with fine hairs that look as if a spider had wrapped it up. *S. ciliosum* is also hairy, but the leaves look like they are covered with bristles rather than webs.

S. giuseppii has red spots on the ends of its lime green, tightly formed leaves.

Hen and chicks species grow for several years before they bloom, producing offsets the whole time. Blooming is a mixed blessing—the unusual blooms add interest to the pots, but blooming also signals the death of the mother plant. Shortly after the flowers fade, the plant from which they grew begins to die. Remove the dead plant from the grouping. The many offsets that the mother plant threw off will quickly grow in to take its place.

Plant *Sempervivum* 'Purple Queen' in a generously rounded pot to achieve a spectacular, mounded display.

Verbena bonariensis
Purpletop verbena

Purpletop verbena makes an excellent cut flower because it lasts and lasts in the vase. The strong purple color makes an excellent contrast to yellow, orange, and red blooms, and it is never overpowering because its form is so open and airy. Butterflies love purpletop verbena. Grow it close to other butterfly-attracting plants for a summer-long show.

Size: 3 to 4 feet tall, 1 to 3 feet wide

Bloom: In early summer, the purple flowers on long stalks appear; the plant blooms continuously until late summer or early fall.

Exposure: Full sun

Soil mix: Well drained, moderate fertility

Companion plants: This plant is so airy that it can be set in front of plants without obscuring them. The deep purple color makes a good contrast to yellow blooms.

Options: The genus *Verbena* includes about 250 species, many of which make good container plants. Of the perennials, look for hoary vervain (*V. stricta*) because the undersides of its green leaves are liberally coated with silvery-gray hairs that add dimension, and the spikes of deep purple flowers can be up to a foot long. It's hardy in Zones 4 to 7, so it's a good alternative for more northern gardens. Blue vervain (*V. hastata*) is also good in the north because it is hardy from Zones 3 to 9. The blooms form from early summer through early fall and are a violet-blue to pinkish purple color. Although less common, you can also see white cultivars. 'Silver Anne' has sweetly scented flowers that open as a bright pink color but fade to silver white as they age. It's hardy in Zones 8 to 11 and must be grown as an annual elsewhere.

Generally, grow verbena as an annual in Zones 3 to 6; started 8 weeks before the frost-free date, it will bloom by midsummer.

Annuals

Annuals are probably the easiest of all plants to grow in containers because you don't have to worry about where or how to overwinter them. You simply plant them every spring, water and fertilize them, deadhead them if they require it, and stand back to watch the show.

The plants featured here represent selections from the designs shown in earlier pages. But don't confine your choices to these plants—almost every annual you can imagine grows well in a container as long as you match the size of the plant with the size of the container and keep it watered and fertilized. Generally, bring pots indoors before the weather cools, and keep them barely moist.

Bidens ferulifolia
Apache beggarticks

Apache beggarticks is a perennial in Zones 8 to 11, but it is often grown as an annual, even where it is perennial. Its primary characteristic is its cheerfulness; the star-shaped yellow flowers and open plant habit make it feel as light as air and as bright as sunshine. Another great quality is its length of bloom. Despite being a perennial, it has as long a bloom period as most annuals.

Size: Varies from 10 to 12 inches tall, 12 to 18 inches wide

Bloom: In midsummer through late summer, successions of blooms form.

Exposure: Full sun

Soil mix: Well drained, moderately fertile, with a pH of 5.8 to 7. Fertilize every 2 to 4 weeks.

Companion plants: Allow this plant its own pot, but pair it with blue, purple, and white flowers.

Options: Apache beggarticks is extremely attractive to the garden's beneficial insects, especially bees and butterflies.

This plant will self-sow in a container, so be prepared to find volunteer seedlings in adjacent pots of perennials whose soil you don't replace the following season.

Brachycome iberidifolia
Swan river daisy

Swan river daisies are wonderful container plants because they are literally coated with blooms. The blooms are striking, too, with bright yellow centers surrounded by clear blue, purple or white petals.

Size: Varies from 12 to 18 inches tall, 10 to 14 inches wide

Bloom: In early summer through early fall, this plant produces hundreds and hundreds of gorgeous, daisy-like flowers.

Exposure: Full sun

Soil mix: Well drained, moderately fertile, moist, with a pH of 5.5 to 7. Fertilize every few weeks while the plant is in bloom.

Companion plants: Grow in a pot by itself because it needs space to become bushy.

Options: To increase the bushiness of these plants, pinch stem tips while they are young. Deadhead to promote reblooming. You can also sheer off the tops of the plants after the first flush of bloom, and they will quickly grow back and bloom again.

This plant really prefers cool conditions and has a tendency to run out when it is hot. To avoid an empty spot in your design, plant successively. In most areas, two seedings, one about 6 weeks before the date of the last spring frost and one in early June to be transplanted into place in mid-July, are appropriate. If you live in Zones 8 to 10, you can add a third seeding date in early July.

Campanula isophylla
Falling stars, Italian bellflower

This tender perennial is generally grown as an annual, even in the zones where it is perennial, if it is grown outside. However, some people use it as a houseplant. Inside, it will live for many years and reward good care with frequent bloom periods.

Size: 6 to 8 inches tall; 10 to 12 inches wide

Bloom: White or blue, star-shaped flowers bloom continuously from midsummer until fall when outside, for 2 or 3 months at a time when kept as a houseplant.

Exposure: Partial shade or filtered light

Soil mix: Well drained, fertile, with a pH of 5.8 to 7. Fertilize every 2 to 4 weeks.

Companion plants: Grow these plants in their own pots.

Options: Favorite cultivars of *C. isophylla* include 'Alba', with its pure white flowers, and the Kristal Hybrids, which include 'Stella Blue', with violet-blue flowers, and 'Stella White,' with white flowers. Plant seeds early indoors. Seeded about 8 weeks before the last frost date, they will bloom in early to midsummer and keep up the show until fall. This species looks particularly good in a hanging basket because it has a naturally graceful trailing habit.

Fuchsia spp.
Fuchsias

Although fuchsias are perennial, in the United States they are most frequently used as hanging basket plants that are replaced every year. Gardeners in frost-free areas can be bolder with them, though. Where it is close to a subtropical climate, certain cultivars have proven to be winter-hardy. In the wild, hummingbirds pollinate these plants, so don't be surprised to see them dipping among your hanging baskets for the nectar.

Size: Varies; most sold for baskets are 12 to 18 inches long, 12 to 18 inches wide.

Bloom: Almost continuously from early summer to fall and through winter if brought inside into an area with bright light

Exposure: Partial shade or filtered light

Soil mix: Well drained, fertile, with a pH of 5.5 to 6.7. Fertilize every 2 weeks when plants are active and blooming well.

Companion plants: Use alone in hanging baskets. Ferns and other foliage plants make a good background for the showy, ever-present blooms.

Options: Although there are more than 100 species of fuchsias and 3,000 to 5,000 cultivars, you are most likely to find a *Fuchsia × hybrida* cultivar. These cultivars have the familiar earring form, and many grow in shades of red, pink, white, and purple. 'Annabel' has won a Royal Horticultural Society Award of Garden Merit award, and once you see it, you'll understand why. This cultivar has double, pale pink and blushed white petals, giving it an ethereal appearance. If you live in the Pacific Northwest, you might be able to overwinter some fuchsias outdoors. Search for 'Tom Thumb'. This plant, which is very popular in Britain, grows to only about 1 foot tall and wide and has red and purple blooms.

Although we think of fuchsias as tropical plants, they do not do well in heat. They prefer temperatures of about 70°F during

the day and night temperatures from 50°F to 60°F. Night temperatures are important for bud initiation; too hot and they won't form. You may also notice that flowering slows and may stop completely when daytime temperatures exceed 80°F. In the fall, if you plan to bring the plants indoors for the winter, gradually reduce watering to prepare them for a winter rest period. Stop fertilizing, too. In spring, repot and gradually increase water and nutrient supplies.

Fuchsias have a legendary—and well deserved—reputation as a magnet for whiteflies. Unless you have an indigenous population of whitefly predators or are running a greenhouse where you can provide a good habitat for them, whiteflies will sooner or later discover your fuchsias. This is one reason that many people grow the plants as annuals; if they bring infested plants into the house in winter, they are sure to spread the problem. Examine your plants carefully before bringing them indoors or, if you are buying them, before bringing them home from the nursery.

Impatiens walleriana
Impatiens, Busy Lizzie

Although this plant is perennial in Zones 9 through 11, most people grow it as an annual. It is, in fact, one of the most common bedding plants because it requires such little maintenance, is so long-blooming, and comes in so many colors that you can usually find a cultivar to suit your design.

Size: Varies from 8 to 24 inches tall, and 8 to 24 inches wide

Bloom: In midspring through fall, red, lavender, pink, white, salmon, and orange blooms cover the plant.

Exposure: Partial shade to shade

Soil mix: Well drained, moderately fertile, with a pH of 5.8 to 6.5. Fertilize every 3 to 4 weeks.

This copper pot sets off the brilliant hue of *Fuchsia* 'Mrs. Popple'.

Companion plants: Plant Impatiens as the underplanting in containers of shade-giving plants, or place their pots in shady areas that need color to provide interest.

Options: Choosing a cultivar may be the biggest problem you ever face with impatiens. In general, these cultivars are members of series: the Accent Series, Deco Series, Elfin Series, Tempo Series, and so on. Choose simply on the basis of color; you'll find that all *I. walleriana* perform well as long as they aren't in bright sun and have reasonably fertile but not soggy soil.

Impatiens differs from other plants because some of the colors of various cultivars clash. You are likely to buy plants in bud, if not in bloom, so check this while you select plants. The combinations some people plant, for example, by putting some of the pinks and salmons together can be garish, so be warned. On the other hand, one of the best things about this plant is its ability to continue blooming without being deadheaded. This makes it practically maintenance free—you plant it and walk away to let it take care of itself. If it begins to look rangy toward late summer, shear it back and let it regrow. It will come back into bloom as long as the soil has a moderate nutrient supply.

Lobelia erinus
Lobelia

Lobelias make one of the finest possible container plants and are ideal for growing in hanging baskets and window boxes.

Size: 4 to 9 inches tall; 4 to 6 inches wide
Bloom: From midspring through summer, clouds of small flowers in shades of blue, white, purple, and pink, some with a white throat, form.
Exposure: Full sun to partial shade
Soil mix: Well drained, fertile, moist, with a pH of 5.5 to 6.8. Fertilize every 2 weeks while it is blooming.
Companion plants: Lobelia is so dainty that it looks good as an underplanting to large, dramatic species such as lilies.

Options: Of the many cultivars available, 'Cambridge Blue' has the clearest blue flowers, and 'Sapphire' has rich, dark blue flowers with a white eye. The Cascade Series is dominated by pink and purple shades and contains just enough whites to make a group sparkle.

Lobelia is one of the easiest plants to grow, and you are unlikely to have any problems with it. If you live in a hot climate or have to situate it in hot, dry conditions, it may stop blooming in midsummer. Plant second and third plantings so you never have a gap during the summer. Plant groups of lobelia together in pots. You can generally fit 5 to 7 plants in a 6-inch pot and 7 to 10 in a 10-inch pot.

Mimulus spp.
Monkey flowers

The brightly colored, sometimes spotted blooms of Mimulus are so cheerful that they draw visitors of all ages. They are bright enough that they can overpower a grouping unless they are combined with equally vivid blooms. Start these plants indoors, 6 or 7 weeks before the frost-free date.
Size: Varies from 5 to 12 inches tall, 10 to 12 inches wide
Bloom: In early summer, white, yellow, orange, or pink blooms form.

Plant Lobelia cultivars, such as this 'Waterfall Light Lavender', toward the edges of their containers so they cascade down the sides.

Exposure: Full sun in northern areas, filtered light in the south
Soil mix: Well drained, moist, fertile, with a pH of 6 to 6.8. Fertilize every 2 to 3 weeks while the plant is blooming.
Companion plants: Bright colored lilies make a good companion.
Options: In most areas, the most common monkey flowers are cultivars of *M. × hybridus* and *M. guttatus*. 'Calypso' is a mixture of yellow, orange, red, and pink blooms. Magic Series plants are also mixed colors and include some soft pastels. Malibu Series plants are quite spotted and are very good in hanging baskets because they are somewhat trailing.

Nemesia spp.
Nemesias

Nemesia strumosa has been a garden favorite for generations. It is a cool-loving annual, so it makes an excellent spring-flowering plant in Zones 6 to 8 and is also a wonderful addition to the winter garden in Zones 9 to 11. Recently, patented cultivars of nemesia have been developed. These are sold as plants rather than seeds and have the advantage of being tolerant of a much broader temperature range; they can survive a light, fast frost and stand up better to summer heat.
Size: 8 to 10 inches tall, 6 to 10 inches wide
Bloom: In early spring, small flowers in a wide range of colors and many bicolors.
Exposure: Full sun
Soil mix: Well drained, moist, moderate fertility, with a pH of 5.5 to 6.8. Fertilize every 2 to 4 weeks.
Companion plants: Started early inside, nemesia can complement late spring bulbs and early summer blooms.
Options: Good cultivars include 'KLM', a blue and white flower with a yellow eye;

'National Ensign', with rose and white flowers; and the Carnival Series, which includes yellow, red, orange, pink, and white flowers that sport spots, streaks, and contrasting colors of the veins. 'Sundrops' is a relatively new cultivar that has a tidier habit than other nemesias and comes in 20 different colors. Patented cultivars now available include 'Blue Bird', 'Compact Innocence', and the Aromatica Series, which, true to its name, is scented. Look online or ask for these at your nursery.

Nicotiana sylvestris, N. alata
Flowering tobacco

Both of these species are blessed with one of the sweetest, most pervasive fragrances in the plant world. It often isn't apparent until dusk, so many people keep blooming plants outside their bedroom windows where the perfume can waft in on evening breezes. Other types of flowering tobacco are not scented but do have masses of open, colorful blooms that liven any garden.

Size: 3 to 4 feet tall, 1 to 2 feet wide
Bloom: In midsummer through fall, masses of blooms appear.
Exposure: Full sun in the north, partial shade in the south
Soil mix: Well drained, fertile, moist, with a pH of 6 to 6.8. Fertilize every 2 to 4 weeks.
Companion plants: Do not pair with other strongly fragrant blooms because you want to be able to fully enjoy their perfume. Trailing petunias look good at their base in a large container and almost echo the flower shapes of N. alata.
Options: N. sylvestris has pendulous white blooms, and N. alata has greenish white blooms, but its cultivars, such as 'Nicki Red' and 'Lime Green', have blooms in much stronger colors, including red, rose, green, and pink. N. x sanderae 'Salmon Pink' is particularly striking because of its soft pink blooms. Other series in this species include the Sensation Mix cultivars, which are also strongly fragrant.

Osteospermum
African daisy

Another cool lover, this plant makes an excellent addition to the spring garden in Zones 5 to 8 and the late winter garden in Zones 9 to 11. The flowers are exotic, with centers that are often in a contrasting color to the petals, spoon-shaped petals in some cultivars, and subtly striped petals in others.
Size: Varies from 12 to 20 inches tall, 10 to 12 inches wide
Bloom: Flowers open in late spring or early summer in most locations; colors range from pinks through whites and yellows.
Exposure: Full sun
Soil mix: Well drained, moderate fertility, moist, with a pH of 5.5 to 6.3. Fertilize every 2 or 3 weeks.

Plant good companions together to make a truly interesting display. Here, *Nicotiana* 'Lime Green', *Lysimachia nummularia* 'Aurea', and *Helichrysum petiolare* 'Limelight' grow together.

Companion plants: Plants look particularly good when showcased among a group of more delicate blooms such as lobelia.
Options: Favorite cultivars include 'Pink Whirls', which have purple to lavender-blue spooned petals around a blue disk; 'Whirligig', with a dark center and spooned white petals with steel-blue undersides; and 'Buttermilk', which has a rich brown center and petals that shade from white to yellow at the tips.

Pinch back the stem tips to four or five nodes soon after transplanting to the final pot. This encourages bushy growth and increases flowering sites. Keep the plants cool and in bright light. They bloom best at 50° to 70°F days and 40° to 60°F nights. Keep them consistently moist, too; when the soil dries, they go into dormancy and have a hard time reblooming. Soggy soil sets the stage for fungal attack, though, so it's important to water only when they need it.

Plants can be deadheaded to prolong bloom but don't require it in the same way that other annuals do because they don't set seed easily. If they look bedraggled, cut back the stems. They will regrow and rebloom quickly as long as nutrient supplies are adequate and temperatures are not too hot and humid.

Pelargonium spp.
Geraniums

The most difficult thing about growing geraniums is choosing what to grow. In addition to the wealth of different bloom colors, leaf forms and plant habits vary tremendously.
Size: Varies from 12 to 18 inches tall, 8 to 18 inches wide
Bloom: In late spring or early summer throughout the season
Exposure: Full sun
Soil mix: Well drained, moist, and rich soil, with a pH between 5.5 and 6. Fertilize soil every 2 to 4 weeks.
Companion plants: Geraniums look good grouped together; choose complementary

LEFT: With a few drainage holes, an old tin can makes an amusing container for small plants such as this lovely scented geranium.

RIGHT: Keep potted petunias deadheaded and trim them back midsummer for a wonderful season-long display.

forms and colors, and place their pots in a prominent place. Alternatively, use a row of the same kind of geranium to create a boundary in the container garden.

Options: Of the many types available, the zonal geraniums (*P. × hortorum*) are the most common in window boxes and other containers. Their name comes from the "zoned" markings on their rounded leaves. One of the nicest zonals is 'Happy Thought'. Its rounded leaves are particularly striking because they have greenish yellow markings in a shape that resembles a butterfly and clusters of single, clear red flowers.

Ivy-leaved geraniums (*P. peltatum*) have leaves that do resemble English ivy. The flowers are looser and less dense than those of the zonal types, and the leaves are smooth and shiny. Of these, 'Amethyst' is always popular. It has pink-purple blooms.

Scented geraniums (*P. graveolens*) are often smaller overall than the other types and diverse in both appearance and scent. Once you begin to grow them, you may discover yourself becoming a collector—they are gratifying all year-round, both inside and out. Many people think that the old-fashioned 'Lady Plymouth' is one of the best rose-scented geraniums, and the Royal Horticultural Society has even given the flower an Award of Garden Merit. In addition to the soft rose scent the flowers

carry, the clear green leaves are variegated with light cream markings, and the flowers are a lovely pale lavender color.

Sanitation is crucial when you are growing geraniums, particularly the zonal types. As soon as flowers fade, snip them from the plant and remove them from the area. If petals drop onto a leaf below, fungal infections will gain a foothold, and the whole plant may become infected.

Petunia x hybrida

Petunia

It's tempting to think that you don't need petunias, simply because they are so common. However, don't overlook this versatile plant. Thanks to the amazing number of cultivars, you can find a petunia in just about any color you want—except orange. You can also find and make the most of scented types and those that look particularly good in hanging baskets.

Size: Varies from 8 to 16 inches tall, 10 to 16 inches wide

Bloom: In early summer until frost, flowers continuously form.

Exposure: Full sun

Soil mix: Well drained, moderately fertile, with a pH of 5.5 to 6. Fertilize once a month while the plant is in active growth.

Companion plants: Place them in a pot by themselves and group them together or with plants whose colors they complement.

Options: The Wave Series petunias are ideal for hanging baskets. Multiflora petunias produce enormous numbers of blooms over the season and are virtually maintenance free; they will even continue to bloom without being deadheaded and

rarely need to be cut back to keep their good looks into late summer.

Of the grandifloras, 'Prism Sunshine' is one of the best. It has large yellow blooms that are shaded white near the tips, giving it a very soft appearance. Other good grandifloras include 'Blue Danube' with double lavender-blue blooms, and the Daddy Series plants with their heavy veination.

Petunias are broadly classified into two groups: the grandifloras and the multifloras. Grandiflora types have flowers as large as 4 inches wide and are physically the more delicate of the two. Multifloras have flowers about 2 inches wide but carry many more of them at a time. Protect grandifloras from wind and rain to keep them looking their best. Multifloras withstand normal environmental conditions, so you can place them anywhere in the container garden.

Deadhead all petunias to keep the flowers coming on vigorously. If they begin to look too leggy in the middle of the season, cut them back, water, and fertilize. They will regrow and rebloom quickly.

Thymophylla tenuiloba
Dahlberg daisy, Golden fleece

It may never be the star of the garden, but this cheerful little annual makes a wonderful accent to contrast with more dramatic blooms. It's also good in a hanging basket because the fernlike leaves are literally coated with the bright yellow flowers.

Size: 6 to 12 inches tall, 6 to 12 inches wide
Bloom: In late spring through midsummer, yellow, daisylike blooms form.
Exposure: Full sun
Soil mix: Well drained, light, moderately fertile, with a pH of 6.8 to 7.2. Fertilize every 2 to 4 weeks.
Companion plants: Plant with other bright-colored blooms, almost as a background to them.
Options: This is an easy plant to grow and is virtually maintenance free once it is established. It will stop blooming in mid- to late summer, but you can start successive plantings to keep its spot in the design filled through the summer.

When crushed, the leaves smell lemony. But they aren't a salad ingredient, so don't make the mistake of thinking that you can use them as an edible green.

Tropaeolum majus
Nasturtium

Nasturtiums are more versatile than you may imagine. Not only do some of these true annuals grow long enough to be good climbers, others are happy to form a nice underplanting. All types are edible. Their flowers, particularly, make a good addition to salads or as a garnish for fish or spreads such as hummus, and their julienned leaves add the right touch to an egg salad.

Size: 1 to 15 feet tall, 1 to 15 feet wide
Bloom: In early summer, and until the frost sets in, continuous red, orange, and yellow blooms form.
Exposure: Full sun to filtered light

Soil mix: Well drained, low to moderate fertility, with a pH of 5.8 to 6.7. Fertilize once a month at most with very low-nitrogen materials; with too much nitrogen, the plants put out huge numbers of very large leaves and few blooms. Aphids are attracted and difficult to eradicate because the plants draw them from long distances.
Companion plants: These plants overpower pastels and soft blues, but look wonderful when combined with other bright, cheery flowers against a background of gray or silver foliage plants.
Options: For the best climbing nasturtiums, look for trailing cultivars of *T. majus*. You will probably be able to find 'Variegatus', a trailing cultivar with cream and green variegated leaves and red or orange flowers. Not all *T. majus* cultivars climb, however. Plants such as 'Peach Melba' are dwarf and bushy. This soft yellow bloom has an orange-red throat that adds interest. The Jewel Series are also derived from *T. majus*. These are also dwarf and bushy but have vividly colored blooms in bright shades of red, yellow, and pink. 'Empress of India' is a striking plant with deep red flowers and purple-green leaves.

Verbena, Tapien Series
Tapien verbena

Tapien verbenas are patented plants and a relatively new introduction to the horticultural world. They differ from standard verbenas by their plant habit, which is low and mat-forming rather than tall and rangy. Many gardeners are using them as ground covers, but you are bound to be impressed by them in hanging baskets.

Size: 6 to 8 inches tall, 12 to 18 inches wide
Bloom: From early summer until frost, small flowers cover the entire plant.
Exposure: Full sun to partial shade
Soil mix: Well drained, moderately fertile, with a pH of 5.5 to 5.8. Fertilize twice a month with a complete fertilizer.
Companion plants: These plants look good near lobelia and nemesia.

Options: Six colors of tapien verbena are currently available: blue-violet, soft pink, powder blue, lavender, pink, and white. The foliage is airy but grows in a tight enough mat that it can smother out weeds when it is grown as a groundcover.

Plants do not require deadheading, and this, in combination with their disease resistance, makes them a truly low-maintenance plant. The only real requirement, aside from routine watering and fertilizing, is that you pinch the stems to encourage branching. It's also important to remove dead leaves from the center of the plant as the season wears on.

Viola spp.
Violas, Pansies

In open garden soil, perennial types of violas overwinter and others self-seed. In the container garden, you can allow this to happen, of course, but you can also grow the plants as annuals, replacing them every year. This gives you the option of controlling your design because you will know the flower color of the plant you're growing

Pretty pots of violas greet the spring each year and last long into summer, if kept cool.

rather than be surprised (as one often is) by self-seeded plants.

Size: 3 to 8 inches tall, 3 to 6 inches wide

Bloom: In early spring, cheerful little flowers open in shades that range from blue to yellow to pink, orange, and purple, many with dark markings on the petals.

Exposure: Filtered light or full sun in the north

Soil mix: Well drained, fertile, moist, with a pH of 5.5 to 5.8. Fertilize every 2 to 3 weeks, depending on performance.

Companion plants: Set blooming pots amid spring-blooming bulbs and, later in the season, pair them with dainty flowers such as lobelia and nemesia.

Options: Of the many types of violas, the purple, lavender, and yellow *V. tricolor,* sometimes known as Johnny-Jump-Up, is a favorite with vegetable gardeners because its small, edible blooms add a touch of cheerfulness to salads or chopped chive garnishes. But not all *V. tricolor* cultivars are used that way. 'Molly Sanderson', which is quickly gaining popularity, is one of the few garden plants to have truly black, rather than deep red, blooms. You'll have to buy started plants of this cultivar because it doesn't come true from seed.

V. × wittrockiana is the plant we know as a pansy. Every year, new cultivars are added to the already enormous list. Choose based on color and markings on their faces. As with so many other flowers, it's hard to go wrong, no matter what you choose, because all pansies give a cheerful look to any garden where they grow.

In cool conditions, violas will bloom throughout the summer. Where it is warm, however, blooming often slows or stops entirely when temperatures average 80°F and above. To prolong the bloom period, cut the plant back severely after the first flush of bloom and move it into a cooler, more shaded spot. This should promote at least a second flush of flowers.

Bulbs

Containers make an ideal home for spring bulbs. Thanks to their portability, you can easily modify the environment and create a bulb garden that comes into bloom both earlier and later than normal. You can force some bulbs, too, and if you bring their pots into a warm environment in succession, you can enjoy these blooms from winter into late spring. Later in the season, summer bulbs provide drama and vivid color. Bulbs are easy to grow and will give many years of pleasure as long as you let the leaves stay in place until they naturally brown and wither. This allows them to manufacture and store the nutrients they'll need to carry them through their dormant period and into bloom the following year.

In the garden, it's common to plant fast-growing perennials such as forget-me-nots as companions to tulips or daffodils. The frothy blue and green forget-me-nots give good cover to the browning leaves of the bulb plant. You can do this in a container garden, too, but it's more practical to remove the pot from the focal area of the garden and tuck it in a corner where the leaves can mature and brown without causing an eyesore. Once the leaves have died back, you can leave the bulbs in the pot, watering them only enough to keep them alive, or take them out of the pot and store them in a cool, dark, and dry place until planting time in fall.

If you live in Zones 7 to 9, you can plant summer bulbs, such as *Agapanthus*, in the fall when you plant spring bulbs, and protect them from freezing over the winter months. In colder areas, plant them in spring. Many of them need a certain number of hours under 40°F, so it's important to keep them in cool conditions over winter months. Let them heat up naturally as the weather warms in spring.

Agapanthus spp.
African blue lilies

If you are searching for a plant with upright, round umbels and a somewhat more relaxed and casual form than alliums, look no further. The ball-shaped blooms are loosely formed, giving an airy feeling, and the leaves are shorter and less dramatic. You'll also find a variety of blues, some with a touch of purple, making them a periwinkle color, and some closer to a soft baby blue.

Potted *Agapanthus*, such as these 'Purple Cloud' plants give a lush, tropical atmosphere wherever they grow.

If you live in a frost-free area, choose an evergreen species. Otherwise, stick to the deciduous sorts.

Size: 1 to 3 feet tall, 1 to 2 feet wide

Bloom: In summer, blue or white umbels form on stalks held high above the leaves. Florets in some species are pendant rather than round.

Exposure: Full sun to filtered light

Soil mix: Well drained, moderately fertile with a pH of 6.6 to 7.5

Companion plants: The blue colors of various *Agapanthus* species are so lovely that it's best to pair them with white flowers or silvery and gray foliage plants.

Options: *A. praecox* and its subspecies, including *minimus*, *orientalis*, and *praecox*, is the most commonly found evergreen species. Bring this plant indoors during winter. Look for the cultivar 'Snowy Owl' for a white bloom. If you want a dwarf, look for 'Peter Pan' or 'Lilliput', both of which grow only 16 inches tall.

African blue lilies make excellent cut flowers, with a vase life up to a week long if they are kept in somewhat cool, moderately lit conditions. If you want to grow a species or cultivar that isn't hardy in your zone, plant the rhizome in spring. Keep the pot inside until all danger of frost has passed and the weather begins to warm.

Allium aflatunense
Ornamental onion

Of the more than 700 species of alliums, *A. aflatunense* is a favorite among gardeners. Give it a deep pot and a central position in your container garden; as soon as it blooms, you're sure to feel that it justifies its position.

Size: 2 to 3 feet tall, 8 to 10 inches wide

Bloom: In late spring, large, round balls composed of hundreds of purple-blue florets rise above the arching, straplike leaves.

Exposure: Full sun

Soil mix: Well drained, fertile, with a pH of 6 to 7

Companion plants: Companions with yellow blooms and a strong structure themselves, such as yarrow (*Achillea* spp.), make these blooms look particularly vivid.

Options: A favorite cultivar is 'Purple Sensation' because its 4-inch balls of florets are such a pure, deep purple. It stands out in any environment and has the virtue of looking good in both formal and informal gardens. For maximum impact, plant several in white urnlike containers, and use them at the entryway to your garden.

Plant these in fall when you plant spring bulbs. For the best results, plant them about 8 inches deep, about 10 to 12 inches apart. Plants bloom best when they are a bit crowded in the pot—don't give them too much room if you want a lot of blooming stems.

Like many plants in the lily family, these plants have been known to irritate the skin of some people. If you tend to have sensitive skin, wear gloves when you handle *Allium* bulbs. No pet would be tempted to eat the flowers; make sure your children don't, either.

Convallaria majalis
Lily of the valley

Lily of the valley has such an enchanting fragrance that you're going to want to have plants inside as well as in the container garden. This species is ideally suited to one of its most common uses, a wedding flower, because the waxy blooms hold up well for long periods of time in a bouquet and also because the little bells on arching stems nod gracefully with every step.

Lily of the valley leaves remain green long after the flowers have faded, giving a restful contrast in your container garden.

Size: 8 to 12 inches tall, 3 to 6 inches wide

Bloom: In mid- to late spring, white or pink, intensely fragrant, with bell-shaped flowers

Exposure: Filtered sun to partial shade

Soil mix: Well drained, moist, moderately fertile, with a pH of 5.5 to 7.5

Companion plants: Pots of delicate blue forget-me-nots are good companions.

Options: Many cultivars are available, but notable ones include C. *majalis* var. *rosea*, which is a lovely soft pink color rather than white. 'Fortin's Giant' is a white cultivar that is larger than most, and 'Flore Pleno' has double white flowers. The leaves persist much longer than those of most spring bulbs. In fall, they will turn yellow before browning, adding color to the container garden.

   All parts of this plant are somewhat poisonous, and the red berries are particularly dangerous, so you may want to remove the flower stems from the plant when the blooms fade.

Crocosmia spp.

Montbretias, Falling stars

Blooming *Crocosmia* is so bright that no matter where you place it in the garden, it will attract a lot of attention—and not just from people. Red cultivars are favorite food sources for hummingbirds, so if you are anywhere near one of their flyways, you're bound to see them dipping in to feed. Butterflies love these blooms, too, so place their pots where butterflies will feel safe enough to come in and feed on the nectars.

Size: 2 to 3 feet tall, 1 to 2 feet wide

Bloom: In the summer months, vivid red, orange, or yellow blooms grow on long, arching branches. Blooms form on one side of the branch, resulting in a graceful, spray-like appearance.

Exposure: Full sun in cooler areas; partial shade in Zones 8 to 10

Soil mix: Well drained, fertile, with a pH of 5.5 to 7.5

Companion plants: This plant deserves a pot of its own and a central spot when it is blooming. Pair it with other vividly colored blooms, but take care to give it enough space so that the graceful form is apparent.

Options: 'Lucifer' is an excellent cultivar. It has clear red blooms and individual flowers as large as 2 inches long. Other good cultivars include 'Golden Fleece', a yellow *Crocosmia* that produces an enormous number of blooming stems, and 'Emily McKenzie', a cultivar with orange flowers with dark markings on the throat.

   The corms of *Crocosmia* are unusual in that they form an underground chain, with the oldest corm at the lowest level and the youngest at the top. They split apart easily, which allows them to spread readily in the wild. In a container, this won't happen. When you repot them in early spring, you can separate a few corms for a new pot or to give to a friend. They make excellent cut flowers. You don't need to deadhead the long stalks when blooming is finished; they are self-cleaning. As fall approaches, attractive seedpods will form all along the branches. Cut them when the pods are fully brown but before they have begun to split open. Spray them with a light coating of varnish and use them in dried winter arrangements.

Potted *Crocus vernus* and *Crocus* 'King of Stripes' are harbingers of the beauty yet to come in your container garden as the season warms.

Crocus spp.

Crocuses

Blooming crocuses symbolize spring for most people, especially since it's not uncommon to see them peeking through the snow. Freezing temperatures are not really good for the blooms, but they will tolerate much cooler conditions than most spring flowers. But spring isn't the only time crocuses bloom; some species, such as *C. sativus*, the saffron crocus, bloom in fall. Fall bloomers tend to be purple or lilac, so they add a welcome contrast to the yellow, orange, and red colors of fall.

Size: 4 to 6 inches tall, 4 to 6 inches wide

Bloom: Early spring or fall. Spring blooms are white, yellow, light orange, or purple and sometimes striped; fall blooms are purple or lilac.

Exposure: Full sun

Soil mix: Well drained; moderately fertile, with a pH of 6 to 7.5

Companion plants: Crocus blooms so early that it's difficult to find companions for it. Instead, make sure to have pots and pots of different crocuses; they will complement each other and add to the show.

Options: If you want an extra early crocus, buy a cultivar of *C. ancyrensis*, such as 'Golden Bunch.' These plants not only bloom very early, they are a rich golden orange color that brightens up the last days of winter. *C. tommasinianus* is another early bloomer that naturalizes well in garden soils. In pots, it will reproduce well as long as the soil is moist but not wet and has a moderate fertility level. Cultivars of *C. vernus* are the easiest to find in neighborhood garden centers in the fall and, fortunately, are also the best to use for indoor forcing.

In addition to *C. sativus*, fall cultivars include *C. speciosus*, which blooms early enough to beat the first snow, and *C. goulimyi*, which is best for warm climates.

Plant the corms only an inch apart; they tolerate crowding and look best when planted in large groups. You won't need a deep container, but look for a wide one so you can grow these plants en masse. Let the corms chill for a minimum of 4 weeks before bringing them into a warm environment. Keep them moist but never wet to avoid problems with fungal diseases.

Dahlia spp.
Dahlias

Dahlias are about as varied as a single genus can be. There are 11 classes of perennial dahlias, based on flower form. These range from blooms with single, flat-leaved petals to those that look like dense balls of petals. Some have pointed petals, some rounded—whatever you're looking for, you can probably find it in a dahlia.

Size: Varies from 8 to 48 inches tall, 5 to 24 inches wide

Bloom: Varies, but midsummer brings blooms in white, pink, red, yellow, pink, and also lavender.

Exposure: Full sun

Soil mix: Well drained, humus-rich soil with a pH of 6 to 7

Companion plants: Depending on type, pair dahlias with other brightly colored blooming plants, or if you want to showcase the dahlias, surround them with soft gray or silver foliage plants.

Options: With more than 3,000 cultivars, dahlias are difficult to select. Whenever you see a plant you like, ask its name. Spend time at nurseries browsing the selections when they are in bloom. Some reliable cultivars include 'Grenadier', an excellent cultivar with double blooms and a bright red color. The leaves are quite dark, giving a strong contrast to the flowers. 'Bishop of Llandaff' is also red and has even darker foliage than 'Grenadier'.

But it is an anemone type rather than a double. 'Hallmark' is a ball dahlia with lovely lavender petals.

Dahlias react well to pinching and disbudding. Keep their growth in bounds by heading back their branches whenever they threaten to overtake other plants. Deadhead regularly to keep plants blooming. You can also cut the flowers for use in bouquets—they look dramatic and last for days.

Hyacinthus orientalis
Hyacinth

The fragrance of hyacinths signals true spring for many people. Later than crocuses and all but the very latest daffodils, they often bloom at the same time as mid-season tulips. The colors of hyacinths tend to be strong, so they easily overpower a mixed grouping. But if you pair them with white cultivars, both plants will shine in the warm spring sunlight.

Size: 8 to 12 inches tall; 6 to 8 inches wide

Bloom: In midspring, tightly packed spikes of red, blue, white, orange, pink, violet, or yellow florets stand stiffly among the leaves.

Exposure: Full sun to filtered light

Soil mix: Well drained, moderately fertile, with a pH of 6.5 to 7.5

Companion plants: Hyacinths look best when planted in groups. As noted, pale-colored tulips can be effective companions, but choose a nonscented tulip because the fragrance of the hyacinths overpowers other scents.

Options: Favorite cultivars of hyacinths include 'Delft Blue', a medium blue cultivar with a wonderful fragrance; 'King Codro',

a double violet cultivar; 'Pink Pearl', a
pink cultivar; 'Edelweiss', a strong white;
and 'City of Haarlem', a clear yellow.
Remember when you shop for bulbs that
the bigger the bulb, the bigger the resulting
flower stalk. Second-year bulbs produce
much smaller flower spikes that are not
as densely packed. Because of this, many
people throw out hyacinth bulbs after they
finish blooming rather than leaving them to
carry over.

Hyacinths are very pest resistant, and
one reason is because they contain slightly
poisonous compounds. Do not eat them.
Some people develop an allergic reaction
when they touch the bulbs, too, so if you
have sensitive skin, use plastic gloves when
handling them.

Lilium spp.
Lilies

Lilies are so dramatic that they easily
become the focal point of your garden
when they are in bloom. Some are
deliciously fragrant, too, making them serve
double duty in the garden.

Size: Varies from 12 to 48 inches tall, 10 to
18 inches wide
Bloom: In early to late summer, depending
upon species, large, showy blooms range
in colors from white through pink, yellow,
orange, red, and purple.
Exposure: Full sun, filtered light
Soil mix: Well drained, fertile, humusy, with
a pH of 6 to 7
Companion plants: Plant them in their
own pots and group them together for the
best effect.
Options: One of the nicest lilies for
container culture is the regal lily (L. regale).
It can produce as many as 25 flowers in a

Choose pots and locations for
lilies, such as these *Lilium longiflorum*
'White American' plants, to
showcase their elegance.

season; the blooms are sweetly fragrant
and trumpet-shaped, and the petals are
white toward the inside but flushed with a
purple color on the outside. The prominent
stamens are bright yellow.

L. rubellum is another fragrant lily that
blooms in midseason. It produces lovely
rose-pink flowers that have a really
pervasive perfume. Just a couple of plants
will scent your whole yard or your home if
you cut them for an indoor arrangement.
L. 'Star Gazer' is a popular cultivar that you'll
find in almost every garden supply shop.
It has numerous large, star-shaped red
flowers with recurved petal tips and dark
spots toward the center. It is not scented
but makes such a spectacular display that
most lily lovers have at least a plant or two.
For a real change of pace, plant L. nanum.
It normally grows only 10 to 12 inches tall
and has pendant, nodding yellow or pink,
unscented blooms. It likes filtered light in
cool climates and light shade in warm ones
and can easily slip into a mixed container
with taller plants.

Muscari armeniacum
Grape hyacinth

Grape hyacinths are cheerful plants. Pay
attention and you'll notice that almost
everyone smiles when they look at
them—the dense little thickets they create
of what look like miniature hyacinths just
make people happy. Do plant them in large
groups; 6 little grape hyacinth plants are
not impressive, but 30 or 40 of them begin
to make a show.

Size: 4 to 8 inches tall, 3 to 4 inches wide
Bloom: In early spring, spikes of deep
purple or white bell-shaped florets will
grow in the center of the bright green,
grass-like leaves.
Exposure: Full sun to partial shade
Soil mix: Well drained, moderate to poor
fertility with a pH of 5.5 to 7.5
Companion plants: Use grape hyacinths as
an underplanting to a huge pot of white or
yellow tulips or daffodils.

These perky little grape hyacinths make a
cheerful contrast to the regal-looking stone
urn where they're growing.

Options: M. armeniacum is the most
common species and the one you are most
likely to find at your local garden outlet.
One of the best cultivars is 'Blue Spike', a
sturdy plant with light blue, double flowers.
M. azureum is also common, although it's a
deeper blue color and spreads extremely
quickly. M. comosum has fringed, double,
light violet-lilac blooms that are grouped
somewhat loosely on the spike. And, if you
want a bright white cultivar, look for
M. botryoides 'Album'.

Narcissus spp.
Daffodils, Jonquils

The variety of daffodils is truly mind-
boggling. According to the American
Daffodil Society, there are 25 species,
divided into 12 classes, and more than
13,000 cultivars. But as far as most
gardeners are concerned, the important
things about the various types are color,
size, and fragrance, as well as hardiness.
There are early bloomers that do well in
any climate, but in Zone 8, late bloomers
do not do well because it's too warm for
the flowers when they bloom.

Size: 6 to 18 inches tall, 3 to 6 inches wide

Bloom: Varied; ranges from white through palest pink and yellow, small cupped and large cupped, fragrant and unscented.

Exposure: Full sun to partial shade

Soil mix: Well drained, moist, fertile, with a pH of 6 to 7.5

Companion plants: Depending on earliness, place beside blooming pots of delicate spring bloomers such as sweet alyssum and Johnny-Jump-Ups. Bulbs also look good massed together; group pots of either the same cultivar or different cultivars that bloom at the same time for a stunning effect.

Options: Of the many cultivars to choose from, 'Tête-à-tête' and 'Thalia' are both excellent for containers. 'Tête-à-tête', a miniature yellow daffodil with standard proportions between the trumpet and petals, is the very earliest daffodil to bloom in the spring. Look for it at the same time crocuses are in bloom. 'Thalia' is a midsize plant with clusters of lovely white flowers, again with standard proportions between the trumpet and petals.

Daffodils need a chilling period of 12 to 15 weeks at a temperature of 40°F, whether you are going to force them for early bloom or let them bloom at a natural time in the outdoor container garden. For chilling, a shed where temperatures remain above freezing and below 45°F is ideal. Pot the bulbs so that their tips are several inches below the soil surface, water them, and let them sit out their time, making certain that the soil stays consistently moist but not soggy.

After the bulbs have had their chilling time, you'll want to gradually warm them if you are forcing them for early indoor bloom. Bring the chilled pots inside once their chilling period is over. If you have planted many pots, you can prolong their season by bringing in only a couple of pots at a time. Warmth will stimulate their leaves to grow. Place them in a location that has a good light source during the day, either on a windowsill or under a good grow light. Prolong their bloom time by keeping them in a cool spot at night.

Tulipa spp.
Tulips

Tulips can look formal or casual, depending on how and where you use them. A long line of columnar pots along a walkway that are filled with tall white tulips is the very essence of elegance. Pots of multicolored tulips scattered among blooming daffodils and other spring charmers are cheerful, bright, and completely informal. Tulips are known for "running out," meaning that they often stop blooming in their second or third year. For a container garden, it's wise to buy new bulbs every year so that you will be assured of having the blooms you want when you want them.

Pot up masses of graceful daffodils, such as these *Narcissus* 'Hawera', to create a truly beautiful spring planting.

Size: 6 to 30 inches tall, 4 to 10 inches wide

Bloom: In mid to late spring, depending on cultivar, upright or reflexed cup- or star-shaped blooms open in every color of the palette save blue.

Exposure: Full sun

Soil mix: Well drained, fertile, with a pH of 6.7 to 7.5

Companion plants: Grape hyacinths or forget-me-nots can make a nice understory to pots of tulips, but remember that they also look striking when planted on their own. To avoid having one plant dying back while another is in full bloom, plant only one cultivar to a container. You can group containers as plants come in and out of bloom over springtime.

Options: Long ago, when "tulipmania" took over Holland and bulbs were selling for astronomical sums, the favorites were those with streaked colors on their petals. At the time, no one knew that the streaking was actually caused by a viral disease. Today, growers routinely destroy any infected bulbs. But don't despair; breeders have created cultivars, often called Rembrandt tulips, with the same sort of streaking. 'Prinses Irene' is an orange-red cup-shaped tulip with dark maroon streaks originating from the bottom of the cup. 'Sorbet' and 'Ice Follies' are both white with red streaks, and 'Orange Bowl' is orange with bright yellow markings.

Other notable cultivars include 'Stresa', a yellow tulip with red streaks. Because it is a Kaufmanniana tulip, it is likely to rebloom year after year, even in a container. After the bloom fades, remove its stem and leave the bulb in place. Water lightly after the leaves have died back and disappeared, until it's time to replant in the fall. 'White Triumphator' is a lily-flowered tulip about 2 feet tall. It can look quite elegant, particularly when planted in a formal-looking container. 'Mariette' is another good lily-flowered tulip; it has rose or salmony-colored flowers that flare at the top. 'Negrita' is in the Triumph class—the kind of tulip you probably think of when you hear the word. It's a dark purple color with a truly classic shape.

Climbers

Climbing plants add drama to a container garden. Their height can serve as a background to other plants or as an architectural feature that adds a focal point, or echoes other features in the landscape.

Many climbers grow best in fairly large pots. For maximum flexibility, plan ahead by setting their pots on wheeled platforms. Similarly, think about trellis choices before you plant. If the plant will grow well on a support that's positioned in its pot, it will never be restricted to a single area. Finally, consider pruning needs and timing, too. If you generally take a late winter vacation, for example, you may wish to buy summer-blooming plants that won't require attention until after they flower.

Campsis spp.

Trumpet vines

Trumpet vines are among the fastest growing climbers. They will completely cover a support in only a few years and provide a screen that is all but "see through" in areas you want to block. But that is by no means their best characteristic. The brightly colored flowers are magnets for hummingbirds. In midsummer, it's not unusual to see two or three hummingbirds feeding from the vine at one time. So if you love hummingbirds and you have a good spot for a vigorous vine, a trumpet vine might be just the plant you want.

Size: 10 to 15 feet in containers

Bloom: Red, orange, and yellow trumpet-shaped flowers form in midsummer and carry on until frost.

Exposure: Full sun to partial shade

Soil mix: Well drained, moderately to highly fertile moist, humus-rich; tolerant to short periods of drought

Companion plants: Nasturtiums planted at the base of the vine and positioned to droop from the container are a lovely companion, as are California poppies and Shirley poppies.

Options: In garden soils, trumpet vines can become a nuisance because they grow so vigorously, but in containers, the plants are much better behaved. Even so, give them their own support outside of the pot, and do not encourage them to grow up the walls of your home or garage.

Favorite cultivars include 'Indian Summer' because of its yellow-orange blooms with vivid red throats. 'Madame Rosy' is a hybrid trumpet vine that, true to its name, has rose-red blooms that begin opening in May and continue until frost sets in. A partially shaded and somewhat cool location enhances the rosy color. 'Flava' has yellow blooms that have a orange tint, and 'Mme. Galen' is an orange-red color. 'Huitan', which was recently patented, has coral red blooms and a compact, nonvining habit. 'Morning Calm' has apricot blooms; don't try to grow this in very cold-winter areas. It is hardy to Zone 6.

Clematis spp.

Clematises

Clematises can be the showiest flowers in the garden. If you search the Web site of a quality nursery for clematis cultivars and species, you're likely to be overwhelmed by the huge selection offered—so many that unless you have a specific color in mind, you'll probably have a hard time choosing just one or two. You can find species that bloom in spring and then again in late summer, as well as those that bloom only in summer. You'll also find fragrant types, bicolored cultivars, and small- and large-flowered plants.

Size: Varies; generally 6 to 20 feet

Bloom: Season, color, and even shape vary. Petals are in general open, with graceful stamens at the center.

These ornate pots and spiral supports perfectly complement the sumptuous appearance of *Clematis* 'Crystal Fountain'.

Exposure: Versatile climbers (originally they were woodland plants), full sun and semishade; keep roots shaded.

Soil mix: Average

Companion plants: Roses are the traditional companion for clematis, although these climbers are happy to grow up almost any support, including a variety of trees and tall shrubs.

Options: Pruning clematis can seem confusing until you understand why you prune at particular times and whether your plant needs light or heavy pruning. Check to see which Pruning Group your plant is in when you buy it.

Early season bloomers are categorized as Group A or 1, and bloom on old wood early in the season. Prune these plants right after they have blossomed to encourage new growth where buds will form for next year's flowers. If the plant is a vigorous grower, you can prune it heavily, but if it is slow, you simply need to cut back the stem tips, crossing branches and old wood and then do some final shaping.

Repeat bloomers bloom in both spring and later in the season, and form flowers on both old and new wood. These are categorized as Group B or 2. Watch your plant to determine when it puts on the greatest display and prune accordingly—right after bloom if the spring bloom is heaviest, and when it is dormant if the late bloom is best. In the case of plants with double flowers, prune after bloom because double blooms form best on old wood. You won't need to prune these back hard—cutting out crossing and crowded wood and shaping should do the trick.

Summer and fall bloomers fall into Group C or 3, and bloom on the current season's growth. You can prune these in early spring, just before they break dormancy. You can cut these back severely and still get great bloom, but leave at least two or three buds per stem—don't cut them to the ground. If you let a lot of old wood accumulate, blooming will diminish. So grit your teeth and prune back hard at least every 2 years.

Favorite cultivars include 'Silver Moon', with pale lavender flowers with gold markings, which is particularly good for hanging baskets. This easy-to-grow plant needs only light pruning in spring. 'Nelly Moser', Group B or 2, as such, blooms heavily in late spring and late summer. It can tolerate light shade. Blooms are large—up to 8 inches across and pink with a darker pink stripe down the center of each petal. Stamens are wine-colored.

C. viticella cultivars are small-flowered but make up for the size of their blooms with enormous numbers of flowers in late summer. These Group C or 3 plants bloom on the current season's growth and can be pruned back heavily when dormant. They betray their Italian heritage by their love of bright sunlight.

C. montana cultivars are known for their vigorous growth and sheer tenacity, so they need to be pruned back hard. Hardy in Zones 6 to 9, they are Group A or 1, plants that bloom on the previous season's growth.

Hedera spp.
English or common ivy (*H. helix*); Atlantic Ivy (*H. hibernica*)

Within the 11 *Hedera* species are literally hundreds of cultivars, sporting five major leaf shapes and colorations varying from a pure, clear green to dark maroon and soft yellow. Some are variegated with white, silver, or gold, and others have light veins on a dark green background. Many are suitable for containers, both inside and out. Be aware that all parts of ivy plants can cause severe intestinal distress if eaten and that some people break out if they touch the sap. If you do not know if you are allergic, wear gloves when working with your plants.

Size: Species vary; vines grow to 6 feet long and more.

Bloom: Inconspicuous

Exposure: Green-leaved types tolerate some shade while variegated ivies prefer more sun.

Soil mix: Well drained, moist, and humus-rich soil.

Companion plants: Ivies complement most other plants but do not share pots well. Use them as the backdrop to a mixed planting for year-round color and interest.

Options: Ivies are easy to grow. As long as you give them enough root room, water, nutrients, and air circulation around their leaves, they will perform well for you. If disease occurs, cut back the affected portion of the plant, thin the stems to increase air movement, and change the placement to a more airy and better lit location. You can prune ivy at any time of the year, so develop the habit of snipping off stems that threaten to take over other plants or garden furniture.

Favorite cultivars for containers include 'Calico', with green leaves variegated with white toward the center and sometimes with pink splotches. This is a slow-growing plant and does equally well inside or out, because unlike many variegated forms, it can tolerate partial shade. 'Congesta' is a nonclimbing form that grows into a small bush with spikelike branches. The opposite leaves stand stiffly out from the stem, giving it an almost prehistoric appearance. 'Maple Leaf' is a good subject for a hanging basket because of its drooping stems on which midgreen leaves grow thickly.

Hydrangea petiolaris
Climbing hydrangea

Climbing hydrangeas make a fantastic show, whether in bloom or not. They attach themselves to supports by aerial roots, so you may need to tie them in place if you are training them up a smooth-surfaced trellis or wall. The deciduous leaves often turn a clear yellow in fall before they drop, adding to the show they give.

Size: 10 to 20 feet, depending on pot size; can grow 80 feet tall in garden soil

Bloom: 6 to 10-inch-wide clusters of buds form in a somewhat flattened dome. The cream-colored center flowers are fertile and characterized by long stamens, and the sterile flowers toward the margins open into four-petaled, pure white blooms.

Exposure: Tolerates partial shade or filtered light in the south; place in a brighter position in northern areas.

Soil mix: Well drained, moist, and fertile

Companion plants: This plant is so spectacular that it steals the show from whatever it sits beside, so you might as well use it as a focal point in your garden.

Options: Once the leaves have fallen, the cinnamon to red-colored peeling bark stands out and becomes a strong garden feature on its own. This good shade-grower is slow to become established, even in good

garden soil. Remember the old adage about perennials that is particularly appropriate when it comes to climbing hydrangeas: The first year they sleep, the second year they creep, and the third year they leap. If it doesn't "leap" in its third year, be patient. Eventually it will put on as much as 2 feet of new growth a year.

Of the cultivars available, 'Firefly' is notable because its leaves have a lime-yellow margin that is most vivid in spring, when they are just opening.

Ipomoea spp.

Morning glories

What can say "summer" better than a morning glory rambling over and under its supports? The genus includes the traditional blue, purple, white, and pink morning glories (*Ipomoea purpurea*) that most are familiar with, as well as moonflowers (*I. alba*), sometimes called evening glories, which open their large white blooms in the evening, just at twilight, letting their

Morning glories can fill a pot and the trellis it holds with so little care that you can depend on them for a mid- to late summer focal point.

fragrance float on the breeze. Cardinal climbers (*I. × multifida*) have slender, finely cut foliage that complements their orange-red flowers. Cypress vine (*I. quamoclit*) also has finely cut foliage and orange-red blooms. And finally, the sweet potato vine (*I. batatas*), is known for its foliage, not its bloom, and is a fantastic addition to any container garden.

Size: 5 to 15 feet in containers
Bloom: Color varies, depending on species and cultivars, but most bloom midsummer until frost.
Exposure: Full sun
Soil mix: Well drained, moist, humus rich
Companion plants: Morning glories and moonflowers do not share space well and need their own containers. Sweet potato vines are a lovely complement to almost all plants with brightly colored blooms. The smaller cypress vines and cardinal climbers can be paired with California poppies for a stunning display.
Options: The two most common cultivars of the sweet potato vine are 'Blackie', a cultivar with leaves that look almost black, and 'Margarita', which has bright lime green leaves. These two look really good together and complement many other plants as well.

Jasminum spp.

Jasmines

The fragrance of jasmine is so sweet that once you've grown this plant, you can't imagine living without it. There are more than 200 jasmine species, not all of which climb or have fragrant flowers. Read descriptions carefully before buying your

jasmine because, no matter how beautiful the plant and how well it climbs and covers the support, you'll enjoy it twice as much if it is also fragrant.

Size: Varies; 5 to 15 feet in containers
Bloom: Most jasmine blooms are white; a few are yellow.
Exposure: Full sun or partial shade
Soil mix: Well drained, fertile, moist
Companion plants: The perfume of fragrant jasmines is so strong that it will overpower any other fragrant plant. Grow them with unscented plants for the most pleasing combinations.
Options: In a good environment, jasmine is rarely bothered by any pests or diseases. If your plant begins to show disease symptoms, prune it to open up the center and allow air to circulate freely around all the branches.

Choose your cultivar and species with location in mind. For example, winter jasmine (*J. nudiflorum*) is the hardiest jasmine and will grow well as far north as protected spots in Zone 5B. The yellow blooms are plentiful but non-fragrant, and the plant will live long if you protect the soil in the pot from freezing solid during the winter.

In many climates, jasmines must move inside for the winter, so they are often planted in decorative "indoor" pots.

Place pots of fragrant sweet peas where you'll be able to appreciate their fragrance and also cut them for the vase.

J. officinale is a favorite in Zones 9 and 10 because of its intensely fragrant white flowers and rapid growth. To grow it in a cooler zone, overwinter it indoors.

Lathyrus spp.

Sweet peas

Annual sweet peas are probably what you envision when you think of these plants because they are more brightly colored than the perennials. These can also be the most intensely fragrant sweet peas. But pay attention to descriptions because some of the newer hybrids that have been bred for coloration are no longer fragrant. In contrast, the old heirloom varieties that are available from many seed companies are both beautifully colored and sweetly perfumed. When in doubt, choose these.

Size: 4 to 8 feet tall

Bloom: Perennials are pale pinkish or white; annuals range in color from pinks to mauves to purples to blues to lavenders to salmon, and many are bicolored.

Exposure: Full sun

Soil mix: Well drained, fertile, and moist.

Companion plants: Sweet peas are showy enough to grow on their own. If you want a companion for their pot, grow sweet alyssum because neither its form nor its fragrance will compete with the sweet peas.

Options: Keep up with trellising these plants. They are light enough to grow well up thin cords, but they reach out with quickly growing tendrils and can get themselves into a tangle before you know it. If you train them to the strings, you have a chance of keeping air circulation high around all the stems and, thus, disease incidence down.

Favorite annual species include *L. odoratus*, with its many fragrant cultivars. Try any of the most frequently available

cultivars, including the pink and white bicolored 'Queen of the Isles', the white with red stripes 'America', the deep maroon 'Black Night', the creamy 'Mrs. Collier,' the purple-blue bicolored 'Cupanis Original', the orange 'Henry Eckford', the white 'Dorothy Eckford', or the pink and white bicolored 'Painted Lady'.

Lonicera spp.

Honeysuckles

Honeysuckle is a favorite plant for anyone who had the childhood pleasure of picking the blooms and sucking out their nectar. While adults may not do this anymore, the sweet scent of the flowers coming from containers is sure to bring back those happy memories. There are about 180 species, many of which are climbers suitable for growing in containers.

Size: 6 to 10 feet in containers

Bloom: White, pink, creamy yellow

Exposure: Sunny and sunless, depending on species type

Soil mix: Well drained, fertile, and moist

Companion plants: Grow in individual pots to show off this plant.

Options: Prune honeysuckles after they bloom because flowers grow on second-year wood. You can cut back severely if you want to keep the plant small and contained, or prune lightly to shape the plant.

Climbing honeysuckle species and hybrids include *L.* x *brownii* 'Dropmore Scarlet' with lightly scented reddish blooms; *L.* x *heckrottii* 'Gold Flame' with fragrant, orange-yellow blooms; *L.* x *americana* with fragrant yellow flowers; and *L. periclymenum* 'Graham Thomas', with highly fragrant white blooms that turn to yellow. Each of these plants is well worth growing for the speed with which it can cover a trellis, as well as the sweet fragrance it provides for weeks at a time.

While not actually a climber, the cultivar 'Winter Beauty' (*L.* x *purpusii*) is also notable. If you tie its branches to supports in a fan form, it can perform well as a backdrop for other plants. It's notable for its red-purple shoots and very fragrant, creamy white flowers that open in late winter or early spring. Blooming persists for as long as 6 to 8 weeks.

Rosa spp.

Climbing roses

Climbing roses may be the most romantic plants you can grow. Beyond choosing the right plant, the trick with climbers is to give them adequate support. Over a few years, a climbing rose plant can grow to be 8 or 10 feet high, even when its roots are in a container, and almost as wide. Think about this when you choose both pot and trellis.

Size: 5 to 15 feet tall; 2 to 6 feet wide

Bloom: Most climbers rebloom; ramblers tend to bloom once a year.

Exposure: Full sun

Soil mix: Well drained, fertile, humus-rich

Companion plants: In separate pots set close to each other, clematis and rose make lovely companions. In the same container, small foliage plants make good companions for roses. Climbing roses also make a good backdrop for the rest of the container garden, particularly if the chosen flower colors are compatible.

Options: Roses don't actually "climb." Those we call climbers have long canes that can be tied to supports, so it seems as if they are climbing them.

Ramblers, which some people consider a separate group, are rose species (R. wichurana and R. laevigata) with thin, whiplike canes that are easy to train.

Other "climbing roses" are particular cultivars in the modern, noisette, tea rose, china, bourbon, hybrid tea, grandiflora, and floribunda groups. In some cases, these have been bred to have long canes; in others, these mutants, or "sports," arose on their own.

Prune climbing roses that rebloom—once on old wood and again on new wood—in late winter or very early spring. Take care not to remove all the buds if you are pruning a rebloomer in winter—just cut out crossing or damaged wood and prune to trim the plant. If the plant blooms only once a year, wait to prune until after blooming has finished because these plants form flowers only on old wood.

Favorite cultivars include R. 'Albéric Barbier', a wichurana rose. This plant is quite vigorous, and its foliage is resistant to mildew. The double blooms are creamy-white with a yellow cast near the center. Some people describe the scent as similar to apples, and some say it smells musky. It blooms only once a season, on old wood. R. 'René André' is a hybrid that was introduced in 1901. One of its parents is R. wichurana and the other is 'L'Ideal', a tea rose. This plant also has double flowers but in soft shades of apricot and pink. It usually blooms only once a year, on old wood, but it can sometimes throw out a few flowers late in the season. The fragrance is soft, and those with poor noses can miss it entirely. R. 'Danse du Feu' is in the "modern climber" group. If you are looking for a true showstopper, consider growing this plant. The large double blooms are red with undertones of orange and a

Plant wisteria in large pots to give their roots adequate space to grow.

bricklike shade, and the foliage is glossy and dark green. The fragrance is almost citrusy. This plant is unusual for a rose in that it is tolerant of a north-facing position and can get by with 4 or 5 hours a day of direct sunlight. R. 'New Dawn' is also a "modern climber" and is considered by many people to be the best possible climbing rose. The plant is extremely disease resistant, making it easier to grow than most roses. Blooms are semi-double to double, pink, and highly fragrant. As the flowers age, the color softens to a pinkish glow. This is a repeat bloomer and has been known to carry a few flowers into the early fall. It's also tolerant of filtered light and north-facing positions and is a strong grower no matter where it is. R. 'Zepherine Drouhin' is a bourbon rose. It lacks thorns, so it is easy to train and prune. The fragrance is just what you think of when you imagine the scent of roses, and its deep pink flowers are a color that many people associate with roses. It is best in low-humidity areas, however, because it is quite susceptible to fungal diseases. R. 'Brite Eyes' is in the new introduction by the breeder of Knock Out™ roses, and is a climber. Gardeners everywhere are cheering the Knock Out™ introductions because these plants are truly vigorous. They are resistant to black spot and tolerant to drought, prosper in high humidity-conditions, and bloom and rebloom throughout a long season. 'Brite Eyes' has salmon-pink single flowers with good fragrance.

Wisteria spp.

Wisterias

ZONE 5-9

The lush beauty of blooming wisteria is matched only by its fragrance. In woodlands where these plants grow wild, their perfume is one of the first signs of spring; it announces their presence long before you see the drooping racemes of pea-shaped flowers among the trees overhead.

Size: 10 feet high in containers

Bloom: Purple or white, less commonly flushed with pink

Exposure: Full sun, but will tolerate partial shade in hot climates

Soil mix: Well drained, moist, and moderately fertile soil.

Companion plants: Tall, spiky plants, such as irises, in complementary shades of purple or white can make a stunning display if their containers are positioned in front of the wisteria pots.

Options: Both Chinese and Japanese wisteria are commonly available. One of the oddities of this plant is that Chinese wisteria twines in a counterclockwise direction, while Japanese wisteria twines in a clockwise direction. Other than that, you might have a hard time distinguishing between the two. All species include both white and purple cultivars. Remember: It's important to keep fertility levels moderate for wisteria. If nitrogen is too high, blooming will be inhibited.

Trellising is also a concern. These plants can get quite heavy. A trellis in the same pot as a wisteria will never have the strength to support it. Set up a separate support before you buy the plant, and make sure to allow enough space for both the trellis and wisteria pot when you arrange your garden.

Prune this plant every year, in late winter or very early spring. Pruning is straight-forward. After transplanting a wisteria into its pot, cut back the leader to no more than about 3 feet tall. All summer long, tie both the leader and laterals to the supports. The following spring, head back the leader several feet if it has grown vigorously— leave about 2 or 3 feet above the level at which the top laterals branch. Also, cut back the laterals to about a third of their length, and cut back the branches growing from the laterals to only two or three buds. Repeat this until the framework of the plant is established. After that, prune back all the laterals to two or three buds at a minimum. You may also need to cut back the leader to keep it in bounds.

When looking for the right wisteria to suit your garden, check first with local nurseries. They will have the plants that grow best in your climate and more than likely will be able to recommend several cultivars with both white and purple blooms.

Grasses and bamboos

Mound-forming and arching, grasses and bamboos tend to look best grown on their own, especially when they have a strong architectural shape. However, smaller varieties can give dramatic height, mesmerizing colors, and graceful movement to mixed plantings.

As a rule of thumb, single-specimen plantings look best when the mature plant is at least two-thirds as tall and wide as the pot in which it lives. Mixed plantings look best when the size, colors, and habits of the individual plants vary harmoniously, and the total mass of the group is at least two-thirds as big as its pot.

For overwintering in areas with freezing temperatures, insulate pots of tender grasses so the roots don't freeze, or move them into a greenhouse or the house for the winter. Many grasses and bamboos will survive outdoors if well covered to protect against frost.

Grasses

Cymbopogon citratus
Lemon grass

Lemon grass is a truly versatile herb. It has a scent and flavor similar to that of a tangy lemon, hence its common name. In its native countries of India and Sri Lanka, it's used in all types of cooking as well as for a light, refreshing tea. Medicinally, the oil extracted from the leaves and bulbs is antiseptic and said to cure athlete's foot. Many "natural" cosmetics use the oil for its lovely fresh scent.

The only disadvantage to this plant is that the edges of the leaves are razor-sharp; they can inflict a cut that's quite similar to a paper cut. Handle it with gloves, and to protect the unwary, set its pot well away from walkways.

Size: 3 feet high, 1 to 3 feet wide
Bloom: Nondescript; lemon grass seeds are usually sterile
Exposure: Full sun, but the plant will tolerate light shade
Soil mix: Well drained, medium to high organic matter, and fertile, although it will tolerate sandy soils if fertile; preferred pH of 5.5 to 7.5 but will tolerate a wider range
Companion plants: Creeping thyme (*Thymus serpyllum*) and lemon thyme (*Thymus citriodorus*) make excellent "understory plants" in a pot with lemon grass.

Extra care: Lemon grass is a sturdy plant that will withstand occasional dry soils and cold temperatures. Bottom leaves have a tendency to brown out in poor circumstances; remove them in early spring and again in early fall.

Festuca glauca 'Elijah Blue'
Blue fescue

Blue fescue is a lovely, mounded plant with thin, wiry, blue-green leaves radiating from its crown. The plant is striking, but it is particularly so when paired with trailing plants or those with white blooms. Use it as the border on a tub planting or the focal point in a window box filled with trailers.

This plant prefers cool, coastal climates but will tolerate hot, humid areas if grown in very well-drained soil and protected from blazing afternoon sunlight. The center of the plant has a tendency to die out within a few years. You'll find that growing it in well-drained situations slows this process, but expect to dig and divide plants at the end of every second year or the beginning of their third year.

Size: 12 inches high, 10 inches wide
Bloom: Early summer. Prune off flower spikes to maintain its showy appearance.
Exposure: Full sun in most climates for the best color; will tolerate light shade. In hot, sunny climates, place it to receive light afternoon shade.

Soil mix: Sandy, well drained, moderate fertility, with a pH of 6 to 7

Companion plants: It's especially effective with blue and purple flowering perennials, such as lavender (*Lavandula angustifolia*) and salvia (*Salvia* spp.), although it can be particularly stunning when grown on its own in a fairly formal-looking, rounded pot.

Hakonechloa macra 'Aureola'
Japanese forest grass

This lovely grass is said to remind people of a waterfall because the long leaves all grow in the same direction—toward the light. The leaves are yellowish with green stripes that turn red in fall if grown in full sun. If grown in shade, the leaves remain a green-gold color. In any situation, the foliage turns a golden brown before dying back in early winter. In gardens, it's often used to border a walkway or create an edge in a flower bed. In containers, it's equally effective when used alone or grouped with plants such as bamboo.

Cut back the foliage in early December. Each year, in early spring, add a generous layer of fully finished manure potting mix to the top of the container.

Size: Varies from 14 to 18 inches tall, 18 to 24 inches wide

Bloom: In mid- to late summer, this plant forms yellow flowers on tall, swaying panicles. In fall, airy, tan-colored seed heads nod above the leaves.

Exposure: Full sun to partial shade

Soil mix: Well drained, fertile, high organic matter, with a pH of 5.5 to 7

Companion plants: Bamboo, blue-leaved hostas, various ferns

Helictotrichon sempervirens
Blue oat grass

From a distance, this European native resembles blue fescue because it also has long, blue-green leaves that grow in a mounded tuft. However, blue oat grass is a larger, stronger plant. Its leaves are longer and broader, and the flowers and seedpods make a focal point in the yard. In 1993, it won the Award of Garden Merit from the Royal Horticultural Society in London because of its striking good looks and easy cultural care.

In late winter or early spring, remove the old leaves, either by raking them off the plant or cutting them close to the crown. This plant tolerates lean soils well and can also withstand occasional periods when the soil is dry.

Size: 18 to 24 inches tall and 24 inches wide

Bloom: Tall, pale blue flowers grow on tall spikes in midsummer. As they transform from blooms to seed heads, they turn a soft tan before becoming brown.

Exposure: Full sun to partial shade

Soil mix: Well drained, fertile soil with a pH of 6.8 to 7.5

Companion plants: Russian sage (*Perovskia*), *Sedum* 'Autumn Joy', and yarrow (*Achillea* spp.); *Campanula* spp., and lavender (*Lavandula*)

Pots that echo the lines of a plant, such as this tall tin can holding a blue fescue, are especially attractive.

Imperata cylindrica 'Rubra'

Japanese blood grass, cogon grass

This plant, native to Asia, could be considered a blessing and a curse. Gardeners love it because of the red tips on its chartreuse leaves and its erect growth habit. And in its native lands, it is known as a versatile medicinal plant. It was introduced to the United States by USDA agronomists who believed that it was a good forage crop. As it turned out, the red cultivar, 'Rubra' can revert to the green species, an invasive plant that forms a dense mat of growth over the soil surface so that no other plants can survive. And it creates a fire hazard in areas of the American Southeast! The only responsible place to

grow it is in a container, and the only way to care for it is to cut off flower heads if they form so that the plant cannot mature the thousands of tiny, wind-blown seeds it is capable of producing.

Size: Normally around 18 inches tall, 12 inches wide. For the healthiest plants, cut the stems back to about 4 inches above the crown in midwinter.

Bloom: Spikes of white flowers with distinct stamens and stigmas can form in spring or fall in temperate climates and year-round in tropical areas. Cut the blooms immediately to prevent seeds from forming.

Exposure: Full sun to partial shade

Soil mix: Well drained, fertile soil, with a pH of between 5.5 and 7.8; tolerates dry soils and high salinity.

Companion plants: This is not a good neighbor; use it alone in containers.

Miscanthus sinensis 'Zebrinus'

Zebra grass

Zebra grass is stunning in any situation. Its long, arching leaves are green with distinct yellow bands running horizontally across them. Light behind the plant makes the plant appear to sparkle as it catches the yellow bands on the leaves that move in the slightest breeze. In garden soils, plants can reach 7 feet tall and 10 feet wide—in containers they won't grow so large, but when placed in a large pot, they can easily form the backdrop to a container grouping. This Asian native turns a rich gold color in fall and the leaves persist until beaten down by winter snows.

Cut the stems of the plant about 3 inches above the ground in early spring to remove old leaves.

Pot up a vividly colored plant, such as this Japanese blood grass, in a container that either softly echoes its hue, as is done here, or contrasts with it.

Size: 3 to 4 feet high, 2 to 3 feet wide, depending on pot size

Bloom: In late summer, silvery or pinkish flowers form on plumes that stand at least a foot above the foliage.

Exposure: Full sun to partial shade in hot, bright areas

Soil mix: Well drained, fertile soil, with a pH of between 5.5 and 7.5

Companion plants: This is an outstanding plant to use with spring-blooming bulbs, if only because the foliage regrows so quickly in spring and therefore provides an effective screen for the browning bulb foliage. In addition, it provides a nice contrast in size, shape, and habit to hostas.

Nassella tenuissima, aka Stipa tenuissima

Feather grass, angel hair grass, silky thread grass

This native of North, Central, and South America is a delicate plant with slender leaves that gracefully blow in the breeze. The foliage is clear bright green in spring but transforms over the season to a buff color. The blooms begin as silvery green but change to gold over the season. Place these plants where sunlight can shine through them for a dazzling display. The flower stalks make a good addition to cut flower arrangements and dried winter bouquets, wreaths, and harvest arrangements. Birds love the seeds and will also pull out leaves to use for nesting material.

This plant grows so quickly that you can grow it as an annual in areas where it doesn't winter over well. Start it early and transplant 2-month-old plants to ensure that it blooms by mid- to late summer. Cut the old stalks a few inches above the ground in early spring or rake out old leaves.

Size: 12 to 18 inches tall, 8 to 10 inches wide, depending on size of pot

Bloom: Early summer. New spikes appear through late summer, and the seed heads persist through early winter.

Exposure: Full sun

Soil mix: Well drained, fertile, light, with a pH of 6 to 7.5; can tolerate dry periods.

Companion plants: Aster × frikartii, Sedum 'Fall Joy', and Dahlia 'Bednall Beauty' are excellent when paired with feather grass, and it's also excellent on its own when its luminous qualities can take center stage.

Pennisetum orientale

Fountain grass

Fountain grass is another Asian native with outstanding ornamental characteristics. The mounded foliage creates graceful arches, and the blooms, which persist from summer through fall, grow on large plumes that sway above the leaves. In the garden, it only grows about a foot tall, so it is much easier to use in a container than some of the larger grasses. For a dramatic effect, situate it so that either morning or late afternoon sunlight can filter through its airy flower plumes—the light bounces off them to create a visual shimmer.

Keep old foliage trimmed for the best appearance. Let the soil surface dry between waterings to protect against fungus problems, and check frequently to see that the crown is not covered with splashing soil. If it is, gently brush it off.

Size: 12 inches high, 10 inches wide

Bloom: In midsummer, pearly white or pink flowers form on plumes that stand at least a foot above the foliage.

Exposure: Full sun or in hot climates, partial shade

Soil mix: Well drained, moderately fertile, with a pH of 5.5 to 7

Companion plants: Sea holly (Eryngium planum 'Blue Dwarf') and Verbena bonariensis both make strong contrasts to fountain grass. It also looks elegant alone; place decorative tubs on each side of a stairway for a striking effect.

Bamboos

Fargesia murielae

Umbrella bamboo

This lovely bamboo is one of the favorite foods of pandas. In its native home in the forests of central China, it grows as a companion to a species of fir (Abies fargesii). As a consequence, it prefers to grow in partial to filtered shade. It's an ideal plant to set close to outdoor lounging areas because, when the wind blows through it, it makes a lovely rustling sound. Unlike many bamboos, it does not have invasive runners. Instead, it grows new stems from the crown and is even slow to do that. The slender stems, or culms, do branch well, however, so the plant makes an excellent screen that soon comes to resemble a lovely green fountain.

This plant is easy to grow in the correct environment. However, in the south or extremely dry climates, it will be difficult enough so that you might want to make a different choice. In fall, it will shed some leaves, although those that remain will stay green throughout the winter months. Mulch with an organic material and apply a slow-release, balanced organic fertilizer every spring.

Size: 6 to 8 feet tall, 1 foot wide, depending on size of pot

Bloom: Rarely; they bloom after 80 to 100 years and then die. Plants around the world tend to bloom at roughly the same time so that fertilization can occur. Flowering occurred in the late 1990s and as a consequence, many nurseries are now selling young plants that are either seed-grown or cloned.

Exposure: Partial shade.

Soil mix: Well drained, fertile, high organic matter, with a pH of 5.5 to 6.5

Companion plants: Grow alone in a pot. Group it with other bamboos and grasses.

Potted bamboos, such as this Fargesia murielae 'Simba', do well with understory plants like this Saxifraga fortunei 'Mount Nachi'.

Phyllostachys aureosulcata, f. spectabilis

Golden groove bamboo

One look at this lovely bamboo, and you'll have no doubt why it won the coveted Royal Horticultural Society Award of Garden Merit in 2002. Its tall, golden culms with dark green to bronze grooves make a stunning addition to a container garden or potted screen. If grown in a sunny position, young shoots are quite red, adding to its decorative value. It's native to the north of China and grows well in all temperate regions.

To keep organic matter high and retain moisture, mulch the soil surface with organic mulch. If the plant is healthy, allow dropped leaves to stay on the surface to decompose. Top dress each spring with fully finished manure potting mix and apply a slow-release, balanced organic fertilizer every spring.

Size: 6 to 9 feet high, 1 to 3 feet wide, depending on pot size

Bloom: Rarely flowers
Exposure: Full sun to partial shade
Soil mix: Fertile, moist, high organic matter, with a pH of 5 to 7
Companion plants: Grow in its own container and group it with black bamboo (*Phyllostachys nigra*) for maximum effect.

Phyllostachys nigra
Black bamboo

The glossy black culms and vivid green leaves of this bamboo make it one of the most sought-after species for ornamental gardens. New growth is protected by multiple wavy sheath blades that, taken together, resemble a decorative arrowhead. Culms are green when they first emerge, turn brown over their first and second season, and don't become black until they are 3 years old.

Fertilize every spring with a balanced organic fertilizer and mulch for moisture retention. High, drying winds damage this plant, even in summer, so place it in a somewhat protected location.
Size: 10 feet tall, 2 feet wide, depending on size of pot
Bloom: None
Exposure: Full sun to partial shade in hot climates
Soil mix: Well drained, fertile, moist, high organic matter, with a pH of 5.5 to 6.5
Companion plants: Grow alone in a pot. Group it with other bamboos as well as camellias and azaleas.

Trees

Small trees look truly spectacular in containers, but bear in mind that young specimens grow rapidly, and you will have to repot them every year into larger and larger pots. Once they are in their final containers, you will need to take them out every year or two to prune their roots and supply them with fresh soil mix. With rare exceptions, you will also want to prune their top growth during their dormant period. This is as important to their health as it is to their appearance. Remember also if you live in a cold climate, where even the soil in a sizable pot can freeze, insulate the pot before true winter sets in. Do not let the soil dry over the winter, either, and if your site is windy, erect a windbreak. More tender varieties will need to be brought into a sheltered but not overheated area.

Plant trees, such as this *Acer palmatum* 'Dissectum Atropurpureum', in pots that allow good root growth to ensure their health and vigor.

Acer palmatum
Japanese maple

The delicate leaves and multilayered habit of this tree make it a standout all through the year. There is terrific variety in this species; from dwarf cultivars that reach only 5 feet high in the wild, to those that grow to 25 or 30 feet. Some are more like bushes than trees, with multiple stems arising from the ground. Leaf colors vary tremendously.

Size: 5 to 20 feet high, 5 to 10 feet wide
Bloom: In spring, the small red or yellow flowers are inconspicuous from a distance except for the haze of color they create along the branches.
Exposure: Filtered light or moderate shade; suffers sunscald when exposed to overly bright conditions.

Soil mix: Well drained, moderately fertile, evenly moist, with a pH of 5 to 6.5

Companion plants: The layered forms of these trees make them ideal plants for any container garden with an Asian theme. Their brilliant colors also complement a group of dark-colored conifers.

Options: Favorite cultivars include 'Osakazuki', which has green leaves during the summer and brilliant red leaves in fall; the dwarf 'Red Filigree Lace', which holds its deep maroon color well into summer and turns bright red in fall; and 'Ukon', another dwarf that has yellow patches on light green leaves that turn a golden yellow in fall.

Acer palmatum var. dissectum is also excellent for container culture. Often called the Japanese Weeping Maple or the Cut-Leaf Japanese Maple, it has finely cut, almost lacy-looking leaves. It, too, varies in summer leaf color from light, silvery green through shades of red and purple. Among the best is 'Crimson Queen', which maintains a deep, dark red color throughout the summer and turns brilliant red, or crimson, in fall. Take advantage of its striking colors and leaves that shimmer in the slightest breeze and make this maple the centerpiece of your garden landscape.

Betula utilis var. *jacquemontii*
White-stemmed birch; Whitebarked Himalayan birch

This birch may have the whitest bark of all birches, so it adds drama to any winter landscape. The bark peels every year, exposing another layer of pure white bark under the first.

Size: 15 to 25 feet tall, 10 feet wide

Bloom: Beige-yellow catkins in spring

Exposure: Full sun

Soil mix: High organic matter, high fertility, with a pH of 5.1 to 6.5

Companion plants: Birch trees look particularly striking when they grow against a dark green background such as an evergreen hedge.

Options: 'Snow Queen' and 'Silver Shadow' are both popular cultivars with very white bark. These trees give year-round interest. In spring, long yellow catkins sway in the breeze and leaf buds open, so that from a distance the tree looks as if it's emerging from a yellow fog. By summer, the light green leaves dance in the slightest breeze, and in fall, they turn a brilliant yellow before dropping and allowing the peeling white bark to take center stage.

Other birches to consider for the container garden are *B. pendula*, also known as weeping birch. Look for the cultivars 'Youngii', which has a habit similar to a weeping willow, and 'Purpurea', with its almost purple leaves. This birch has a much wider temperature range than *B. utilis jacquemontii*, tolerating conditions from Zones 3 to 9 and also tolerates more variation in soil fertility and pH. It is one of the last trees to lose its leaves in fall.

Chamaecyparis pisifera
False cypress

If you want a cypress in your container garden, a dwarf *C. pisifera* is your best choice. Standard false cypress can grow to heights of 30 feet, but containerized dwarf cultivars are often only between 3 to 5 feet high and wide.

Size: 3 to 10 feet tall; 3 to 5 feet wide

Bloom: Inconspicuous bloom in spring

Exposure: Full sun to partial shade

Soil mix: Wide variation. It grows best in well-drained, moist, moderately fertile soils but tolerates a wide range of conditions with the exception of alkaline soils—those it does not tolerate.

Companion plants: This attractive tree looks lovely next to almost any other plant, so you can use it in groupings or as a focal point on its own.

Options: One of the best cultivars for containers is 'Sungold'. When grown as a dwarf in the pot in full sun, the foliage emerges as bright gold and softens to a lime green as it matures. It does not

tolerate wind or poorly drained soils, but any trouble you take over it will be amply rewarded. This plant is classified as a "threadleaf" type because the foliage is extremely thin and the branches weep, making it an ideal subject for the center of an ornamental garden.

Crataegus spp.
Hawthorns

Hawthorns are extremely common in Great Britain, where they have been used as hedging for generations. They have thorny branches and a thick, bushy habit, but you're more likely to grow them because of their lovely flowers and red berries that provide winter food for visiting songbirds.

Size: 5 to 10 feet tall, 3 to 7 feet wide

Bloom: In spring, clusters of white flowers form. Their fragrance is not universally loved, so be careful where you place the tree. It's likely that you want it some distance from a dining area.

Exposure: Full sun to partial shade

Soil mix: Well drained, moderate fertility, with a pH of 5.5 to 7

Companion plants: Do not grow this plant close to other members of the rose family because it will share pests and diseases. Instead, surround its pot with small-flowering plants that feed beneficial insects.

Options: Check with suppliers to learn the hardiness of the species you are considering, and take the cautious route, forgoing any temptation to "make your own" infusions as hawthorn is a very strong medicinal plant.

Dicksonia antarctica
Tree fern

Often known as the Tasmanian Tree Fern, this unusual plant brings a touch of the exotic to any landscape it graces. *D. antarctica* is the most hardy *Dicksonia* species, but even so, it will grow only in a limited range in Victoria, BC, as well as protected areas of the Pacific Northwest and into California. It prefers a maritime climate with high humidity levels throughout the year and few temperature extremes, either hot or cold. In the wild, it is native to areas that do not exceed 65°F during the summer. The safest low temperature is about 20°F, but if your climate gets this cold, it's wise to give it winter protection.

Size: 8 to 15 feet tall, 3 to 5 feet wide

Bloom: Inconspicuous

Exposure: Partial to full shade

Soil mix: High humus content, good fertility, with a pH of 5.6 to 6.5

Companion plants: In the wild, epiphytes take root and grow on the long rhizome that forms the trunk. You can mimic this in your container garden by growing a staghorn fern, mosses, or an orchid on the trunk of your tree fern.

Options: What we think of as the trunk of a tree fern is actually a rhizome covered with the remains of past growth. Because of this, the diameter grows quite slowly—from 1 to 3 inches a year. Fronds develop in flushes that give a layered appearance. Let fronds brown and drop off of the plant naturally because their old stems serve to protect the underlying rhizome from cold and drying. If you live where temperatures are routinely higher than about 80°F, give the plant shade to keep it cool and moist.

Ilex spp.

Hollies

The much-used term "holly bush" includes more than 300 species and many times that number of cultivars. Many hollies have glossy green leaves with four or five spines along the margins and red berries, but some have purple or dark blue berries and are spineless or have only one spine at the end of the leaf. Size is variable, too, making it easy to find a holly suitable for your container garden.

Size: Varies; 2 to 80 feet tall, 2 to 10 feet wide in the wild

Bloom: Hollies bloom in spring, generally with white or pinkish flowers. Flowers are either male or female, and most species require that female flowers be fertilized to produce berries.

Exposure: Full sun to filtered light

Soil mix: Well-drained, moist, fertile soil with a pH of 5.5 to 6.5. Fertilize every 2 weeks during the spring and summer with a half-strength solution of liquid seaweed and fish emulsion. Stop fertilizing in late summer or early fall.

Companion plants: Evergreen hollies add winter interest to a grouping of deciduous shrubs and trees or when placed in front of a group of conifers.

Options: If you don't have space for both a male and female plant and want berries, look for a dwarf 'Burford' holly, *I cornuta* 'Burfordii', because it fruits without pollination. Among the best Japanese hollies for container culture are: 'Stokes', a dwarf that won't exceed 5 feet tall; 'Rotundifolia', with rounded leaves and a top height of 6 feet in a container; 'Convexa', with rounded leaves and a height of about 3 to 4 feet; and 'Helleri', a low-growing holly that makes a good edging plant for a container garden. Excellent Chinese hollies include *I. cornuta* 'Rotunda' because of its rounded shape that

This *Dicksonia antarctica* is perfectly complemented by the mix of annual bedding plants that share its huge, decorative urn.

doesn't require pruning, height of 2 to 3 feet, and greater heat tolerance than most hollies. It lacks berries, though, so don't grow it if you're after bird food and winter color. *I. cornuta* 'Carissa' grows 3 to 4 feet tall in the soil and has one spine per leaf.

Juniperus communis
Juniper

ZONE **2–8**

Junipers are among the easiest plants to grow because they are tolerant of so many conditions. You can find junipers that grow in an upright, cone-shaped habit or those that form prostrate mats on the soil surface. Some cultivars are blue-green, some are gray-green, and some are gold. Investigate local nurseries to learn which junipers and species are commonly grown in your area.

Size: 2 to 10 feet tall, 2 to 8 feet wide

Bloom: In spring, inconspicuous yellow flowers form; male and female flowers are on separate plants. The seed cones look more like berries, and the male cones drop after shedding their pollen.

Exposure: Full sun to partial shade; tolerates wind and can be used as a windbreak for more delicate plants

Soil mix: Fine in a wide range of soils, from dry and sandy to moist and clay filled, with a pH of 4.5 to 8.5. Fertilize each spring with a well-balanced material such as fully finished manure potting mix.

Companion plants: Use junipers as a backdrop for more vividly colored plants, or let their lovely plant habits serve as focal points in your garden.

Options: Of the many cultivars available, look especially for 'Depressa' if you want a low-growing juniper. This cultivar has blue-green needles and is tolerant of difficult growing conditions. Even in the best of situations, the plant rarely grows taller than 4 feet; in a container, it usually tops out below 3 feet tall, although it can be maintained at 2 feet quite easily. 'Depressa Aurea' is a gold-colored cultivar. In winter, rather than the brown of 'Depressa', its leaves turn bronze.

Two other *J. communis* cultivars that are particularly notable are 'Pencil Point', with silver-blue needles and a height of 6 feet, and 'Gold Cone', a golden version. *J. scopulorum* 'Skyrocket' is another excellent choice if you want a blue-green, cone-shaped plant. If a ground-hugging juniper would suit your landscape, look at slow growing *J. horizontalis* 'Wiltonii', sold as blue rug juniper. *J. procumbens* 'Nana' is widely loved for its ability to thrive in almost any situation in Zones 4 to 9. If it has space, the plant will spread out, but if it doesn't, it will form a mound.

Malus floribunda
Japanese crabapple

ZONE **4–8**

This plant deserves its botanical name of "floribunda" because the flowers are indeed abundant. In spring, this tree can't help but be a focal point. Its decorative value persists through the summer, too, as the yellow crab apples that festoon the branches develop a soft pink blush. Birds love these fruits, so they add bright spots of color in fall as they come to dine.

Size: 10 to 15 feet tall; 10 to 15 feet wide

Bloom: Early spring. Buds are red but the blooms are pale pink when they first open. They fade to white as they mature. Throughout, they perfume the garden with a sweet, delicate fragrance.

Malus 'Adirondack' is an ideal crabapple for container-growing because it is naturally small, unusually disease-resistant, blooms lavishly, and has bright red fruits that persist into December.

Exposure: Full sun

Soil mix: Well drained, fertile, moist, with a pH of 5.5 to 6.5

Companion plants: Apple trees require cross-pollination to form fruit. In your container garden, you will need a compatible tree if you want fruit. Ask the nursery to select it; they will know which trees bloom at the same time your *M. floribunda* is in bloom.

Options: If you are looking for a plant that can stand up to conditions in Zones 8 and 9, *M. angustifolia* is a good choice. *M. sylvestris* grows best in cooler conditions, so it's a good choice if you live in a northern area. *M. fusca* is sometimes known as Oregon crabapple and is well adapted to conditions in the Pacific Northwest. This wealth of species means you will find crabapples to suit your conditions.

Olea europaea
Olive

ZONE **8–10**

Olive trees add a touch of the exotic to your container landscape. The long leaves are an unusual tone of gray-green, and as the tree ages, the trunk becomes twisted and gnarled.

Size: Varies; Container cultivars: 4 to 15 feet tall, 4 to 12 feet wide

Bloom: Small, cream-colored flowers grow in drooping clusters from the leaf axils on the previous year's growth. Many cultivars are self-infertile and require a pollinator tree to produce fruit.

Exposure: Full sun

Soil mix: Extremely well drained soil, with moderate to low fertility, and a pH of 7 to 8. These plants thrive on limestone and require high calcium levels. In the wild, trees grow on low-fertility land, but in a container, you'll need to supply a balanced fertilizer every 2 to 3 weeks when the tree

A potted olive tree (*Olea europaea*) easily becomes the focal point in any garden.

you are most likely to prize it for its environment flexibility and low maintenance requirements.

Size: 4 to 10 feet tall, 3 to 6 feet wide

Bloom: Both male and female flowers are on the same plant. The yellow blooms in early spring are inconspicuous; the cones are about an inch or two long and grayish brown in color.

Exposure: Full sun to partial shade

Soil mix: Well drained, moist, fertile, with a pH of 5.5 to 7. Provide a well-balanced fertilizer every 3 or 4 weeks during the growing season.

Companion plants: Brightly colored foliage or blooms show up nicely against the deep green of this pine.

Options: Excellent cultivars for containers include 'Compacta', which is about 3 feet tall and rounded; 'Gnom', which grows to 12 feet tall and is bushy; and 'Pumilio', a 2-feet-tall prostrate form that can easily spread for 10 feet along the soil surface. It makes a striking statement when planted in a long narrow container that defines the perimeter of an area. 'Teeny' is even smaller and rounder than 'Compacta', and 'Mops' is about the same size. 'Slowmound' lives up to its name, slowly growing into a dense mound about 3 feet tall.

is in active growth and every couple of months during the winter period.

Companion plants: Many people grow roses in shades of pink and yellow near olives because the colors of the rose blooms and the olive leaves bring out the best in each. Use companions in separate pots; few plants like to be as dry as olives do.

Options: 'Arbequina' is one of the best olives for container culture. This plant is self-pollinating and produces a nice crop of small fruit that can be pressed for oil—if you are that ambitious. It also has a lovely weeping habit that is a standout in any garden. More cold tolerant than most, it requires winter temperatures in the high 20s to thrive, so it's best to leave it outside until nights are about 28°F.

'Little Ollie' is a patented dwarf cultivar that grows no higher than 6 feet. Rather than a single trunk, it grows multiple stems, so it looks more like an olive bush than an olive tree. It does not fruit, so it is a good plant for those who are allergic to the pollen.

Pinus mugo
Pine

This pine is popular for its many naturally rounded, bushlike cultivars. Branches hold their needles for 4 or 5 years, giving it a density that makes it an excellent screening plant. The needles are somewhat sharp, so the plants are often used as barricades under windows. In a container,

Salix caprea
Goat willow

This European cousin to the American pussy willow (*Salix discolor*) has a showier catkins and is a common container plant, thanks to its oval gray-green leaves, yellow-brown wood, and large yellow or gray-green catkins in spring. Besides being a good ornamental and a valuable addition to cut flower arrangements, this plant is bee-friendly. The catkins produce a great deal of nectar and pollen and give the bees an abundant early food source.

Size: 6 to 15 feet tall, 3 to 6 feet wide
Bloom: In early spring, both male and female plants bloom. The fat male catkins are yellowish in color, and the more slender female catkins, which are less showy, are gray-green. The female seed capsules and tiny seeds with fine, silver hairs add late-summer interest.
Exposure: Full sun to light shade
Soil mix: Moisture retentive, fertile soil, with a pH of between 6 and 7.5. Fertilize every month during the growing season with a well-balanced nutrient source such as manure potting mix or a combination of liquid seaweed and fish emulsion.
Companion plants: Whites and soft pastel colors make the gray-green leaves stand out.
Options: Goat willow is listed as an invasive species in some regions of the mid-Atlantic, so be careful about keeping it contained. If you want a weeping form, look for 'Kilmarnock', a male cloned plant, or 'Weeping Sally', a female cloned plant. They can be grafted to the top of an erect willow stem to produce a small, single-stemmed tree with pendant branches at the top. If either of these plants grows from its own roots, it will creep over the soil surface.

Herbs
Small trees look truly spectacular in containers, but bear in mind that young herbs are among the most gratifying plants for the container gardener. They add beauty and fragrance anywhere you place them and are also indispensable in the kitchen. Like homegrown tomatoes, homegrown herbs are so good that you'll never go back to store-bought once you've grown them. They have the added advantage of being very easy to grow. You might have to protect a few species from frost, but other than that, herbs tolerate a wide variety of conditions and require only minimal care.

Most herbs will die back in extreme cold but survive if the roots don't freeze. Insulate pots or take dormant plants into a sheltered spot that's just warm enough to keep the soil and roots from freezing, preferably in cool, bright conditions.

Allium schoenoprasum;
A. tuberosum
Chives, garlic chives

Chives are one of the true gifts of the container garden. It's such a pleasure to snip fresh chives onto a finished dish or separate the florets and sprinkle them over a salad or entrée that needs a dash of spice and, perhaps a lovely white or purple garnish. No matter what kind of chives you grow, you'll never tire of this plant.

Garlic chives have a somewhat different flavor than common chives. They have thick, flat leaves as opposed to the hollow, circular leaves of common chives, and their flowers differ, too. They form in umbel-shaped clusters at the top of stiff, long stalks and are white rather than purple. As well as being a tasty addition to recipes that could use a little zip, they are so pretty that they can easily be used as fillers in a cut flower arrangement.

Size: 12 to 18 inches tall, 4 to 8 inches wide
Bloom: Common chives have purple blooms; garlic chives have white flowers.
Exposure: Full sun in cool regions, filtered light in Zones 8 to 11
Soil mix: Well drained, fertile, moist, with a pH of 5.8 to 6.8
Companion plants: Chives make an attractive understory plant in large tubs containing shrubs or trees. When they are in bloom, beneficial insects use their nectars as a food source, so they perform double duty in the container garden.
Options: After common chives flower in spring, cut the plants back to an inch or two above the soil surface and let them regrow. Garlic chives flower in fall; cut them back as well (as they be rampant reseeders). In mild climates, they will regrow before winter sets in, and in cold ones, this prepares them for the frosty weather coming up.

LEFT: *Pinus mugo* 'Winter Gold' gives year-round interest in a pot. Here, it's complemented by an understory planting of *Heuchera* 'Obsidian'.

LEFT: An elegant pot as shown here, can make ordinary garden chives look as decorative as an ornamental lily.

Anethum graveolens
Dill

Dill is a fast-growing plant that can serve double duty in the container garden. Not only do a few plants provide you with all the dill leaves and seeds you'll need for the season, the small flowers are favorites of the tiny wasps and other beneficial insects that prey on aphids and other soft-bodied garden pests.

Size: Varies from 1 to 2½ feet tall, 6 to 8 inches wide

Bloom: This member of the *Umbelliferae* family blooms in umbrella-shaped flower clusters on tall stalks held above the foliage. Once the plant blooms, growth will slow, so it's best to grow some plants for foliage, snipping off flower stalks before they elongate and saving some for seeds.

Exposure: Full sun

Soil mix: Well drained, moderately fertile with a pH of 5.8 to 6.8. Don't fertilize with a high nitrogen material.

Companion plants: Dill is pretty enough to serve as a lacy filler in ornamental

containers, but you'll need to keep it from flowering if you want it to last through the season. When it does flower, it feeds many beneficial insects.

Options: Dill can grow entirely too tall for its width. To keep it from falling over, tie it to stakes that you set inside the pot. If this seems like too much trouble, grow one of the dwarf cultivars that are too short to fall over.

Coriandrum sativum
Cilantro/coriander

When you eat the leaves of this plant, you're eating cilantro, but if you eat the seeds, you're eating coriander. And, if you're enjoying a recipe from South America or the Far East, you could be eating the roots, because they're also considered a delicacy. Cilantro grows very quickly—you can generally start harvesting individual stems about 40 days after planting it. It won't reach full size until it is 2 months old, but you'll increase the eventual harvest if you cut off the oldest stems every few days. Once you have this herb at hand, you'll probably find yourself adding it to everything from beans and rice to omelets to Asian dishes.

Size: 1½ feet to 2½ feet tall, 6 inches wide

Bloom: White flowers form in umbels at the top of tall stalks.

Exposure: Full sun in northern areas; partial or filtered shade in hot, dry climates, particularly in the afternoon

Soil mix: Well drained, moderately fertile with a pH of 5.8 to 6.8

Companion plants: Cilantro is a wonderful plant to grow as a habitat for beneficial insects—they all love it. It grows so quickly that you can tuck it on the edges of various pots filled with ornamentals and harvest it just as they are beginning to need the space.

Who would guess that this bronze fennel, surrounded by annual baby's breath in its pot, was destined for the kitchen?

Foeniculum vulgare
Fennel

Fennel is a huge plant when it grows in the wild. Fortunately, growing in a pot dwarfs it, and it becomes a perfectly manageable plant in these conditions. Like dill, it's grown for both its seeds and leaves, although many people also eat its stems, which are more tender than you might expect. Decide what you want—stems, leaves, or seeds—before the season because your choice may affect its location and, in the north, even the planting time.

Size: 2 feet tall, 1 foot wide

Bloom: Another *Umbelliferae*, this plant produces numerous small umbrella-shaped flower clusters at the top of its flower stems. Bloom begins in early summer.

Exposure: Full sun in the north; tolerates filtered light in hot, dry climates

Soil mix: Well drained, moderately fertile, with a pH of 6.6 to 7

Companion plants: Like all umbellifers, this plant feeds beneficials. It also imparts a lacy look to mixed groups of ornamentals and can be grown for that reason alone.

Options: Bronze-colored cultivars taste just as good as the green ones do but have the added advantage of making a dramatic statement in a vase or mixed ornamental tub. Try them for a spot of unusual color, and add some long stems to cut flower arrangements. Use the seeds in tomato sauces for an authentic Italian flavor. They also season meats, especially sausage. Leaves resemble anise because they taste more like licorice than any other flavor.

Laurus nobilis
Bay laurel

Bay laurel trees make an excellent focal point or background plant in a container garden because of their dark green, glossy foliage and elegant habit. A well-pruned row of bay laurels in formal-looking pots

A potted bay tree can be pruned and trained as a decorative standard for your container garden or left to grow more naturally.

When drying bay leaves, place them on elevated screens. Let them curl because when you use them in cooking, you will be breaking them into small pieces anyway. Bay leaves can be sharp and, even when broken into small pieces, can irritate tender tissues. Prevent problems by using them whole and removing them before serving or by placing broken pieces in a tea ball or piece of cheesecloth tied into a bouquet garni.

Lavandula spp.

Lavenders

Lavender adds so much to your container garden that you're going to want to include it, even if space is limited. Its fleshy gray-green or silver-green leaves and upright plant habit remain beautiful throughout the year, with the long-lasting spikes of pink white, blue-purple, or lavender flowers.

Lavender is a fairly well known ingredient in English breakfast tea, but few people know that you can use the flowers in baked goods and fruit preserves. The leaves make a strong-tasting tea that has calming properties—mix them with chamomile to make them palatable for children. You can count on a good 5 years' pot life if you take reasonable care.

Size: Varies from 1 to 3 feet tall, 1 to 1½ feet wide

Bloom: Spikes of tiny fragrant flowers can grow to a foot long in some cultivars. In others, they are 8 to 10 inches tall. Depending on cultivar, they range in color from white to lavender, to a blue-purple hue, to various shades of pink.

Exposure: Full sun; tolerates partial shade in hot, dry climates.

Soil mix: Extremely well drained and moderately fertile with a pH about 6.8 to 7. Top-dress with manure compost or apply a well-balanced fertilizer every spring.

can make an excellent border to a garden, too. Bay laurel does not tolerate freezing temperatures well and is stressed by cold winds, even when temperatures are above freezing. Place this plant in a sheltered spot if you keep it outside during the winter months in Zones 8 and 9. You can begin harvesting leaves in the second year of growth, but remember to take only a few until the tree is about 1½ to 2 feet tall.

Size: 3 to 10 feet tall, 3 to 6 feet wide

Bloom: Small yellow flowers form in spring. Plants have male or female flowers and berries form on plants bearing female flowers.

Exposure: Filtered light or full sun, followed by partial afternoon shade

Soil mix: Well drained, rich, moist, with a pH of 4.5 to 8, but it thrives with a pH close to 6.2

Companion plants: Bay laurel is so striking that it looks good growing next to just about every flowering perennial.

Options: This plant responds beautifully to pruning, which is why so many topiaries in warm climates are bay laurel trees. Prune the tree each late winter or early spring to make certain that the top growth never becomes too great a burden for the root system.

Companion plants: Lavender is an excellent subject in a mixed herbal planting. Its small flowers also feed many beneficial insects, so when it's in bloom, move the pot close to plants where aphids are feeding.

Options: The finest fragrance comes from cultivars of English lavender, *L. angustifolia*. When you buy plants, be certain to check the species; shy away from *L. × intermedia* because the fragrance is truly inferior.

To save lavender for sachets and potpourris, cut both leaf and flower stems just before the flowers open. Bring them inside and dry them by laying them flat on screens that are elevated on bricks. You can also hang them, but flower buds sometimes drop when plants are hung, particularly if you leave them until they are bone dry. To store them, pack the stems in ziplock bags with a packet or two of silica gel to keep them from rehydrating.

Ocimum basilicum
Basil

It's a real treat to have a pot or two of various cultivars of basil. Bought fresh, this herb can be expensive, but you can grow enough in a small window box to flavor all your sauces for the year and make pesto to your heart's content.

Size: Varies from 6 inches to 2 feet tall, 6 inches to 1 foot wide

Bloom: Blooms feed beneficial insects, but once you let the plant bloom, growth slows and the plant may even die. Wise gardeners often grow some basil for the insects and some for themselves.

Exposure: Full sun

Soil mix: Well drained, fertile with high humus levels and a pH of 6 to 7.5. Do not apply high-nitrogen fertilizers because they make the plant more susceptible to some diseases and disorders. Maintain constant moisture for best growth.

Companion plants: Basil is an excellent companion to tomatoes and peppers. As an ornamental, purple or mottled cultivars add a spot of color to a grouping.

Potted parsley is a truly gratifying plant to grow because it looks good enough to set in front of an ornamental garden and is also a mainstay of most herb gardens.

Options: Basil is easy to grow as long as you provide lots of water and fertilize with a balanced substance such as fully mature manure potting mix or potting mix tea. Encourage a bushy habit by pinching off stem tips as the plant grows. Branches at the internodes form easily and will soon give your plant a lovely form. Pinch off flower stalks as soon as you notice them, too; do not let them get so large that the buds are distinct. Many people grow frilly leaved purple or light green cultivars for additions to their cut flower vases. If you are growing these types, add a few sprigs to arrangements for added color and fragrance.

Basil is said to repel flies. Try keeping a pot on the patio to see if your flies dislike the odor. When flies become bothersome, pinch off a leaf or two and crush it.

Petroselinum crispum
Parsley

Parsley is a staple on the weekly shopping list. However, it's an added item on the grocery bill, so many people pass it by. The solution is to grow it yourself. A couple of well-tended plants will give you at least a full season's worth of leaves and, if you live in a warm region, a full year or more.

Parsley lovers often grow both a curly cultivar and an Italian flat-leaf cultivar. Flat-leaf parsley has a stronger, more distinct flavor that stands up to cooking better than the curly parsley does. But the curly type is a lovely edible garnish, so grow it to decorate your plates restaurant-style.

Size: 8 to 18 inches tall, 8 to 12 inches wide

Bloom: Plants will try to go into bloom in midspring of their second year. Pinch out the flower stalks to extend the harvest until your newly planted parsley is ready to pick.

Exposure: Full sun in the north; partial shade or filtered sun in hot, dry areas

Soil mix: Well drained, fertile, high humus, with a pH of 5.8 to 6.8. Fertilize every 10 to 14 days with a well-balanced fertilizer such as diluted fish emulsion or potting mix tea.

Companion plants: Parsley is an excellent edging plant for a large container, especially if you keep outer leaves picked so the plant habit remains attractive. When it blooms, its flowers feed many beneficial insects.

Rosmarinus officinalis
Rosemary

Rosemary has the capacity to grow into a wonderful shrub. Its natural habit is lovely in an informal setting, and it takes so well to pruning that it's equally effective in a more formal design. Rosemary does not tolerate freezing temperatures, so it must come inside for the winter. But that shouldn't stop you from letting it grow into a shrub; put its pot on a wheeled platform to move it around as the weather decrees.

Size: 2 to 6 feet tall, 1 to 3 feet wide

Bloom: Clusters of tiny pink or purple flowers form in late winter to early spring.

Exposure: Full sun

Soil mix: Extremely well drained, moderately fertile, with a pH of 6.5 to 7.5. Side-dress with fully finished potting soil each spring.

Companion plants: Rosemary shrubs are so commanding that they really need a pot to themselves. However, if you grow one of the prostrate forms, you can use it to add dimension to a mixed group of conifers. When the plants are in bloom, beneficial insects flock to it.

Options: Rosemary plants are killed by excess watering more frequently than they are killed by neglect. Make certain that their potting soil drains freely, and water them only when the top inch of the soil surface has dried.

For a recipe, snip off the tip of a branch or two. However, if you want to harvest enough to dry for sachets or potpourris, search along the stem to find the beginning of the current season's new green growth. When you find it, move your fingers about two or three nodes up into it and make your cut there. If you cut into the woody part, the nodes may not send out any new branches, so pay attention when you cut.

Use rosemary as an aromatic herb in the bath. Let the water run over dried leaves or a green sprig as the tub is filling. The clean, fresh fragrance is invigorating rather than calming. If you have dark hair, you can also use a strong infusion of rosemary leaves as the last rinse after shampooing to give your hair a lovely fragrance and brighten its natural highlights.

Salvia officinalis
Sage

Sage, with its gray-green leaves and busy habit, can be a beautiful addition to an ornamental garden or a focal point in a grouping of herbs. The plant has a tendency to get lanky if left to its own devices, but just a little pruning encourages a lovely rounded form. For a treat, grow a pot of *Salvia apiana* beside a pot of common culinary sage; the contrast in the color of the leaves makes each stand out.

Sage is versatile. You can cut whole branches to use as the foundation of an herbal wreath, or dry the leaves to use in sachets and soothing footbaths. Dried leaves also season poultry stuffings and gravies.
Size: Varies from 12 to 30 inches tall, 10 to 24 inches wide

Bloom: Whorls of pink, purple, blue, or white flowers sometimes form on tall stalks in late spring or early summer after the plant is a year old. They are edible and make a pretty addition to a salad mix; don't use more than a sprinkling because their flavor is strong.
Exposure: Full sun
Soil mix: Well drained, moderate fertility, with a pH of 5.8 to 6.5. Every spring, apply a layer of fully finished manure compost to the pot if you don't transplant into a new soil mix.
Companion plants: Blooming sage feeds beneficial insects, so you can move its pot close to plants that are hosting aphids or other soft-bodied pests.

Thymus spp.
Thymes

There are a huge number of thyme cultivars—light pink, rosy red, pure white, and all shades of lavender and purple flowers, or delicate gray, dark green, silver, golden, yellow-bordered, smooth or fuzzy leaves. Whatever sorts you choose, you can include new cultivars every year. Just remember that while thyme plants remain vigorous for many years in the wild, they often lose their vigor in a container.
Size: 2 to 12 inches tall, 8 to 24 inches wide
Bloom: In midsummer, hundreds of tiny flowers coat the stem tips.
Exposure: Full sun in Zones 5 to 7 but prefers filtered light in Zones 8 and 9, particularly in midseason
Soil mix: Extremely well drained, moderate fertility, with a pH of 6.5 to 8.5
Companion plants: Thyme is an excellent companion to itself. Plant a large shallow container with a variety of creeping thymes, each with differently colored foliage, for a focal point in the container garden. When

growing upright thymes, move flowering pots close to any plants with insect problems because beneficial insects love the sweet, tiny blooms.
Options: Thyme cultivars are divided into two categories: bush plants and creeping plants. The best known creeping thymes may be the various cultivars called Mother of Thyme (*T. serpyllum*). There isn't only one kind of Mother of Thyme—look for the cultivars 'Albus', 'Coccineus', and 'Roseus' for a bed with white, red, and rose-colored blooms. If you want particular flowers or leaves for their ornamental value or kitchen cultivars, buy plants. Most cooks prefer cultivars of English thyme (*Thymus vulgaris*) and lemon thyme (*Thymus x citriodorus*). Cooked lemon thyme rarely holds its flavor, but fresh adds a clean, lemony taste. Sprinkle it over fish or salad. Before you buy a plant for the kitchen, take a nibble. Even within the same cultivar, flavors vary. Thyme has other household uses, including being useful as an insect repellent. Rather than using moth balls for woolens, tuck sprigs of thyme between the layers of your clothing. It's also a soothing addition to a bath. Oil of thyme is an antiseptic, although it takes a lot of thyme to get much oil.

Thyme thrives in pots of all sizes and shapes. Grow it in a huge pot if you want enough to dry for winter use, or gifts for nongardening friends.

Vegetables

If you have gourmet tastes when it comes to vegetables, you'll love growing your own in containers. All it takes is a little time and attention to produce vegetables that you either can't get outside of a large city market or that cost so much you wouldn't think of buying them. This is one area where container gardening truly shines, and once you begin, don't be surprised to find yourself sneaking an elegant oriental eggplant into a tub of ornamentals or transforming all your window boxes into gardens of multicolored salad greens.

Soil quality matters when it comes to vegetables. The better the soil, the better the vegetable. Choose a manure compost-based potting soil. It should smell good—more like rich topsoil than an ordinary potting soil. Almost all vegetables like moderate to high fertility, too, and the best fertilizers for them are those used by organic growers: specially formulated dry fertilizers with "OMRI approved" on the label, fish emulsion, liquid seaweed, and other liquids, all of which should have "OMRI" on the label.

Some vegetables will overwinter in containers if the soil doesn't thoroughly freeze. Cover them if a light frost threatens.

ORGANIC PEST CONTROL

You may see some pests on your vegetables. Try to avoid problems by mixing your pots to confuse flying pests looking for a big plot of their favorite food and by growing small-flowered plants that feed beneficial insects that prey on many of the pest species. These good companions include herbs in the parsley family, such as dill and cilantro, and flowers such as various salvias, sweet alyssum, and scabiosa.

PESTICIDES: A WORD OF WARNING

If you have to use a pesticide, look for one with the "OMRI" label and follow the directions to the letter. Remember that, aside from biological controls, if something can hurt an insect, it can also hurt you; wear protective clothing, and take care to store materials where pets and children cannot reach them.

Allium cepa, A. fistulosum
Scallions

Scallions are easy to sneak into pots holding other plants because they take so little space. Their upright blue-green leaves give nice form to a planting, and their strong odor acts as a deterrent to many flying insects, so they are a useful addition to a planting.

Size: Varies; generally about 8 to 12 inches high, ½ inch wide
Bloom: None
Exposure: Full sun to filtered light
Soil mix: Well drained, fertile, high humus, with a pH of 6 to 7
Companion plants: Annuals; vegetables except for legumes
Options: Plant green onion seeds in early spring for green onions about 2 months later. For continuous crops, keep planting a few seeds every week or two until late summer. You can cover the last of the green onions to protect them against the first frosts, and keep harvesting them until winter has truly set in.

Beta vulgaris var. cicla
Swiss chard

Swiss chard is one of the prettiest greens you can grow. Many cultivars have white ribs and wrinkled green leaves, but some modern types have bright orange, gold, purple, red, and magenta ribs. This is a truly versatile green, too. Start chard from seed and you can pick leaves when they are only a few inches long for a colorful addition to the salad bowl, or let the plants grow to full size and cook them as you do spinach.
Size: Varies from 12 to 24 inches tall, 10 to 18 inches wide

Indeterminate cherry tomatoes, such as this 'Tasty Tom' thrive in containers and yield well, as long as you remember to keep them supported as they grow and remove extra suckers.

'Bright Lights' Swiss chard adds a decorative note to the container garden as well as a tasty, nutritious one to the dinner table.

Bloom: None

Exposure: Full sun

Soil mix: Well drained, fertile, high humus content, with a pH of 6 to 6.8

Companion plants: A mixed grouping of Swiss chard with almost any flowering plant is lovely. Try growing red and yellow nasturtiums with it for a spot of "hot color" in the container garden.

Options: Steam the Swiss chard leaves for the best flavor. You'll get good results if you cut out the ribs and steam them for several minutes before adding the leaves. To taste, dress the leaves with vinegar, lemon juice, or butter.

Swiss chard is also an indicator of air pollution. Its wrinkled leaves will become even more wrinkled and look distorted when air quality is poor. In very bad conditions, the ribs also become somewhat distorted and twisted. If your plants exhibit these symptoms, confine your container

vegetables to the fruiting crops because they take in fewer airborne pollutants.

Capsicum annuum
Pepper

Green peppers, red peppers, orange peppers, purple peppers, sweet peppers, stuffing peppers, hot peppers, pickling peppers, and ornamental peppers—you'll never run out of peppers to try! Despite the huge variety of pepper seeds that are available these days, you see few exotic peppers at the store. This, as well as the price of red and yellow peppers, is a good reason to set aside a few pots for peppers.

Size: Varies from 12 to 30 inches tall, 12 to 24 inches wide

Bloom: Small white flowers with prominent yellow centers form in early to midsummer.

Exposure: Full sun in all but the very brightest, hottest areas. If fruit is not shielded from afternoon light by the leaves, it may develop sunscald—a disorder that opens the way to various fungi that promote rotting. Use thin material to shade the plant, as discussed on page 177.

Soil mix: Well drained, moderately fertile, humus-rich, with a pH of 5.5 to 6.8. Fertilize with a tomato fertilizer once bloom begins and every other week after that. Crushed, dried eggshells make excellent mulch for these calcium lovers.

Overwintering: Peppers overwinter well in a brightly lit and moderately warm environment. Cut back on water, provide good air circulation, and let the plants rest during winter. Once all danger of frost has passed, repot them in new soil and place them outside again. They'll bloom quickly and give you an extra early crop.

Companion plants: Unfortunately, peppers draw many pests, including aphids, spider mites, whiteflies, striped and spotted cucumber beetles, and tarnished plant bugs. Diseases include verticillium wilt, fusarium wilt, early blight, late blight, and various viruses. To protect the plants, surround them with edible purslane or a tiny basil such as 'Spicy Globe'. You can also place pots of nasturtiums that you grow for the edible flowers adjacent to the pepper pots; often they will act as a trap crop because they are more attractive to the aphids that fly by.

Options: Peppers in pots sometimes become so heavy with fruit that their stems break from the stress. Prevent this by staking any plants that seem in danger, tying their stems to supports outside the pot. For maximum pepper yields, pick the first couple of peppers that form on each plant when they are about three-quarters of full size. This stimulates the plant to create more flowers.

Colored peppers are simply ripe peppers. If you leave them on the plant until they are completely ripe, they are

susceptible to sunscald and various fungi. Use the farmer's trick of picking them when they are half colored. Bring them inside and set them in an area that's well lit but not sunny and hot. They will continue to ripen and within a few days to a week, you'll have beautiful, blemish-free red or yellow or purple or chocolate-colored peppers.

Cucumis sativus

Cucumber

Fresh cucumbers are so much better than those you'll find at the store that they may become one of your favorite container plants. You can grow standard slicing cucumbers or, if you're feeling more adventurous, one of the more exotic types such as round, yellow, lemon cucumbers; a long striped cultivar; or a new seedless cultivar that's suitable for growing outside.

Size: Varies; bush: 1½ feet tall, 3 feet wide; vines: 1 foot tall, 6 to 8 feet long

Bloom: Yellow flowers form in early summer. Standard slicing cucumbers have both male and female flowers and are insect pollinated, but many of the newest cultivars are parthenocarpic—that is, they

produce seedless fruit without pollination. In some cases, if a flower on such a plant is pollinated, the resulting fruit is misshapen and tastes bitter. When growing these cultivars, keep them inside a greenhouse or tightly enclosed by insect-grade row-cover material. If you can't go to that trouble, read the plant description carefully, and avoid those types that say they should be grown under cover.

Exposure: Full sun

Soil mix: Well drained, fertile, high nitrogen content, with a pH from 6 to 6.8

Companion plants: Radishes are good companions because they mature quickly enough that they'll be out of the pot before the cucumbers need the space, and they also repel some of the worst cucumber pests. Set pots of small-flowered plants such as French marigolds around the plants to feed beneficial insects.

Options: Cucumber vines need trellising when you grow them in a container. If you are using a half barrel, you can set up a V-shaped frame in the pot and train the vines to grow up it. Another practical system is to place the container close to a trellis or wall from which you can hang strong strings. Tie the plants in place so their tendrils attach to the supports where you want them to be. Trellised cucumbers have three major advantages over those you let sprawl: The fruits grow straight because they hang down, the fruits are less likely to rot because they are not in contact with the soil, and it's much easier to pick the fruits because they are so readily visible.

Cucurbita pepo

Summer squash

Summer squash is fantastically productive—even in a pot. But use a big container; half-barrels are about the right size for a hill of top-quality squash. Leave space around

the pot, too, because the leaves will extend beyond it as the plants mature.

Size: 3 feet tall, 5 to 7 feet wide

Bloom: Bright yellow flowers begin forming only a month or so after planting and develop rapidly into squash. Flowers are either male or female; flying insects carry pollen from the male flowers to the female flowers. If your squash is on a screened porch where no insects fly, use a small paintbrush to pollinate the female flowers every morning—ideally, after the sun has risen and the air is warm. The flowers are edible, too. If you don't need all the male flowers that form, find a good recipe for them and treat yourself to exotic appetizer.

Exposure: Full sun

Soil mix: Extremely well drained, very fertile, and moisture retentive. Maintain a pH of 6 to 6.8. Begin with a mix rich in manure compost, and fertilize every week after the first month with liquid seaweed or compost tea.

Companion plants: Radish, sweet alyssum, cilantro, and dill, planted in nearby containers or on the perimeter of the squash container. Let the cilantro and dill bloom so that beneficial insects can feed on them.

Options: Pick the squash when they are still small for the very best flavor. This also helps to keep the plants productive; once seeds mature in a squash, the plant stops flowering at the same rate.

Lactuca sativa

Lettuce

Lettuce is such a good container crop that once you discover it, you'll never go back to store-bought again. Check a good seed catalog for cultivars: you'll find a huge variety of lettuces that are too delicate or too fancy to ever end up at the grocery store or even at most farmers' markets. You could spend a mint trying them all, so

Salad crops and small vegetables make great container plants that you'll find yourself picking from almost daily, so plant them in succession.

restrict yourself to a few types, such as a butterhead, a bibb, a romaine, a red leaf, and a green leaf, that are bred for particular seasons—spring, midsummer, and fall.

Size: Varies with cultivar; ranges from 4 to 14 inches tall, and 6 to 14 inches wide

Bloom: Do not let lettuce bloom unless you are saving seed from an open-pollinated variety.

Exposure: Full sun in spring; filtered light or partial shade in summer; full sun in fall

Soil mix: Fertile, humus rich, high nitrogen, with a pH of 5.8 to 6.8

Companion plants: Plant blooming sweet alyssum in pots next to spring lettuce containers for a food source for beneficial insects, and keep some small-flowered plants in bloom at all times during the season. Many lettuces are decorative and can be used as edging plants on tubs of ornamentals and also make good companions to violas and other edible flowers in window boxes.

Options: Lettuce can be eaten at full size or as "baby greens." In hot weather, they often get bitter if allowed to mature, so this is the time to rely on salad mixes (see page 178). You can prolong harvest of mature heads by giving the plants shade. Make a wire frame over the container, and suspend burlap or commercial shade cloth over it. Plants grown under shade will be much sweeter and more succulent than those grown in the open. Remove the frame and shade when the weather begins to cool down.

Raphanus sativus
Radish

What says spring more clearly than a radish? You can plant them in very early spring, and because they are in a container, cover them well or bring them inside on chilly nights. If you have children, plant some of the novelty cultivars that produce red, white, and purple radishes in only a month. For the gourmet in the family, plant a long French cultivar, too.

Size: 6 to 10 inches tall, 2 to 4 inches wide

Bloom: Don't let radishes bloom unless you're saving seeds or growing a specialty rat tail cultivar for its spicy edible pods.

Exposure: Full sun

Soil mix: Well drained, fertile soil, with a pH of 5.5 to 6.8

Companion plants: Radishes are excellent companion plants for squashes because the squash vine borer does not like their odor and steers clear of plants surrounded by lots of radishes. Because of their small size and very fast maturity, radishes can be planted in the "empty" spots in containers holding perennials that are growing into the space.

Options: In hot, dry weather, radishes become even spicier than usual and also develop bitter undertones. In containers, radishes are unlikely to develop pest and disease problems because the soil mix will be fresh and clean. If the leaves develop fungal problems, plant your next crop with wider spacing to allow for more air circulation. The long daikon radish requires a very deep pot and high fertility if it is to do well in a container.

Solanum lycopersicum
Tomato

Home-grown tomatoes are a luxury. You can choose the cultivars you like best, whether for their wonderful flavor, novelty looks, or early production. Spend some time researching tomatoes, and make it a habit to

grow at least one favorite every year and one you've never before tried. It could be that your favorite tomato will change as you try new cultivars.

Size: Varies; bush: 2½ to 3 feet tall, 2 to 2½ feet wide; indeterminate: 4 to 8 feet tall, 1½ to 2 feet wide

Bloom: Yellow flowers form in early summer. They are often self-pollinating, but you can help them along by wiggling the flower clusters every morning after the sun has risen and the air is warm.

Exposure: Full sun except in warm areas in Zones 8, 9, and 10 where they need afternoon shade from mid to late summer.

Soil mix: Well drained, moderately fertile, high humus content, with a pH of 5.5 to 6.8. Supplement fertility with compost tea or fish emulsion and liquid seaweed every week to 10 days after the blooms begin to open.

Companion plants: Grow basil at the perimeter of the container and small-flowered plants nearby.

Options: There are pros and cons to growing both determinate, or bush, cultivars and indeterminate, or staking, tomatoes. Bush tomatoes are likely to hang over the edges of whatever container you give them. This makes them prone to being bumped into and injured, so you'll probably end up tying them up anyway. Indeterminate tomatoes are much easier to trellis if you plan on it from the beginning. Hang a string from the ceiling of your porch or an outside support, and tie the plant to it as it grows. Remember to remove the suckers growing between the main stem and leaf axils to keep the plants in bounds and allow air to circulate around the leaves. It's possible to "double leader" the plants by letting the sucker just below the first flower cluster develop; tie this branch to a separate string that leads away from the first so the leaves of the two leaders aren't touching.

We all want vine-ripened tomatoes, but the best way to get high yields of these fully flavored fruits is to pick them shy of being completely ripe. Pick them when they are one-half to three-quarters colored, and let them sit in a well-lit area that's warm, not hot. Don't store tomatoes in the refrigerator, either; at temperatures of 40°F and below, the cells burst, ruining the texture of the fruit.

Solanum melongena

Eggplant

Eggplants are lovely enough to have a central spot in the ornamental garden. If you explore available cultivars, you'll see a choice including classic oval purple eggplants, round pink ones, long white ones, skinny purple ones, white-and-pink striped fruits, and even an orange cultivar. Both the leaves and plant habit are lovely, too, so this is a plant you won't want to ignore.

Size: Varies from 1½ to 3 feet tall; 1½ to 2 feet wide

Bloom: White or pink-purple flowers form in early to midsummer.

Exposure: Full sun

Soil mix: Well drained, moderately fertile, high humus, with a pH of 5.8 to 6.8. Fertilize weekly after the first flowers form with a material high in trace elements; a mixture of fish emulsion and liquid seaweed or potting mix tea is a good choice.

Companion plants: Set small-flowered plants close to eggplants to provide a food source for the many beneficial insects that attack aphids.

Options: Eggplants naturally grow as a determinate bush that doesn't need staking. However, commercial growers often tie them to stakes in the field because the plants react so adversely to wind that their yields fall. You can do this in a container, too. Place a stake in the container when you transplant, or tie the plant to a support next to the container.

Solanum tuberosum

Potato

Potatoes in a pot? You might be surprised to find out how easy it is to grow your own spuds on your balcony or terrace. Given their high price as well as their generally smaller size, specialty fingerling potatoes are a great choice for a container. Types such as Russian Banana are known for their high yields and great cooking quality. Go online to search for specialty potatoes—you're sure to find some that you'll want to grow.

Size: Varies from 24 to 30 inches tall, 24 to 30 inches wide

Bloom: Not all cultivars bloom but many do. Depending on the color of the potato, flowers can be white, pink, or violet. After the blooms drop, a careful person can reach under the center of a plant that produces large potatoes and pull off one or two small "new potatoes."

Exposure: Full sun in Zones 3 to 7; filtered afternoon light in Zones 8 to 10

Soil mix: Well drained, fertile, humus rich. A pH of 5.2 to 5.8 is ideal for potatoes, but they tolerate a pH as high as 6.5.

Companion plants: Potato plants take some time to reach full size. Use the edges of their pots for baby lettuces and greens for salad mixes, or plant some early radishes when you plant potato tubers.

Options: Many people plant potatoes up to a month before the frost-free date. The plants can withstand cold weather,

certainly, and you can cover them when frost does threaten, but you won't gain time by doing this because growth is slow and, even in containers, the plants will be more susceptible to diseases if they are stressed. Instead, wait to plant until night temperatures are 50°F. The plants will grow rapidly at this temperature and be stronger and more able to resist diseases.

Wait to harvest potatoes until 2 weeks after the tops have died back in late summer or early fall. This assures that the potato skins will thicken up enough so that they'll keep for some time; otherwise, they will be thin-skinned new potatoes that must be used within a few weeks of harvest. If temperatures are getting cold enough so you are worried that the potatoes themselves will frost, knock the tops over and let them brown and dry. Cover the pots if it does frost while you are waiting.

Various species

Salad mix, mesclun

Salad mix is one of the best reasons to have a container garden. In fact, you can skip the tomatoes and forgo the basil, but if you ignore salad mixes, you are denying yourself a treat that you simply can't buy. The mixes at stores and farmers' markets can be lovely, of course, but they are never as good as those you grow yourself. Your home-picked mix will be as fresh as produce can get, and you can mix the proportions of various crops to suit your own tastes exactly.

Size: Plants grow in dense rows and average no more than 6 inches tall when cut.

Bloom: Harvest when plants are tiny and immature unless saving seeds.

Exposure: Full sun in spring; filtered light or partial shade in summer; full sun in fall

Soil mix: Fertile, humus rich, high nitrogen, with a pH of 5.8 to 6.8

Companion plants: Salad mixes are composed of plants that serve as good companions to each other. Place pots of blooming herbs such as dill and cilantro close to them to feed beneficial insects.

Containerized eggplants, such as these 'Ping Tung Long', 'Fairy Tale', and 'Listade de Gandia' make a gorgeous display, on or off the plant.

Small fruit

Warmed by the sun and ripened to perfection, homegrown grapes and berries are some of the most satisfying crops you can grow. And surprisingly, these fruit are also among the easiest plants to produce on a small scale. Give them the right soil mix, the appropriate environment, a suitable container, and just a modicum of care, and they'll flourish. Your success with small fruit may inspire you to expand your plantings. If you ever have an excess, these fruits are easy to freeze or make into preserves that bring a welcome touch of summer to the winter table.

Fragaria vesca; Fragaria x ananassa

Alpine strawberries; June-bearing and day-neutral strawberries

Strawberries grow as well or better in containers as they do in open soil. They are ideally suited to container conditions because their roots are shallow, and their nutritional needs are easy to meet with liquid fertilizers, particularly fish emulsion and seaweed. Beyond that, frost, which can be the banc of open-ground berries, is no problem in a container because you can either bring it inside or cover it whenever temperatures threaten to plunge to blossom-damaging levels. Soilborne diseases such as the red stele that damages garden-grown berries aren't likely to attack berries in a potting soil, and you can generally catch pest infestations right in the beginning, when they're easy to control. All around, you're likely to find that growing strawberries in containers is far easier and more convenient than growing them in the garden ever was.

Keep strawberry plants for 1 to 3 years. If you live in the north, protect the roots of the plants from freezing by bringing the pots into a protected area or insulating them well. In areas where the soil won't freeze, leave them outside, unprotected.

Size: 6 to 12 inches tall, 8 to 12 inches wide

Bloom: Early spring brings clusters of white flowers. Five white petals surround a prominent yellow center that's made up of tiny true flowers. The strawberry fruit is formed when each of these flowers is fertilized; if pollination is poor, the ovule won't plump up and the strawberry will have sunken, tough spots. Bees and other flying insects pollinate strawberries, so it's important to allow them into the area where you're growing the berries—don't screen them out!

Exposure: Full sun when blooming and fruiting. In northern areas, allow full sun all season; in tropical regions, give the plants partial shade during midsummer heat waves.

Soil mix: Well drained and humus rich with high fertility. Supplement fertility by spraying liquid seaweed on plants every 2 or 3 weeks from the time you can see the developing buds until just before the first blooms open. Apply approximately a cup of potting mix tea or diluted fish emulsion to each plant once in early summer and then again in late summer on plants you're holding over the winter.

Companion plants: Strawberries are heavy feeders and also grow quickly enough so that they don't share space well. Plant companions in separate pots, set close to the berries. Sweet alyssum and flowering cilantro, basil, thyme, and mints will feed the many predators and parasites that attack aphids, so they all make good companions.

Options: June-bearing plants fruit only once a season—in spring or early summer, depending on climate and cultivar. In contrast, day-neutral plants fruit throughout the summer. Many people think that June-bearing cultivars, particularly the old-fashioned ones, are the best tasting, so they plant only those. But if you have the space, it's nice to plant both types of berries so you'll have a few throughout the year. Grow day-neutral plants in hanging baskets if space is at a premium; let one or two runners form, and fruit will literally drip from these pots.

From berries to leaves, alpine strawberry plants are smaller than the other types. Many people consider them the best-tasting berries, though, and also like the looks of their mounded forms and crisp little leaves in a row of decorative 6-inch pots.

No matter what kind of strawberries you are growing, pinch off all or most of the runners as soon as you notice them. If you don't, the plants will put more energy into their runners than their fruit.

Drainage is as important as soil fertility. Make certain that the soil is damp, but don't water more than necessary. If frost threatens once the plants are in bloom, cover them until the danger is over.

Ribes hirtellum and *R. uva-crispa; R. nigrum; R. sativum, R. rubrum, R. petraeum*

American and European gooseberry, black currant; red and white currant

A pot of 'Red Lakes' currants will yield enough fruit for a small batch of jelly or to make a tasty addition to other preserves.

These staples of the European garden fell out of favor in the United States when it was discovered that they were alternate hosts of the fungus that causes blister rust (*Cronartium ribicola*), a serious disease of white pines. Today, disease-resistant species of gooseberries and white and red currants are available, and the federal ban on growing them has been lifted. However, states where white pines are a significant part of the ecosystem still outlaw them, so check with local nurseries or your state Department of Agriculture before ordering.

Size: 3 to 5 feet tall and wide

Bloom: In early spring. Like the fruit, they form in drooping clusters, but the flowers are small and nondescript.

Exposure: Full sun in Zones 3 to 5; filtered afternoon light in Zones 6 and 7

Soil mix: Slightly acid soil with high levels of organic matter. In late winter to very early spring, fertilize each plant with about 3 cups of a high-nitrogen material such as soybean meal. Cover this with a thick mulch to prevent flies from being drawn to it.

Companion plants: Use separate pots because it's best to cover the soil surface with thick plastic to prevent the larvae of fruit flies from burrowing down into the soil to complete their life cycle after the fruit drops. Plants that provide food sources for hover flies (or syrphid flies) and parasitic wasps are good choices for nearby pots.

Options: Plant these species in early spring or fall. When you plant, prune back the stems to about 10 inches long and cut out any damaged or crossing branches. Ribes species fruit on 1-, 2-, and 3-year-old wood. In late winter, while the plant is still dormant, prune out old branches and any new growth that is weak or badly located. Each year, prune so the center of the bush is open, and don't keep more than 8 to 10 stems per plant for best health and yields.

If the plant begins to lose vitality for what seems like no reason, repot it. After you take it out of its old container, prune the roots (see page 181 for more information). This will stimulate new root growth and give the plant a boost.

Vaccinium corymbosum; V. angustifolium

Half-high blueberry; lowbush blueberry

ZONE 3-8

Blueberries are an ideal container plant. You'll need more than one cultivar for the best pollination, so plan on having at least three but, more sensibly, six bushes. Their small shiny leaves are decorative at any time of year, so that may an excellent choice as a foundation planting. Unfortunately, birds love blueberries, too. Completely cover them with a tight plastic mesh cloth a few days before the first berries ripen.

Size: Half-high blueberries: 2 to 3 feet tall, 2 to 3 feet wide; lowbush blueberries: 1 to 3 feet tall, 3 feet wide—or as wide as they can grow in the container

Bloom: Early spring; clusters of white, waxy-looking, bell-shaped flowers

Exposure: Full sun

Soil mix: Acid (pH of 4 to 5), high humus, high fertility, and very well drained. Test the soil every spring and fall and adjust the pH accordingly. Fertilize with manure compost or, if the pH is too high, cottonseed meal. Lower it by applying elemental sulfur to the soil. Do not use fish emulsion or other materials with nitrogen in a nitrate form.

Companion plants: Few plants like soils with a pH of 4 to 5, so grow their companions in nearby pots. Summer-blooming nicotianas make lovely companions. You can enjoy their fragrance as you harvest the blueberries.

Options: High bush berries are too big to grow well in a container, so half-highs, which are literally about half as big, are a good choice for container gardens. Lowbush berries look superb in a grouped container garden because of their low, spreading habit.

Prune half-high plants each year, in late winter or very early spring, cutting out old wood, and cut back the branches to leave three to five buds per branch. Thin the branches enough so that light and air can reach the center of the plant. Thin stems of lowbush berries every year, too. As soon as

These grapes are thriving in their pots. Prune them for productivity or trellis them as a decorative element; either way, you'll love what they do for your garden.

all types go dormant in the fall, trim off the laterals where the berries formed.

When the plant has grown into the largest container you want to give it, you'll need to begin root pruning (see page 181). If yields of lowbush berries decline despite root pruning, cut off all the stems in late winter, and give them a year to regrow and rejuvenate themselves. Pay attention to the pH and adjust it when necessary. If soil-borne pests and diseases become a problem, wash the soil off the roots when you prune them, and repot them with a completely new soil mix. Do this in late winter, just before you expect regrowth to start, and the plant will make a speedy recovery.

Vitis labrusca; V. vinifera

American grapes; European grapes

ZONE **5–9** ❀ ◗◗ **3–5**

Grapes can be relatively easy or quite challenging, depending on the types you grow and the location where you grow them. American grapes are well suited to the cooler areas of the United States as well as southern Canada, while hybrids containing both European and American parentage are suited to California and the Southwest. Pure European strains are not as pest and disease resistant as the hybrids or American grapes, so they are much more challenging to grow.

Size: 10 to 12 feet tall, 3 to 5 feet wide, depending on support system

Bloom: In spring, clusters of small, inconspicuous flowers form.

Exposure: Full sun

Soil mix: Fertile soil with excellent drainage and high levels of organic matter. Side-dress each vine with 1 to 2 pounds of fully finished, well-balanced manure compost each late winter or early spring.

Companion plants: In nearby pots, grow small-flowered plants to feed the many biological controls of aphids and mealybugs.

Options: Provide a large container such as a half barrel so roots will have adequate space. Trellises or some other type of support system is mandatory for grapes, as is careful pruning. Potted grapes could be trained up an arbor or on a sturdy support sunken into the soil.

Vines will bear the following year from buds growing on the 1-year-old wood. American grapes tend not to fruit close to the trunk, so remember to leave enough buds on the shoots to get a good yield. Continue pruning and training in this way for many years of productivity.

Repotting a trellised grape plant is easier said than done. In most cases, it makes more sense to continue to add potting mix to the container each year and leave the roots in place.

Fruit trees

Small fruit trees make excellent container plants. Not only are they productive, most of them have fragrant blooms, outstanding foliage, and—thanks to your good pruning (see below)—a pleasing form and strong presence all through the year. Because they are living in small quarters, they never yield as much as in-ground trees, even if they are the same cultivars on the same rootstocks. But even so, you'll get enough fruit to make them a worthwhile addition to your container garden.

The choice of a container is important. As the plants grow, you'll need to keep potting them into larger containers until you reach the maximum, which is usually about the size of a half barrel. The weight of such a pot is enormous, so it's a good idea to keep it on a wheeled platform if you plan to move it around.

Pruning fruit roots

You can't leave a mature tree in its final container for long; every year or two, you'll have to remove it and prune its roots to keep it growing and fruiting vigorously. For this reason, it's best to use a plastic container with smooth interior walls.

Containerized dwarf apples give such great yields that you'll wonder why you haven't planted them sooner.

1 In late winter, when the tree is still dormant, tip it over and apply pressure to the pot as you roll it back and forth over a firm surface. This helps to break the bond between the roots and the pot and enables you to slide the rootball out of the container.
2 Take a look at the rootball. You will have to choose whether to remove up to a third of the bottom or several inches from the bottom and all vertical sides of it.
3 Decide this by determining where the largest concentration of small feeder roots is—if they are at the bottom, cut off about 2 inches from all sides of the root ball. If they are at the sides, remove up to a third of the bottom of the root ball.
4 In either case, remove large roots that no longer have small laterals and feeder roots growing from them, and tease out the soil surrounding most of the remaining roots.
5 This gives you a good enough view of the roots to do selective pruning of any that have lost vigor or are threatening to strangle the trunk or other roots.
6 Place an appropriate layer of new soil in the container, and ask a friend to help you position the tree back into the center of it.
7 Fill the spaces around the root ball with potting soil, using the handle of a wooden spoon to gently push the soil into any voids.
8 Water well and add more soil mix as needed to bring its level to within 2 inches of the top of the pot.

Prune the top growth after root pruning and repotting a deciduous tree. This reduces the need for feeder roots when the first leaves develop and also helps to open the tree so that sunlight can enter the canopy and ripen the fruit.

Citrus spp.
Citrus

Small citrus trees make excellent container plants no matter where you live. Some citrus—Meyer lemons (*Citrus limon* × *C. sinensis*), kaffir limes (*Citrus hystrix*), and kumquats (*Fortunella margarita*) are naturally small enough to thrive in containers. And many other citrus types and cultivars are available on dwarfing rootstock that makes them well suited for life as a container plant. In the north, bring citrus trees indoors before frost. In mild-winter areas where frost is rare, leave citrus outside. If frost does threaten, cover the trees with blankets until the danger is past.

Size: Varies from 3 to 10 feet tall, 2 to 5 feet wide

Bloom: Fragrant white flowers in late winter and early spring

Exposure: Full sun for at least 8 hours a day; wind-free area

Soil mix: Special citrus soil mixes are available at some nurseries. If you can't find such a mix, make your own by adding equal parts of sand and redwood or cedar shavings to a high-quality potting soil. The mix must drain very well to keep citrus healthy. These plants require high levels of nitrogen as well as ample trace elements. Fertilize them monthly, cutting back on nitrogen during the winter months when growth is slower. Liquid seaweed is an excellent foliar feed all through the year because it supplies necessary trace elements in good balance. Remember to spray early enough in the morning so that droplets will dry before the sun is strong.

Companion plants: The soil around the roots must remain open, so it's wise to plant companions in separate pots placed close to the tree. All of the small-flowered plants that feed beneficial insects are wonderful companions.

Options: Watering these plants can be tricky. Citrus do not do well with soggy soil. Let the soil surface dry out between waterings, and use your finger to check the soil at lower depths to make sure the plant really needs more water. When you do water, always do so thoroughly.

Pruning is necessary even on dwarf trees. Keep the center of the tree open by removing excess foliage there, and cut back any branches that cross each other or interfere with the easy circulation of air around the foliage. Pinch back the tips of new growth in spring and summer. Citrus fruit often develops on the tips of small branches; don't remove them when you prune unless the tree looks as if it's bearing too heavily for its own good. Repot citrus every year. When you do, shave off at least

In a warm climate or bright sunspace, potted lemon trees can be as productive as they are beautiful.

an inch from all sides of the rootball, and tease out as much soil as you can from its interior. When you replace it in the pot, keep the root collar above the soil line. Do not cover any of the trunk with soil, and make sure that the crown of the plant is covered only lightly. It will develop fungal diseases if you bury it.

Ficus carica
Fig

Many people believe that figs yield best when their roots are constricted, as they often are by rocks on the sunny hillsides where they are native. Others say pruning makes all the difference. But everyone agrees that figs are one of the easiest fruits to grow in a container.

Size: Varies from 5 to 10 feet tall, 3 to 8 feet wide

Exposure: Full sun for at least 8 hours a day

Soil mix: Good drainage is the key to good fig growth. They grow well at a pH of 6 to 7.8 and thrive with moderate, rather than rich, fertility levels. Add a top dressing of about 2 inches of manure compost in the spring, and use liquid seaweed as a foliar feed about once a month when the plant is actively growing. Root prune fig trees every second or third year, adding new soil mix when you do.

Companion plants: Group small-flowered ornamentals and herbs around the tree to feed beneficial insects.

Options: Common garden figs are self-fruiting, so you need only one. If fruit drops early, the tree may be too hot and dry. Start watering more frequently and thoroughly. Figs drop fruit when they get too little light, too, so try give it nothing more than a little afternoon shade if you are trying to cool it down. Fruit forms on the previous year's wood, so prune in late winter or very early spring. Some cultivars, such as 'Mission', also produce fruit on the current season's growth in fall. To encourage this, prune in late fall in southern areas or very early spring in more northern areas. Prune for shape and also to allow air and light into the

This potted 'Brown Turkey' fig has the support of a wire espalier to ensure its health and productivity.

center of the tree. Wear protective gear, including gloves and goggles, when pruning because the sap of the fig tree can irritate the skin.

Malus spp.
Apples

Dwarf and "columnar" apple trees add fragrance and beauty to a container garden. In fact, many gardeners grow them simply for the architectural structure they add to a grouping or, in the case of columnar trees, to create a visual "fence" at the edge of a property line. But don't ignore the fruit! Sweet apples from a couple of containerized trees can fill lunch-boxes and dessert menus for weeks at a time. In cold zones, move the pots into an unheated garage or shed over winter. In more

southern areas that get occasional frosts, you can probably get away with just insulating the pot.

Size: Varies from 7 to 10 feet tall, 2 to 4 feet wide

Bloom: Early spring brings delicate white or pink blooms with a pervasive, sweet fragrance.

Exposure: Full sun

Soil mix: Apples prefer well-drained soil with moderate fertility. Too much nitrogen encourages pests such as aphids, so it's best to keep nitrogen moderate in comparison to higher levels of potassium and phosphorus. Calcium is also important, as is a balanced mix of trace elements, so weekly foliar sprays of liquid seaweed are beneficial. Potting mix tea is also good as a foliar spray or root drench, applied once a month during spring and through midsummer. Hold back on all fertilizers when late summer comes because the tree will fare better through the coming winter if it doesn't have much new wood.

In late winter, after root pruning the tree and repotting it in a new soil, add a topdressing of about 2 inches of fully finished manure potting mix to the container and water thoroughly. As it breaks down, it will feed the microorganisms that supply nutrients to the plant and keep the soil friable. Add earthworms to the soil mix if they are not already present.

Companion plants: Plant small-flowered annuals and herbs in nearby pots to feed the many beneficial insects that prey on aphids. As well, most apple cultivars require a pollinator—another apple or crabapple that blooms the same time and has compatible pollen. The nursery where you buy your tree will recommend, and probably sell, an appropriate pollinator. These plants don't have to sit right beside each other because flying insects such as bees will carry pollen from one to the other.

Options: Buy trees that are adapted to your particular climate. For one thing, they will be more pest and disease resistant, and for another, they will have an appropriate "chilling" requirement. Most fruiting trees must experience temperatures of 32° to 40°F for a certain number of hours each winter in order to break dormancy. Plants bred for northern conditions have a longer requirement than those bred for the south.

Columnar trees make great sense in pots because their growth habit makes them quite stable in the pot. If you grow these in a small (18- to 24-inch) pot, feed them every 2 weeks or so to make up for the smaller pot size. Root prune as usual, but remove less of the root system than you do when the tree is growing in a larger pot.

If you are growing a dwarf tree, you'll need to prune it. You can choose a single leader design or an open design. If you are in an area where you can leave the tree outside all winter, you can also train it to an espalier. Prune as recommended for whichever design you decide upon and, if the tree seems unsteady because of the small root size, use wires to support it during the season.

Fruit trees can be too productive for their own good. After the customary "June drop," when trees drop a percentage of the fruit they've set, take a good look at the remaining apples. It's better for the tree's long-term health and productivity to thin them even more. On all but columnar trees, make sure that eating apples are at least 4 to 6 inches apart and cooking apples are 6 to 9 inches apart. Don't let the apples on columnar trees touch each other—touching fruit is an invitation to codling moths and several diseases. Other than that, you can leave the fruit that remains after June drop.

Glossary

A

Acid: Lacking in lime; associated with peaty and sandy soil; pH value below 7 (see also pH).

Acid lover: Also known as *ericaceous*, a plant that prefers an acidic soil.

Alkaline: Opposite of acid, high lime content; pH value above 7 (see also pH).

Alpine plant: Plants that grow naturally below the snow line and above the tree line in mountainous areas.

Annual: A plant that grows from seed and completes its life cycle in one season.

Aquatic: Plants that grow in water, with all or some of the leaves submerged.

B

Bedding plant: A plant that is used for a temporary, seasonal display only.

Biennial: A plant that completes its life cycle in two years.

Biological control: A natural predator, parasite, or disease.

Bulb: A fleshy underground structure from which plants such as tulips, lilies, and daffodils grow.

C

Clay: Versatile material for containers, including terra-cotta; ideal for its natural porosity.

Coir: Environmentally friendly alternative to peat made from coconut waste.

Conifer: A tree such as a spruce, fir, and pine that bears cones and is usually evergreen.

Corm: A fleshy storage structure from which a new plant will grow. In contrast to bulbs, corms are solid structures.

Crown: Point where root system gives rise to the stem.

Cultivar: A variety of a plant that has been developed through breeding.

Cutting: A section of a plant that is used for propagation. Cuttings can be taken from roots or stems at various stages of growth.

D

Deadheading: Removing spent blooms after flowering to encourage the development of new flowers.

Deciduous: A tree or shrub that loses its leaves, usually in autumn.

Dibble: A pointed tool that is used to make holes in soil where plants can be inserted.

Dormant period: The time when a plant ceases to grow, usually autumn and winter.

Dwarf (and semi-dwarf): Smaller variations of standard-size growth.

E

Espalier: A tree trained to produce several horizontal tiers of branches from a vertical main stem.

Evergreen: Plants that retain leaves throughout year.

F

Fibrous roots: Roots that are wiry and multibranched.

Floating row cover: A synthetic cover used to raise the temperature and protect plant and container from frost. Allows air and rain through.

Floret: One of many small flowers, sometimes in a cluster, sometimes in other formation.

Formal: Classically derived geometric design or arrangement.

Frost-free climate: A climate where frost does not occur.

G

Galvanized: A metal that has been rust-proofed.

Glazed: Polished or patterned coating for containers that is impervious to the passage of water and nutrients.

Green wood cutting: A cutting taken from a stem that is in a quickly growing, vegetative state.

H

Habit: The form or shape a plant takes as it grows.

Half standard: A tree or shrub trained so that it has a clear stem measuring 3 to 4 feet.

Harden off: Acclimatizing greenhouse-grown plants to the open air.

Hardwood cutting: A cutting taken from a stem when the wood has fully hardened for the winter.

Hardy, half-hardy: Hardy plants can withstand hard frosts. Half-hardy plants can survive limited cold and need removal to frost-free areas.

Herbaceous plant: A plant with soft, nonwoody stems. In cold climates, the top growth of herbaceous plants generally dies down over winter.

Herbs: Aromatic plants generally used in cooking. Also used for alternative medicines and aromatherapies.

Horticultural fleece: See Floating row cover.

Humidity: The amount of moisture in the air.

Hummock-forming: Plants with a rounded low-growth habit normally on exposed areas such as coastal sites.

Humus: Organic residue of decayed organic matter in the soil (i.e., leaf mold compost or animal matter.)

Hybrid: A plant that was produced by crossing parents of different species.

I

Informal: Relaxed planting or design.

Interplanting: Mixing different plant species in the same bed or row, or combining plants that bloom at different times of the year.

L

Leaching: Occurs when compounds such as salt, lime, and fertilizer are washed through the soil by rain or excessive watering. A concrete container can leach lime into the soil.

Lime: A compound of calcium added to soil to make it more alkaline.

Loam: Medium-textured soil with roughly equal parts of clay, sand, and silt; usually rich in humus.

M

Mature wood: Wood that has hardened and then developed fully formed bark.

Microclimate: Localized climate defined by its immediate surroundings.

Mulch: A layer of organic or inorganic matter placed on top of the soil that can suppress weeds, retain moisture in the soil, and in some cases feed plants.

N

Nutrients: Natural chemicals and minerals necessary for plant growth, such as nitrogen, phosphorus, and potassium.

O

Organic: Creating a healthy, fertile environment without the use of manmade fertilizers and pesticides.

Oxygenators: Submerged pond plants that add oxygen to the water.

P

Peat: Nonsustainable resource now considerable unsuitable as a base for potting medium.

Perennial: A plant that lives for several years.

pH: The measure of the acidity against alkalinity in the soil.

Pinching out: The removal (usually with finger and thumb) of a shoot at its growing point to encourage the development of lateral shoots.

Planter: A large container, often for trees and shrubs.

Pollination: The transfer of pollen from a male flower to a female flower. Pollination can be carried out by insects, water, wind, or the gardener's hand.

Pot: Alternative name for a container, often used to define small ones.

Pot-bound: Pot-grown plant, taking up all the available space in its container, sometimes with roots coming through the drainage holes.

Potting: The act of placing the plant into the container.

Potting medium: A soil mix for plants made from various materials including loam, sand, peat, coir, and leaf-mold. Mixes are suitable for specific types of plants or situations.

R

Rambler: A vigorous trailing plant with a scrambling habit.

Recycled: Creative reuse of objects for plant containers (must have drainage holes).

Root: The plant's underground support system.

Root ball: The combined root system and surrounding soil/compost of a plant.

Root pruning: The cutting of live plant roots to control the vigor of a plant.

Rootstock: The root system onto which a cultivar is budded or grafted.

S

Semihardwood: Partially mature stem.

Semiripe cutting: A cutting taken from wood that has begun to mature.

Shrub: Branching perennial that has woody stems.

Softwood: Actively growing stem, soft and sappy.

Softwood cutting: A cutting taken from a stem when it is in its rapid first growth.

Species: The individual plant type within a group or genus of plants.

Standard: A tree or shrub trained so that it has a clear stem measuring at least 6 feet.

Stem: The main shoot of a tree.

Sustainable: Refers to natural resources that renew themselves readily, so that they can be harvested without harming the environment.

T

Temperate: Describing a zone roughly midway between tropical and arctic.

Thinning: The removal of branches to improve the quality of those remaining.

Topdressing: Removing the spent, top layer of soil and replacing with fresh material.

Topiary: Creative hedging, including clipping of geometric or representational shapes from small-leaved evergreens such as box, yew, or privet.

Trailer: A plant with stems that hang down.

V

Variegated: Plant parts (usually leaves) marked with a blotched irregular pattern of colors such as gold or silver on a base color of green.

Variety: A plant within a species that grows naturally in the wild.

W

Winter annual: A plant that lives only one year, generally germinating in midsummer and forming seeds and dying the following spring.

Wire frame: Used in hanging baskets, either galvanized or plastic-coated.

Woody plant: A plant that develops woody tissue.

Z

Zone: In this book the regions of North America are broken down by minimum air temperatures in winter to help you determine where a containerized plant will survive outdoors.

Hardiness zones

Remember that hardiness is not just a question of minimum temperatures. A plant's ability to survive certain temperatures is affected by many factors, such as the amount of shelter given and its position within your garden.

Australia and New Zealand

Europe

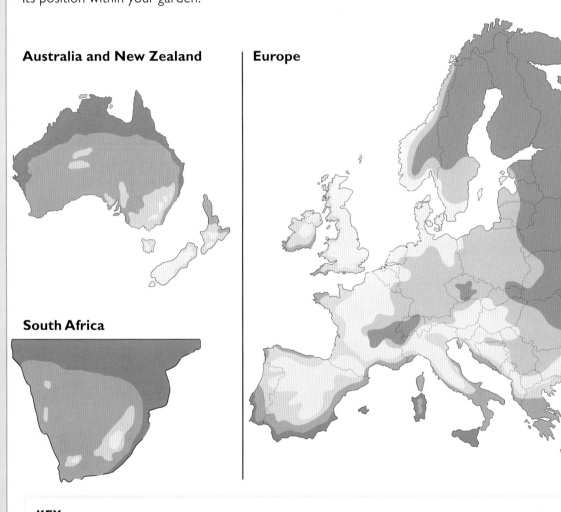

South Africa

KEY
Average annual minimum temperature

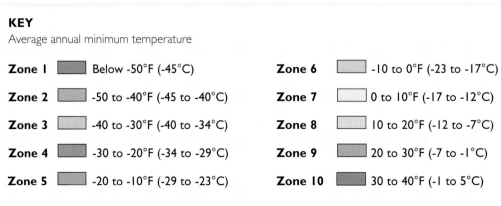

Zone 1	Below -50°F (-45°C)	**Zone 6**	-10 to 0°F (-23 to -17°C)
Zone 2	-50 to -40°F (-45 to -40°C)	**Zone 7**	0 to 10°F (-17 to -12°C)
Zone 3	-40 to -30°F (-40 to -34°C)	**Zone 8**	10 to 20°F (-12 to -7°C)
Zone 4	-30 to -20°F (-34 to -29°C)	**Zone 9**	20 to 30°F (-7 to -1°C)
Zone 5	-20 to -10°F (-29 to -23°C)	**Zone 10**	30 to 40°F (-1 to 5°C)

United States of America

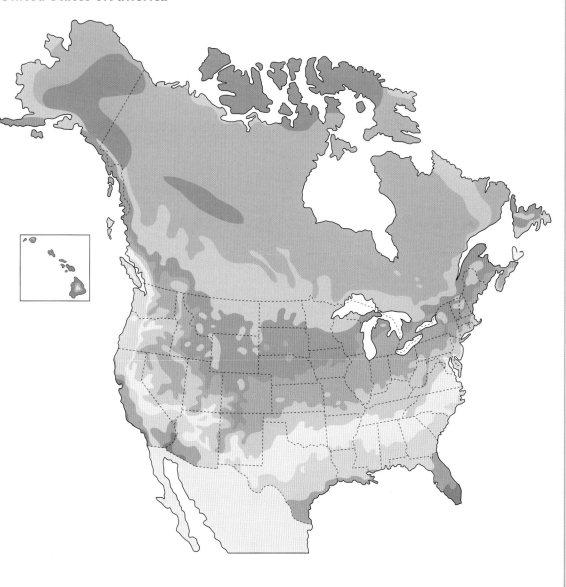

Index

Credits

Quarto would like to thank the following agencies for kindly supplying images for inclusion in this book:

Key: l left; r right; b bottom; m middle; t top

GAP Photos www.gapphotos.com
pp. 11bl, 14–15, 16, 18, 19bl & br, 20m, 21bl & br, 23, 25bl, 2nd & 3rd from left, 26bl & br, 27bl, 3rd from left & br, 28–29, 30–31, 32–35, 36, 37m & r, 38m, 39–40, 43, 44, 45r, 46, 47b, 48–49, 51, 53b, 55, 57b, 59tl & b, 61tr & br, 62l & m 70, 72b, 75t, 78, 79t, 80–81, 83, 84t, 86–87, 89t & b, 91bl & 91t, 92–93, 95, 96–97, 100–101, 111, 118, 120–122, 125, 217tl, 129–131, 136–183

Garden Collection www.garden-collection.com
pp. 1, 2–3, 4, 6–7, 13, 16/17b 17r, 19m, 20l&r, 21m, 24, 25r, 26 2nd & 3rd from left, 27 2nd from left, 27l & r, 41, 44bl, 45l, 47t, 52t, 55b, 57t, 59tr, 61l, 71l, 72tr, 73–74, 76–77, 82, 84b, 88b, 90b, 91b, 98, 99, 172

Bridgeman www.bridgeman.co.uk
pp. 9, 11t, 11br

Christie's Images www.christiesimages.com
pp. 10, 12

Shutterstock www.shutterstock.com
p. 42, 132-135

Photolibrary www.photolibrary.uk.com
pp. 68–69

All other images are the copyright of Quarto Inc.
While every effort has been made to credit contributors, Quarto would like to apologize should there have been any omissions or errors—and would be pleased to make the appropriate correction for future editions of the book.

Joanna Harrison would like to thank:

Miranda Smith for her excellent contribution throughout the book, and for providing the hardworking plant directory.
Paul Gingell and Elaine Day at the Burford Garden Company, for giving us help, support, and access to their fabulous selection of containers and plants (Burford Garden Company, Shilton Road, Burford, Oxfordshire, OX18 4PA, UK, E: info@burford.co.uk).
John Fryer and Guy Dagul for their invaluable advice.